The Lost Paths

The Lost Paths

*A History of How We Walk
From Here to There*

JACK CORNISH

MICHAEL JOSEPH

PENGUIN MICHAEL JOSEPH

UK | USA | Canada | Ireland | Australia
India | New Zealand | South Africa

Penguin Michael Joseph is part of the Penguin Random House group of companies
whose addresses can be found at global.penguinrandomhouse.com

First published 2024
001

Map illustration © Ian Moores, 2024
For picture credits see page 364

Set in 12/14.75pt Bembo Book MT Pro
Typeset by Jouve (UK), Milton Keynes
Printed and bound in Great Britain by Clays Ltd, Elcograf S.p.A.

The authorized representative in the EEA is Penguin Random House Ireland,
Morrison Chambers, 32 Nassau Street, Dublin D02 YH68

A CIP catalogue record for this book is available from the British Library

ISBN: 978–1–405–95128–9

www.greenpenguin.co.uk

This book is dedicated to all those who fight for public access and to preserve our paths – past, present and future.

And to my nephews, Max and Charlie – I look forward to walking alongside you, whatever path you choose in life.

Contents

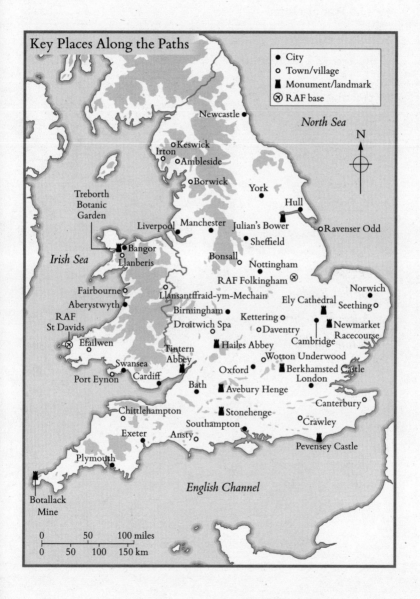

Key Places Along the Paths

- ● City
- ○ Town/village
- ▮ Monument/landmark
- ⊗ RAF base

North Sea

N

Newcastle

Keswick
Irton
Ambleside

Borwick

York

Hull

Treborth
Botanic
Garden

Liverpool   Manchester   Julian's Bower

Ravenser Odd

Sheffield

Bangor
Llanberis

Bonsall

Irish Sea

Nottingham

RAF Folkingham ⊗

Fairbourne

Llansantffraid-ym-Mechain

Norwich

Aberystwyth

Ely Cathedral   Seething

RAF
St Davids

Birmingham
Droitwich Spa

Kettering
Daventry

Newmarket
Racecourse

Cambridge

Efailwen

Hailes Abbey

Swansea
Port Eynon   Cardiff

Tintern
Abbey

Wotton Underwood

Oxford   Berkhamsted Castle

London

Bath   Avebury Henge

Chittlehampton

Stonehenge

Canterbury

Southampton   Crawley

Exeter   Ansty

Pevensey Castle

Plymouth

English Channel

Botallack
Mine

| 0 | 50 | 100 miles |
| 0 | 50 | 100 | 150 km |

The Lost (and Not So Lost) Paths of England and Wales

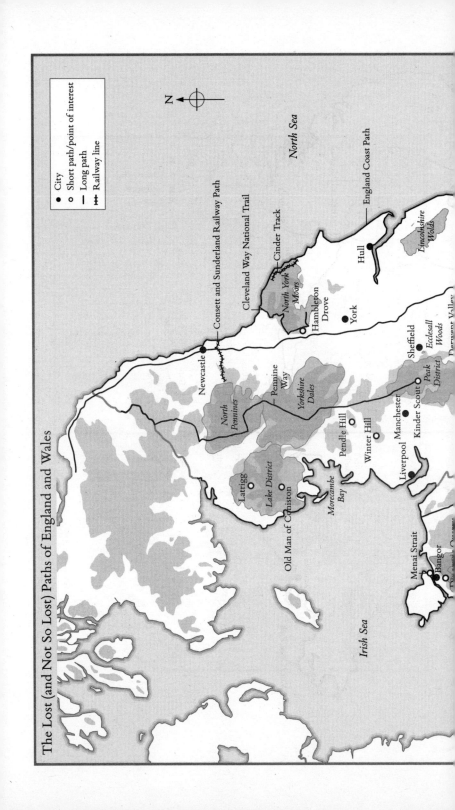

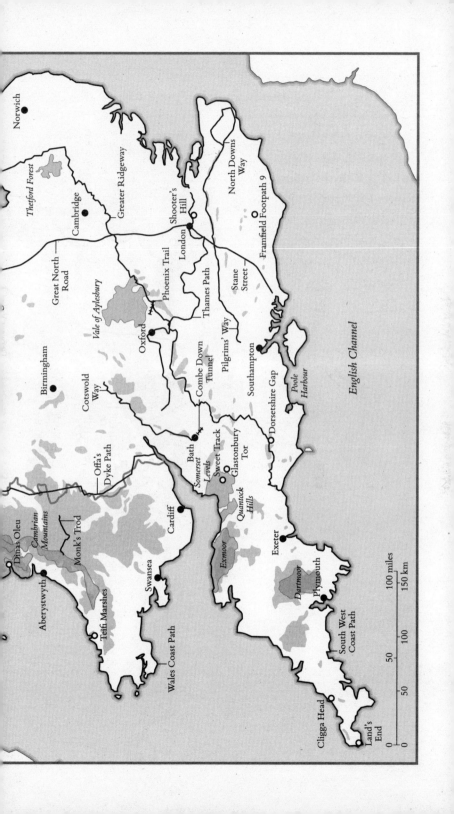

Introduction

At first glance, it's not exactly the most exciting photograph I've ever taken. A photo of my trousers, dew-soaked from early-morning walking through a wheat field, and my boots, moulded and cracked to the shape of my feet. But at this very spot, on a scree-strewn grey lane near the English–Welsh border, I'd walked exactly 500 miles. Behind me, a trek which had taken me along high cliffs, through woodlands, down valleys, over punishing hillsides and along city streets. Standing on that Shropshire lane, my feet were a bit sore, but I felt truly, overwhelmingly happy – a moment worth capturing.

That summer I walked a total of 1,550 miles, over 100 days, on a looping and meandering journey from Land's End to John O'Groats. In England and Wales, my guides through unfamiliar land were the green dashes of rights of way shown on my Ordnance Survey map (although I stepped foot on just a tiny fraction of this 140,000-mile network).[1] These public rights of way didn't magically appear on our maps. In 1949, the National Parks and Access to the Countryside Act was passed, a piece of legislation described by one Member of Parliament as 'an epoch-making measure . . . a charter for the British people after their very long struggle to obtain rights of access to the natural beauty of this country'.

---

1 Rights of way come in a variety of flavours: footpaths (just for walking), bridleways (for walking, horse riding and cycling), restricted byways (for walking, horse riding, cycling and driving a horse and cart) and byways open to all traffic (including motorized vehicles).

Rights of way have existed for centuries, passages for people to negotiate their landscapes. But they were undrawn, kept in the minds of locals – walkers, riders and landowners. It wasn't until the 1949 Act that these paths were required to be legally recorded. The legislation compelled councils to create 'definitive maps', to set down our paths on paper. To ensure that the public knew their rights and that these rights could be stoutly defended from obstruction or encroachment.

The creation of these maps was a great communal effort. From the early 1950s, civic society swung into action. Groups of ramblers could be seen out on the ground, carefully mapping the paths they used. They were joined by cyclists, horse riders, boy scouts, anglers, countryside protection societies and ordinary members of the public. It wasn't just paths in use at the time which were considered – from the archives were pulled ten-foot-square tithe maps drawn and painted on parchment, railway plans many feet long were unrolled, and hundreds of years of parish records were leafed through. Committees and sub-committees were formed which pored over the evidence. Local newspapers reported on parish council meetings across the country. On the agendas, alongside requests to repair the seats around the cricket pitch, local plans to celebrate the Festival of Britain, the installation of street lamps and the provision of bus shelters, was public access to the countryside. Local people were invited to schoolhouses and village halls to discuss and claim *their* paths. Thousands of miles were walked and thousands of miles were mapped, but many paths were missed, often through accident, with some as the result of deliberate subversion.

The origins of this book can be traced back to my walk across the country, to the hundreds of individual paths – the footpaths, country lanes, moorland tracks, wide bridleways and urban alleyways. Coming home on the Caledonian Sleeper, I contemplated what to do next. A strangely perfect answer came a few months later when I saw an opportunity to work at the Ramblers, Britain's walking charity. To help in some small way to protect the paths which had served me so well.[2] I set up and ran a new project – Don't Lose Your Way – an effort to right the wrong, to put back on the map and reclaim for public use paths which had been forgotten in England and Wales.[3] This work was all the more vital ahead of a government-imposed deadline for recording our historic paths. I met a band of inspirational volunteers, dedicated to preserving and protecting public access, and I fell in love with the extraordinary which can be found in the most 'ordinary' of paths.

Years ago, I came across a phrase from the American writer Alfred Barron: 'an old path electrifies . . . weary legs'. It's stuck around inside my head and propelled me to walk the paths, to discover and rediscover their long history. This book is the result. It is an account which, like our path network, branches and diverts and doesn't follow a strictly linear timeline. Our history can be told along our paths – a messy, interleaved story of creation, transformation, loss and reclamation.

2 You can read more about the Ramblers in the Appendix on page 367.
3 The recording of rights of way on definitive maps applies to England and Wales, hence why this book neglects Scotland, where the majority of access to the countryside comes from a right of responsible access (often called the right to roam). There are many wonderful books written, and surely more yet to come, about the paths of Scotland.

Land

1.   Ancient Highways

Solemn, enigmatic monuments lay scattered and stand proud across the ground of England and Wales. Traces of a remote past – the Stone, Bronze and Iron Ages.[1] Sites which attract the curious, the nostalgic and the spiritual. To pace the breadth of stone circles or clamber up grassy mounds, the remains of long-abandoned forts. Grand prehistoric landscapes can be found in remote places, seemingly frozen in time, free from the developments of the modern world. On Dartmoor, where circles, menhirs, cairns and cists rise from plains and slopes of grass and heather. In Wiltshire, at Avebury, a whole land of stones, arranged in circles and avenues; and earth and rock piled up high like at Silbury Hill, the largest man-made mound in Europe. A day's walk south, the world-famous Stonehenge, imperiously grounded next to a busy A-road. Near-neighbours are the Iron Age fortifications which crouch and dominate, such as the vast complex of Hambledon Hill, where walkers climb the encircling ramparts to gaze down across Dorset. Other prehistoric imprints are perhaps less famous and less obvious to the casual observer. Dips and gullies, ranging in subtlety, have left their mark on the ground. Crop marks hazily shine through the surface when the conditions are just right. All these features, big and small, offer tantalizing glimpses

---

1 The Stone Age is broadly defined as running from 12,000 BC to 2200 BC and is split up into the Palaeolithic, Mesolithic and Neolithic. The Bronze Age is from 2200 BC to 800 BC and the Iron Age from 800 BC to AD 43. These times are collectively defined as prehistory, before written language, before the Roman invasion of Britain.

into how our ancestors once lived with and worked the land, telling stories of ritual, strife and community.

The intended purposes of these landmarks is remote from life today. The ramparts and battlements of Iron Age hill forts no longer serve as protection from warring neighbours. Henges, circles and standing stones have, for the most part, ceased to be places of worship or ceremony. Instead, it is the paths leading to, between and around these monuments that continue to act as a connection between our present and this distant past. Paths are the oldest part of our collective heritage still in use for their original purpose. The humble act of walking reveals a remarkable legacy stretching back to prehistory.

Any study of prehistoric England and Wales which only surveys or maps preserved archaeological sites, the stone circles and impressive fortifications overlooks the place of movement. It leaves the story of prehistoric individuals and groups on foot largely untold, ignoring, in the words of anthropologist Tim Ingold, the unfurling of life that can be found 'not in places, but along paths'.

Wild animals were the first path makers. When hunting for food and water, animals push, shove and break through long grass and thick vegetation, finding the easiest contours, the best places to cross and negotiate difficult terrain and rivers. The earliest humans in Britain were able to follow in their wake. These Palaeolithic and Mesolithic people lived in a patchwork landscape. Much more wooded than modern Britain but interspersed with open land and scrub.[2] The lives of these largely nomadic hunters and gatherers were vitally linked to the animals which

2 This was also a time when Britain wasn't an island but was joined to continental Europe. This connecting land, known as Doggerland, was flooded entirely by 6500 BC. Patterns of movement and settlement are now washed

rustled through undergrowth and grazed the grassland.[3] Our ancestors used the animal tracks, which became, over time, people tracks, and along these paths they collected nuts, seeds, herbs and berries and followed these slight paths to water, where fish could be caught and shellfish gathered. From the paths they stalked, trapped and killed their prey, including deer, elk, hares and seals.

These earliest paths are the most difficult to tease out, having been lost in the noise of subsequent generations. In a few extraordinary places, though, the precise footsteps of our ancestors have been captured and preserved. In 2014, at Port Eynon in the Gower Peninsula in Wales, a storm stripped back the sand to reveal a layer of hidden peat. First whole tree trunks emerged, then a series of slightly irregular rounded impressions on an ancient surface. These are the imprints of feet left in boggy ground by a group of adults and children, placed some 7,000 years ago. Running alongside the human footprints were traces of wild animals – red deer, boars and young aurochs (and a solitary print from a wolf or dog).[4] The animal and human prints are moving in the same direction, the remains of a Mesolithic hunting party.[5]

---

under the North Sea and the Channel, ground which saw some of the very earliest loss of paths.

3 Recent excavations have uncovered concentrations of artefacts associated with the Mesolithic period, which suggest that people did stay in some places for short periods of time. So perhaps some of these people were not entirely nomadic, but by no means could they be described as settled. It is likely that they may have moved between sites on a seasonal basis.

4 The aurochs are the extinct oxen of Europe, from which our modern cattle are most likely descended.

5 Happisburgh in Norfolk takes the prize for the oldest footprints in Britain – in fact, the oldest hominid footprints anywhere in the world outside Africa. By analysing pollen samples, we can demonstrate that prints left here between

Around 4000 BC, Britain saw the first widespread domestica-
tion of plants and animals, the production of pottery, the
building of monuments and nomadism starting to give way to
settlement. The monuments of this age served as fixed points in
the landscape of prehistoric communities, significant places
along the paths. Avebury henge, a massive complex at nearly
three quarters of a mile around, is formed of a series of banks
and ditches which swaddle a later medieval village. Inside, Britain's largest stone circle comprises ninety-eight standing stones.
There are four breaks in the henge, through which modern
roads run. Two of these have long processional paths leading up
to them – old ways flanked with standing stones (the West
Kennet and Beckhampton Avenues). The break in the east aligns
with an old track called Greenstreet, which carries on up to a
ridge one and a half miles away – evidence that Avebury henge
was specifically placed at a crossroads. The exact purpose of the
henge, and of the paths so intimately connected to it, continues
to be a source of speculation and discussion. Given the huge
amount of work involved in its construction (the outer circle
has stones that weigh up to 40 tonnes), the henge almost certainly played an important ritual or ceremonial role in the lives
of the people who walked the paths to come here.

And yet, from this age of settlement we also start to see more
concrete evidence of mobility and the first tentatively datable
paths. In the late 1990s there was a fight over the decision to build
a second runway at Manchester Airport. Protestors, dubbed 'eco-
warriors' by the press, set up camp at the proposed site, chaining
themselves to treetops while digging (and living in) a network of
underground tunnels and chambers. This battle was ultimately
lost, but before the contractors started work, archaeologists came

---

850,000 and 950,000 years ago were made not by *Homo sapiens* but by the early
human species *Homo antecessor*.

in to survey and dig the site. They excavated a path, worn down by the passage of centuries of feet, at the very bottom of which lay objects from the Bronze Age – a clear indication that the erosion by people had taken place before these items had collected there. This distinctive, dated path from the Neolithic is now buried somewhere under a two-mile concrete runway, lost for ever.

The village of Ansty is spread along a road which runs through the chalk hills of central Dorset: a well-ordered ribbon of housing where you can't quite work out where one village stops and another begins. Ansty means 'path for one' or 'narrow track' – an appropriate place to venture out to walk one of the reputed (and disputed) great highways of prehistoric England. It is mid-morning, and this walk begins like many others being undertaken on this bright June day across the country. I walk alongside my friend Liv, dodging the occasional car, from green lane to bridleway and then footpath. Fields, untidy hedgerows, tarmac and grass. We stop to greet two long-faced rams and then, turning at a farm gate, we press on straight, directly up the face of the chalk hill to the top of an escarpment.

Behind us is the verdant Blackmore Vale, the land of Tess of the d'Urbervilles, Hardy's 'engirdled and secluded region, for the most part untrodden as yet by tourist or landscape-painter', where 'the fields are never brown and the springs never dry'. Looking north we are facing the direction of some of the islands of prehistoric settlement which dot Dorset. Under two miles away is Bulbarrow Hill, the remains of an Iron Age hill fort, and five miles further still over the downland, the assertive features of Hambledon Hill.

Facing away from this vale, we look south into a valley of chalk, scooped out like the bowl of a dessert spoon. Across this amphitheatre a thin corona of cloudy summer sun tops the distant

hills, a glowing line across the horizon. We make our way along
the narrow hilltop and I can see where recent walkers have made
their own paths, negotiated their own ways, step by step along the
steep bank. I choose the wrong route, larger steps required to
overcome thick solid tussocks, although it does mean that I stumble across, and almost on, a heath spotted orchid, pink-hearted
and creamy white against the dusky green grass. Moving along
this escarpment, on the strip of land between two valleys, we are
walking the path which for centuries was most associated with
prehistoric people on foot: a ridgeway.

This route is marked out on the Ordnance Survey map as the
Wessex Ridgeway, and occasionally on posts by the path with
plastic waymark discs emblazoned with an upright, serious-
looking dragon (perhaps a nod to where this path begins, on the
south coast near Lyme Regis, where it climbs directly up Drag-
ons Hill). This long waymarked path is part of a much longer
posited ridgeway, a sash that splits south and eastern England –
from the Dorset coast to the East Anglian Wash. This longer
path has been named the Greater Ridgeway (sometimes the
Greater Icknield Way). Under this Greater umbrella, a meandering line has been traced on the map, a collection of modern
long-distance leisure paths.[6]

The idea of this long prehistoric path captured the imagination
of romantics, writers, poets and antiquarians of the nineteenth
and early twentieth centuries. They regarded this Greater

6 This long chain of paths starts with the Wessex Ridgeway, and then connects with the Ridgeway National Trail near Avebury in Wiltshire. The
Ridgeway then runs through four counties to Buckinghamshire at which
point the Icknield Way takes over, ending just outside Thetford in Norfolk.
The 'Greater Ridgeway' then makes a distinct northward turn. Here it
becomes what looks like a straight line through the landscape on a path called
the Peddars Way (or perhaps on an alignment roughly parallel to the Peddars
Way), which reaches the North Sea.

Ridgeway as *the* primordial path. Travel writer H. V. Morton, when addressing the East Anglian stretch of the path, writes of it being 'planned before history began'. A path which has seen 'the stone weapon give way to metal', which has 'nursed the dawning of civilisation . . . first a savage trail, then a road'. For the Victorian writer Richard Jefferies, it was a special path for significant journeys in prehistory:

A broad green track runs for many a long, long mile across the Downs, now following the ridges, now winding past at the foot of a grassy slope, then stretching away through cornfield and fallow. It is distinct from the waggon-tracks which cross it here and there, for these are local only . . . The origin of the track goes back into the dimmest antiquity; there is evidence that it was a military road when the fierce Dane carried fire and slaughter inland, leaving his 'nailed bark' in the creeks of the rivers, and before that when the Saxons pushed up from the sea. The eagles of old Rome, perhaps, were borne along it, and yet earlier the chariots of the Britons may have used it – traces of all have been found; so that for fifteen centuries this track of the primitive peoples has maintained its existence through the strange changes of the times.

Many of these romantic writers pieced together this path, hundreds of miles long, from what they could see in the landscape. They plotted barrows, stone circles and henges, ascribing them a significance in relation to the Greater Ridgeway – monuments as ritual markers on the path. They saw prehistoric man (and it always was 'man') striding along the ridges, passing these sacred places and avoiding marsh, bog and swamp in the valleys below.[7] Perhaps this man would be carrying a small collection

7 The idea of prehistoric swamps perhaps came down to these romantics from the Roman historians. Herodian writes that 'most of the regions of Britain are

of stone axes, or some other valuable items, in his bag to trade at
the furthest end of this long continuous track. To poet Edward
Thomas these men were 'early nomads' walking from island to
island of high ground on a path which 'ran along the back of
each one and branched over the spurs . . . highways of great
length, like that trodden by Launcelot, "far o'er the long backs
of the bushless downs" to Camelot'.

Considering this ancient track, I turn towards the trees at the
end of the escarpment, where a series of terraces has been cut
into the ground next to the path. These are strip lynchets (from
the Old English *hlinc* – 'ridges', 'bank' or 'rising ground').[8] They
have been formed over many years for cultivating the ground,
either deliberately created or through the action of hundreds of
years of ploughing and pushing the earth down into lines which
band the side of the hill. These distinctive marks help define the
features they surround, exposing the shape of farmsteads, enclosures and their paths – the trackways of this small community.
This chalk landscape holds indentations well, and there are further features scattered around this area which give clues to
prehistoric settlement. Along the ridge is the ghost of Nettle-
combe Tout, another Iron Age fort, formed with a long rampart
and a ditch ten feet deep.[9] The top of the next valley along is
braided by a series of cross dykes which cut across the valley
ridge. These Iron Age earthworks were likely to have been

---

marshy, since they are flooded continually by the tides of the ocean' and that
'the barbarians are accustomed to swimming or wading through these waist-
deep marsh pools'. Cassius Dio writes that the tribes of Britain 'inhabit wild
and waterless mountains and desolate and swampy plains'.

8 The same word, via Scots, leads to 'links' to describe a golf course.

9 The prominent fort also features briefly in *Tess of the d'Urbervilles* : 'If Tess
were made rich by marrying a gentleman, would she have money enough to
buy a spy-glass so large that it would draw the stars as near to her as Nettle-
combe Tout?'

defensive, blocking the approaches to the fort, or perhaps marking the territory of the people who inhabited this area.

And beyond, over the gently rippling chalk downland to the south-east, eight miles towards the fractal inlets of Poole Harbour, can be found the largest unenclosed pre-Roman settlement in Britain. Archaeologists have uncovered a community who lived together in the late Iron Age, in hundreds of densely packed roundhouses alongside outbuildings and animal pens. This settlement is named Duropolis after the local tribe. The Durotriges were, like most Iron Age people, farmers and probably controlled a territory which stretched from the River Axe in the west to the Avon in the east. The location of Duropolis is important in giving more complexity and nuance to the picture of prehistoric Britain than the idea of the Ridgeway implies. It is not high up at the top of the hills but set on gently sloping ground. When the Romans came, they found people spread widely across a varied landscape, not just encamped on high ground.

On the ridge above Ansty, we leave the sun, plunging into leaf-darkened woodland and an extraordinary meeting of paths. Here there is a depression in the escarpment and the Wessex Ridgeway joins us again, dipping briefly with the ridge. There is a disorientating star-shaped junction of paths known as the Dorsetshire Gap. On the map, four clear rights of way come together, but spinning around from one to the other it is difficult to keep track of them. They are deep holloways, natural geological depressions greatly aided in their depth by the pounding and scraping of generations of feet and hooves. Corridors galleried with moss-creeped beech and ash wind away from the Gap, sinking out of sight. Wooded depressions in the soil that recall a line from George Eliot's *Adam Bede*: 'hollow-shaped, earthy paths . . . paths which look as if they were made by the free will of the trees and underwood, moving reverently aside'.

This is a world almost turned upside down, a place where you look up, not down, to see tree roots; where the beginnings of the undergrowth and leaf litter is ten feet above your head, and the ground slants at extraordinary angles. Climbing carefully to the top of one of the banks, taking the obvious way where someone or something has gone before, I take some photos of Liv, her figure far below, dwarfed by the immensity of the surroundings. It feels as though the sun may never reach the furthest depths of the holloways, that the leaves, if it weren't for the free-draining chalk soil, would never fully dry. The actual walked paths are thin at the bottom of the holloways, hemmed in by just-wilting wild garlic. The V-shape of these deep paths suggests that they have been formed by the passage of single people (or perhaps small groups) or horses rather than carts or herds of animals.

We walk back and forth down the paths, always drawn back to the centre of the Dorsetshire Gap. This is a meeting point of paths, a place for continuing journeys. The settlements that have been uncovered in the neighbouring lonely valleys and beyond suggest a landscape which, at least in the Iron Age, was alive with activity, with people moving between farmstead and field and between settlements and fortifications. Rather than a point on a signature ancient highway which stretched unimpeded across southern England, the Dorsetshire Gap is part of this complex prehistoric network – local, regional, national and international.

Our understanding of this web of paths emerges more clearly with the aid of modern archaeological techniques. We no longer have to rely on mapping large impressive monuments in the landscape to piece together our prehistoric history. Through analysing the isotopes found in bone and teeth, we can see evidence that animals were driven across Britain, over significant distances, to henges in Dorset and Wiltshire, and that a man buried close to Stonehenge in the third millennium BC had journeyed from what is now Germany. Analysing DNA has enabled us to see indications that early Neolithic farmers had genetic links with central Europe and the Iberian Peninsula. We also understand much more about the economies and societies of our prehistory. A stone axe would be unlikely to travel from Norfolk to here in Dorset on one long journey but instead made its way slowly across England, passed between people over years and sometimes generations. An object which would be used to cement relationships between a succession of neighbouring groups – exchanged from one hand to another, carried along one path to the next.

In the Dorsetshire Gap we are all alone, hidden in the trees, the only walkers seemingly for miles. But a plastic box to the side of this crossroads bears witness to others having come before. Alongside an abandoned beer bottle, a notebook has been left, a record of visits to the Dorsetshire Gap. This is one notebook in a long chain which goes back to at least the 1970s, taken away when full to be stored carefully somewhere. The recent notes record long attachment to the Gap ('I have been coming here for forty years or so, on and off. It's always beautiful. Always healing') and discovery of this place ('Londoners enjoying the air, the view, the peace and a walk with our kids'). There are touching messages in the time of Covid, intrusions of the world away from these woods: 'Good luck and good health', 'stay safe' and 'I'm writing this with gloves on', and a more worrying one: 'DO NOT TAKE THE BILL GATES CHIPPED VACCINE – IT WILL BE THE MARK OF THE BEAST'. To this last one, I can only agree with the comment left in the book by a subsequent visitor: 'NEED ANY MORE TINFOIL?'[10]

Perhaps it was the realities of modern pandemic Britain that broke the spell keeping us in the Dorsetshire Gap. Taking a

10 I received my second vaccine exactly thirty-seven days after visiting the Dorsetshire Gap, a wonderful blast of Pfizer.

bridleway south-west, if anything the path drops even more impressively into the earth, and for 800 feet or so we are walking in a hart's-tongue-fern-lined canyon, emerging into the open air in the bottom of this scoop of land. The recorded rights of way run along and up the bulging and swirling contour lines, smooth serpentine paths. But even around the Dorsetshire Gap, paths have disappeared from the map.

The Ordnance Survey map from 1900 shows lost bridleways and footpaths on these chalk hills. One of these lost paths heads straight for the deserted medieval village of Melcombe Horsey and the manor of the same name. This land used to belong to the Binghams, who give their name to the parish, a family which married into the Turbervilles, the surname claimed, with a slight change, by Hardy for the eponymous Tess. We are now standing where the old path came down from the escarpment, where a community disappeared maybe 600 years ago. A large farmhouse with a scattering of outbuildings is all that remains, next to the neat plot of complex lumps and pitted earth. The whole abandoned village lies under a grass coat. An access road now runs from the farm out of the valley. The modern tarmac is to the right of two lines of trees which appear to mark the course of an older path. This leaves a wide high bank of grass stained with soft lines of where people have walked before, under the shade of russet copper beeches.

'Once a highway, always a highway'; this legal maxim governs the saving of lost and forgotten paths. All public rights of way are highways – footpaths just as much as your local high street or the A1. A landowner who blocks a seemingly inconsequential stretch of footpath is obstructing the King's Highway.[11] To

---

11 Upon the death of Elizabeth II in 2022, the Queen's Highway automatically became the King's Highway, in the same way that senior lawyers went from

legally reclaim our lost paths we need to demonstrate use by the public in the past, evidence of use that can stretch back to time immemorial. However, the past has its limits. The term 'time immemorial' feels like it should describe something so distant in the past that we can't quite grapple with it, something indubitably ancient. In fact, the Statute of Westminster of 1275 defined time immemorial to a precise date, 6 July 1189, when Richard the Lionheart acceded to the throne. Any evidence of use before this date is disregarded in efforts to save and reclaim lost paths.[12]

The path from the abandoned medieval village of Melcombe Horsey heads directly to the Dorsetshire Gap, a meeting of two prehistoric paths – part of the same network but separated by thousands of years. Continuity comes from human instinct. In one island, 80,000 miles square, people have settled in not *too* dissimilar places and they have needed to communicate, hunt, farm

---

being QCs to KCs. The King's Highway has an interesting intersection with the mythology of the Greater Ridgeway. The Icknield Way section of the Greater Ridgeway can trace its foundational legend back to the twelfth century, when historians turned their thoughts to the history of our paths and tracks. Henry of Huntingdon, in his *Historia Anglorum*, writes of 'four highways' of England, with regal protection 'on which no one should dare attack his enemy'. Three of these are identifiably Roman roads: Ermine Street, the Fosse Way and Watling Street, and the fourth is the mysterious 'Ichenild'. Geoffrey of Monmouth, writing in the same decade, embellishes the legend of Icknield Way further. He assigns the creation of the 'four highways', as physical routes and zones of protection, to Dunwallo Molmutius, a mythical ruler who 'excelled all the kings of Britain in valour and gracefulness of person'. The protection that these highways supposedly offered was part of an entirely mythological package of fundamental laws laid down by King Molmutius.

12 There is a certain irony that this date for claiming public rights of way was set at the beginning of the reign of a king who hardly ever rode the paths and roads of England. It is estimated that on becoming king he only spent about six months in the country.

and trade. Our oldest paths are spread across the map, in the valleys and on the ridges – paths used in prehistory folded into and under our current rights of way and road network. 'Modern' paths we follow for a summer stroll in Dorset may have under them strata of thousands of years of movement, reaching much further back than time immemorial.

2. Animals

The meadow is broad, and drifts of common bent grass give a purple-hued smudge to the horizon. We create our own path through, heading towards a ten-foot-wide woodland-flanked track. The woods are reassuringly thick – coppiced oak alongside maple, aspen, birch and hawthorn. Along with my friend Anna, I am searching for two things: the grey scaly bark and spiked leaves of the wild service tree, growing somewhere in these ancient woodlands, and a lost, almost forgotten lane.

This is a small surviving patch of Bernwood Forest, in Buckinghamshire's Vale of Aylesbury. A royal hunting ground established by the Saxon kings. In my mind this ancient forest would have extended for hundreds of miles just like this: thick, green and dense. Monumental. In reality this land was more akin to a royal reserve, with woods of varying density interspersed with open ground, the perfect environment for the royal pursuit of deer and wild boar.[1] It is from Bernwood Forest that we have the earliest surviving depiction of an English village.[2] It's a map which puts hunting at its heart (older sources link the village's name, Boarstall, to this hunting; however, more modern historians trace its derivation to the Old English for 'the site of a stronghold' – burh-stall). Shown are a church and a tower, some fields, a small network of roads and houses in hedge-ringed plots. To the sides are the surrounding great forest, deer walking and resting amid the trees. Several oversized figures are depicted in

1 The etymological root of 'forest' is *foris*, which just means 'outside'.
2 The map is dated to at least 1444 but may be much older still.

the foreground. One is kneeling: Nigel the Forester of Bernewode. He is presenting the head of a fearsome boar impaled on a sword. A beast which had terrified the people of the forest. The man accepting this bloody gift: Edward the Confessor.

Bernwood Forest was Edward's favourite hunting ground; Kings Henry II and John were also fans. This was a place reserved for them, land for the king's use. The royal connections persist in its place names. To the west is Kingswood. There are myths and memories of a track between the trees somewhere near this hamlet, a path called Rosiman's Waye – named after the supposed mistress of Henry II, Rosamund Clifford. It is said that Henry built a complicated maze in the park at Woodstock in Oxfordshire to hide his beautiful mistress from Queen Eleanor (who was pregnant with Henry's seventh child when the affair is reputed to have begun in 1165), but the queen found out and managed to negotiate the twisting paths of what was known as the Bower of Fair Rosamund. She confronted her rival and forced her to choose death by dagger or a bowl of poison. Rosamund took the poison and died at the heart of Henry's maze. The tale of Rosamund's death is almost certainly a fantasy, a slandering of Eleanor as a callous murderer by later chroniclers. It's a fairy-tale archetype – the jealous older queen poisoning her younger rival, set in a landscape of folk horror, shadowy woods and dark labyrinthine paths.

This part of Bernwood is today called Ham Home Wood, one of the patches of the royal forest which survives in Oxfordshire and Buckinghamshire. As important as their historical significance is, their role now as precious habitat islands – small niches which support rare hoverflies, moths, butterflies and beetles. The wood clings to the north side of Akeman Street, a Roman road linking up with Watling Street and the Fosse Way, a connection between the Roman settlements at Cirencester (Corinium Dobunnorum) and St Albans (Verulamium). Along the eastern side of the wood, there is a narrow strip of land which runs clear of the trees and northward up Oving Hill – marked on my Ordnance Survey map as 'Oxford Lane (Track)'. The border between wood and lane has all but disappeared, with blackthorn drifting across the boundary and grey willow suckering on both sides. I can't get up the lane; a dense thicket of nettles and a gate now bar the way to public access. Yet hundreds of years ago this lane, passing through the venerable Bernwood, would have been thundering with the sound of hooves, my view from this roadside obscured in a swirl of dust. The Oxford Lane was once a local drove road, intended for transporting animals, one of hundreds of similar paths that connected pasture and field to village, town and city.

I've been led here by Bruce Smith, who has been 'collecting' (and walking) drove roads across England and Wales since 2005. Bruce has traced sections of the Oxford Lane cutting across Northamptonshire, Oxfordshire and Buckinghamshire – some now major and minor roads, others recorded public rights of way and others simply lost. Turning from the gate, we venture towards Wotton Underwood village to see if we can find any continuation of the Oxford Lane south of Akeman Street.[3] It's a hunt in the landscape for part of this old path, to walk in the footsteps and hoof prints which have come before. The area is crossed by recorded public rights of way, patterns of movement from the last few centuries which have stood, captured in time, on the map and on the ground. We walk on a concrete path through the centre of the community, the fluffy seeds from a row of poplar trees turning the path from grey to white. A small smattering of houses and a church collect around the grand

---

3 The 'Underwood' is a further sign of the parish's relationship with Bernwood. Previous names for this community include 'Wotton juxta Bernewode' and 'Wotton subtus Bernewode'.

Wotton House, a solid rectangular manor. This doesn't have the feel of a typical English village; the homes are huddled together but isolated from the rest of the world at the centre of this grand estate. In their own secluded bubble. Along this path once stood a row of cottages and smallholdings. In the early eighteenth century, the lord of three local manors, Richard Grenville, built the first Wotton House, overseeing hundreds of farmers on his sprawling lands. Three decades later, his son of the same name was elected to Parliament and obtained an Act to enclose the land. Some 1,668 acres of 'common fields, Lawns, Wastes and uninclosed [sic] Grounds', along with many of the residents, were swept away.

People's homes and livelihoods were replaced with a new, fashionable 'natural' landscape, in this instance a wide avenue, grotto and lake designed by the most in-demand landscaper of the time, Lancelot 'Capability' Brown. A later owner of the Wotton Estate, the third Duke of Buckingham and Chandos, revived the village somewhat by building a school and a post office.[4] He also used the estate to indulge his passion for railways, building several lines across it (one of these lines, the Brill Tramway, would become part of the London Underground for two years in the 1930s before it closed for good). On our walk we stumble across a narrow-gauge track, part of the Wotton Light Railway – a private line owned and operated by a high court judge as a hobby.

Given so many centuries of change, it is no wonder we can't find a trace of the Oxford Lane. Perhaps it did run here before

4 The school was closed in 1968 after a further period of decline for the village. A plaque in the church bitterly describes the change: 'This school and its predecessor served Wotton children from 1790 until 1968. After 1948, when the estate was sold, the character of the village entirely changed. Most of the villagers were unwillingly turned out of it, and the number of scholars diminished until the school could no longer continue.'

the land was enclosed, or maybe it linked into the network at Akeman Street. The lane's ultimate destination, thirteen miles to the south-west, was Oxford, a city whose fortunes had, by the seventeenth century, become intertwined with the university. Indeed, it is likely that the final destination for the animals was to be the tables of Oxford college dining halls.[5] But first, they had to go to the city's slaughterhouses. Originally the killing and butchery would have happened right on the street, specifically the prime pedestrianized shopping avenue of Oxford – Queen Street (then, unsurprisingly, known as Butcher's Row). By the fourteenth century, the butchers had been relocated away from the city centre streets. First to the shambles just outside the city walls, where they slung the 'entrails of Beasts' into a nearby stream (an act described as an 'extreme negligence'), and then to Oxford's new covered market.[6]

We are hidden away from the gory slaughter of the animals we eat and also from how they are transported to our plates. In an age when our food arrives by lorry, plane and delivery van, it is difficult to imagine the sheer number of animals that were being moved on the ground in past centuries and the impact they had on the everyday rural landscape. Drovers' roads are most associated with great herds of cows but they also carried sheep for their wool (and meat), and geese and turkeys, with their feet protectively dipped in tar and covered in sand – driven to London from August onwards in time for the Christmas dinner table. Pigs struggled up the paths, barely managing to walk ten miles a day, and donkeys were ferried over from Ireland to join

5 Perhaps they were served alongside the turbot in lobster sauce, veal pie and fruit fool at the legendary banquet given for the Duke of Portland at Christ Church College in 1793.
6 'Shambles' is an archaic name for a slaughterhouse, a word preserved in the name of a famously picturesque street in York. The Shambles of York, like Queen Street in Oxford, no longer has any butcher shops.

the menagerie.[7] Sometimes drovers rode on horseback (the cow-
boys of Britain) and they usually travelled with dogs to keep the
animals in check. Welsh drovers favoured corgis, a breed chosen
for their comical closeness to the ground, which meant they
could avoid the kick of a bullock. There are even tales of drovers
travelling home by coach and letting their dogs find their own
way back across the country, where, along the way, they would
be fed and watered in the drovers' inns. One dog, Carlo, was
recorded as being sent back to Wales with a pony's harness on its
back, his owner having sold the pony, and a note for innkeepers
asking for him to be looked after on the way. The skills of the
drover's dog are evident in an incident relayed by Delabere
P. Blaine in his *Encyclopaedia of Rural Sports*, which saw a dog
drive a pack of sheep and oxen nine miles to market in Alston in
Cumbria – completely unaccompanied.

The number of animals involved is staggering – almost 19,000
cows alone passed through Carlisle in 1663; Daniel Defoe
recorded 150,000 turkeys travelling from Norfolk to London in
1724; and a single tollbooth in Wiltshire registered payment for
over 14,000 pigs in 1830. These great forced migrations would
have been unmissable in the open countryside. In *Far from the
Madding Crowd*, Thomas Hardy describes the experience of
sheep converging on a fair: 'When the autumn sun slanted over
Greenhill this morning and lighted the dewy flat upon its crest,
nebulous clouds of dust were to be seen floating between the
pairs of hedges which streaked the wide prospect around in all
directions.' To add to the visual spectacle would be the noise:
the cries of the beasts, the barking of dogs and the cracking of

7 Another animal which perhaps used the Oxford Lane was the famous
Aylesbury duck, flocks of which were driven the forty miles to London from
their homeland in the Vale of Aylesbury.

whips.[8] The sound of the drovers themselves was described in one account as 'something out of the common, neither shouting, calling, crying, singing, hallowing or anything else, but a noise of itself . . . made to carry and capable of arresting the countryside'.

Now, in slightly quieter times, I am exploring the suburbs of Daventry in Northamptonshire. Five thousand years ago, the Scots pine was driven out of England by a warming climate and retreated to its native Scotland as well as more remote parts of Wales (as John Evelyn wrote in *Sylva*, his 1664 treatise on forestry, 'the worst land in Wales bears (as I am told) large pines'). Standing in front of a nursing home in Daventry, I'm looking up at two Scots pines which appear to be well over 200 years old. With their tall evergreen canopies rising high above the more common deciduous trees, these pines are an indication that there was once an inn for drovers here, the Wheatsheaf. The cones of these trees may have been carried in the pockets of the drovers on journeys from Wales or Scotland. Pines were planted as welcome waymarkers, letting fellow drovers know they could stop for the night (or planted to signal good pasture and safe river crossings). Inside an inn such as this, drovers could expect to find a comforting fire, a hot meal (on one drove road leading to a fair, the inn had 'vast stores of provisions, notably gigantic pies with standing walls of crust of preternatural toughness and thickness') and ale (the financial accounts of a drover in 1841 record a pint costing 3p). After a meal and drink, the head drover would retire to bed, but the lowlier members of the droving party would often not stay inside, banished to spend the night in a nearby barn or huddled up under a hedge.

8 While whips were used on large animals, such as cattle and donkeys, sticks would have been used to 'persuade' sheep along. The 1890 census lists quite a few 'ankle beaters', the men who wielded the sticks.

This largely forgotten inn, with its majestic pine trees, is now marooned, divorced from its history. It stands at a point on the Oxford Lane almost thirty miles from Wotton Underwood and thirteen miles to Oxford (it is also possible that the Oxford Lane went further north than Daventry but we simply don't know). Daventry has long been a crossroads in a much larger story of our paths. Defoe, in his 1720s tour of Britain, identified it as 'subsisting chiefly by the great concourse of travellers on the old Watling-street way'. Today Daventry is a key node in a system of global trade. The Daventry International Rail Freight Terminal (blandly acronymized to DIRFT), opened by Princess Anne in 1997, is a massive road and rail terminal on the western edge of town. Mushrooming around the terminal are gigantic distribution centres of up to 1 million square feet – a home for Amazon, Sainsbury's, Tesco and DHL (described by Jonathan Glancey, the *Guardian*'s architecture correspondent, as 'one of the most extraordinary places in contemporary Britain . . . the modern equivalent of medieval tithe barns').

Trade routes, which now depend on connections around the globe, began to spread within Britain from at least the early medieval period and probably before. The most well-known routes brought cattle from the Scottish Highlands and the mountainous interior of Wales – places that, according to Adam Smith, 'seem destined by nature to be the breeding countries of Great Britain' – to the south of England for sale. One of the earliest records we have of these routes is of two Scottish men, Alan Erskyn and Andrew Moray, who were given the freedom of the king to drive horses, oxen and cows south to England in 1359. The journeys lasted months, with drovers passing through hundreds of small communities. The drover often presented as a remote, romantic figure as he strode behind the herd dressed in his smock or thick tweed, legs clad in leather or woollen stockings (sometimes with an extra outer wrapping of brown paper).

These were skilled men – one record from 1742 calls droving an 'art and mystery' – with the men needing to know how to handle all the animals in their care, a shrewd eye for a deal and a good sense of the land and countryside; their skills even extended to knitting as they walked along behind the animals.

While on the whole they were treated with respect, this was tempered by some suspicion. The drover was an outsider, his life potentially subversive. Rootless people seemed a threat to the countryside's settled order, an idea that informed the long history of 'vagrancy' laws in Britain from the aftermath of the Peasants' Revolt to the present day. It was one of the earliest vagrancy laws that saw long-distance droving become a formalized trade. From the reign of Elizabeth I, drovers had to be licensed and able to prove that they were fit and proper men who could be trusted to wander the country's paths and roads. The conditions of achieving a licence are a picture of Tudor ideals of good character. A drover would be male, a homeowner (it wouldn't be seen as wise for the poor to move around too much) and married (to try to avoid any romances blossoming with local women on the way).

This respectability meant that the drovers' journeys, and their paths, became avenues for supporting the wider economy. A drover travelling from Wales to London carried large amounts of money, either in the form of the animals themselves (on the way down) or as hard cash (on the way back). They were also entrusted with other people's finances – rents from Welsh estates were carried to landlords in London, and the drovers became government agents by conveying Charles I's 'Ship Money' tax to the capital.[9] The routes often took drovers through remote, dangerous territory, and stories abound of them being robbed.

9 Ship Money was levied by Charles I on the coastal counties of England to pay for a strengthened navy during peace time. It was a hated tax that

The *Berkshire Chronicle* reported a theft in 1859 which 'caused a good deal of excitement' and saw an Irish drover robbed of £23 and thrown in a pond. Five years earlier, would-be thieves tried to commit a 'daring highway robbery' on Mr Richard Vowe Webster but they were left empty-handed as the drover had had the foresight to 'put his purse in his mouth'.[10]

Eventually, in order to avoid transporting large sums of cash, drovers began accepting and carrying notes promising cash in exchange – in effect, the start of our modern banking system. In 1799, David Jones, a successful Welsh drover and cattle dealer, started the Banc yr Eidion Ddu (the Bank of the Black Ox), featuring the eponymous beast on the banknotes. Other drover banks included the Craven Bank in North Yorkshire, which displayed the Craven heifer (a large rotund ox standing in front of Bolton Abbey), and the Bank of the Black Sheep in Aberystwyth (where the number of sheep on the note corresponded to the value in pounds).[11]

It wasn't just money that the drovers carried, but passengers too. In Wales, there is evidence of prisoners being strapped to cattle to take them from Harlech on the Gwynedd coast to court in Welshpool (a journey of at least sixty miles). More happily there was also a tradition of young men travelling with drovers to see, understand and explore the country – a slightly more pedestrian version of the European grand tour – an experience

---

contributed to resentment against the king and which, in part, led to the English Civil War and Charles's ultimate downfall on the scaffold in Whitehall.

10 As reported in the *Leicestershire Mercury*.

11 In his book *Hard Road to London: A Graphic Account of the Lives of the Welsh Drovers*, Idris Evans also speculates that the famous Lloyds Bank prancing black horse has a droving origin. The black horse, in 2015, was given 'an emotive backstory' by the ad agency Adam & Eve, which included ploughing a field, serving in the First World War and delivering a happy couple to a church – but droving was conspicuously absent.

which seemed to have been enhanced by the 'rustic' mode of travel and companions. At other times passengers accompanied the drovers for safety rather than exploration. In the 1850s, Jane Evans from Caeo in Carmarthenshire travelled with drovers down to London so she could set sail for the Black Sea. Jane was to join Florence Nightingale and Mary Seacole nursing soldiers in the Crimean War, though it's interesting to note that some accounts record her as being a drover herself and, indeed, the first female of the profession.

The roads and paths of the drovers were understandably one of the country's most important conduits for information. Drovers brought letters (for a price), gossip and news (especially political news from the capital) to the small, often remote communities they passed through. In places they also brought their language – to this day the thatched drovers' inn in Stockbridge, Hampshire (now a private Grade II listed house), has painted across it the Welsh words *GWAIR TYMHERUS PORFA FLASAS CWRW DA A CWAL CYSRUS* ('good grass, pleasant pasture, good beer and a comfortable bed').

While London was the prime destination for most long-distance drovers, they were not averse to trading their wares along the way. This meant that markets and fairs were crucial nodes in the drovers' network, and the two had rather different functions. The market was, in a modern sense, a place for one's weekly shop. Fairs, on the other hand, were exciting events held annually or perhaps several times a year. It was the fair that most drovers aimed for, where they would join with local traders, farmers and inhabitants from the area. They often started as quasi-religious festivals – pagan, then Christian – sometimes taking place right in the churchyard, during the octave (the eight days following a saint's day, and often the saint associated with that parish). They blossomed into something much more secular – events to make money, to mix with people from outside of your immediate community and, in true British fashion, to enjoy yourself.[12]

Almost anything could be bought at the fair; indeed, in some places, some items couldn't be bought outside of it. With the sheer scale of wheeling and dealing (at one fair in Halifax in the nineteenth century, a man was seen to count out nearly £1,000 pounds after a deal), it's not surprising that disputes, fighting and theft were common. Fairs had their own form of justice: the piepowder courts. These tribunals were established during the time of the fair to settle disputes and punish wrongdoing; fines, the pillory and the seizure of goods were common punishments. The odd name of these courts comes from the mode of travel by which most, drovers included, arrived at the fair – on foot. 'Piepowder' is mangled from the French *pieds poudrés* for 'dusty feet' (in France, *pieds poudreux* is still sometimes used to describe a vagabond – similar to our word 'tramp').

Over time the commercial focus of these fairs waned and fun came to the fore. While they remained at their traditional locations, connected by the drove roads, from the nineteenth century the great sale of livestock was largely replaced by waxworks, boxing, freakshows and theatrical displays. In the twentieth century, budding technologies were maximized for entertainment, such as early cinema (attractions included Biddall's Royal Bioscope and Arnold Bros Picturedome) and electrical displays (Dr Walford Bodie, with his assistant La Belle Electra, demonstrated his 'electric chair' – apparently passing 30,000 volts through his body), and an audience in Yorkshire enjoyed rides in their first motorcar in 'Mrs Hannah

12 In Scotland, these fairs were known as trysts – a word whose origin branches off from the etymological tree of 'trust' – a safe place to meet or wait. Perhaps this meeting of people from between communities still lingers on in the modern meaning of a meeting of lovers.

Waddington's Motorcar Switchback'.[13] Some fairs live on – the Nottingham Goose Fair (historically the destination for thousands of geese driven from the Fens) still attracts about half a million visitors a year.

In the Quantock Hills in Somerset, the passage of the drovers has left a marked impression, with signs of the past ever-present. A path follows a ridge along the hills, passing a Bronze Age barrow and stone cairns. From it, one can look down north and west to the village of Nether Stowey and a thickly forested wood marked with evocative and intriguing names – Dibble's Elbow, Knacker's Elbow and Dead Woman's Ditch.[14] This ancient route was first used as a herepath, a Saxon military path, but it is the drovers who have left the greatest mark here, quite literally. The track itself has been scoured out, with two distinctive levels. The deepest, several feet down, has been worn away by the passage of the hundreds of thousands of animals that walked here over centuries. The higher level, just above, is still visibly worn away and hollowed out when compared to the surrounding ground. I like to think that this is where the drovers themselves would have walked – they certainly wouldn't have wanted to get caught in the deep ditch below with their cattle. Bordering the way is an extraordinary hedge of beech. Once these trees would have been an effective barrier to stop

13 Another 'wonder' from Dr Bodie was the now-standard trick of performing 'bloodless surgery'. He eventually ran afoul of the medical profession who sued him for using the titles 'Doctor' and 'MD'. Despite claiming that 'MD' stood for 'Merry Devil', Bodie lost the case and was later chased out of a Glasgow performance by 1,000 rioting students to the cries of 'Bodie, Bodie, Bodie, Quack, Quack, Quack'.

14 It was in Nether Stowey that Coleridge, despite his usual association with the Lake District, wrote two of his most famous poems: *Kubla Khan* and *The Rime of the Ancient Mariner*.

animals escaping but now, having been left to grow unmanaged, they have contorted into shapes of sinewy and bulging wood, like flexing muscles frozen in time.

The path of drovers in the Quantocks is clear; yet in other places, they are less immediately distinctive. Although, the clues are there (if you know what you are looking for). As they had to be suitable for transporting huge numbers of beasts, the tracks were often very wide (sometimes up to 100 feet), with extensive verges to allow the animals to graze as they walked. In many places, minor and major routes of the modern network overlay now lost drove roads like a palimpsest. In Thomas De Quincey's *Autobiographic Sketches*, for instance, he writes of 'vast droves of cattle' walking along the Great North Road, now the A1. But even where dusty earth has been replaced by tarmac, the traces of a drove road can still be seen: passing places on country lanes and lay-bys may have been 'slip-fields', overnight stops for pasture and rest if the drover couldn't reach more comfortable surroundings before night drew in. Our modern roads also carry names from the past – Welsh Lane, Cow Lane or Bullock Way. Halfpenny Field shows where cattle were grazed for half a penny per animal per night on their long journeys.

We are used to our roads linking places – routes which go between where people live in villages, towns and cities. But, with the exception of markets and fairs, drovers often preferred to steer clear of the local population. Their paths frequently veered away from village centres in order to avoid local, and potentially inferior, animals breeding with theirs. Drovers also often took to high ground to circumvent the cost of using the toll roads in the valleys. Many of our most cherished country paths and walks – those high up in remote and beautiful landscapes – were inadvertently provided for us by their use by drovers. It was on one of these scenic paths that Dorothy and William Wordsworth were striding in the summer of 1802.

They had started early on a walk in the Hambleton Hills of North Yorkshire, stopping by a small stream to rest. Dorothy recalls in her journal, 'We sate [sic] a long time by this water, and climbed the hill slowly. I was footsore, the sun shone hot, the little Scotch cattle panted and tossed fretfully about.'[15]

I'm walking in the footsteps of the Wordsworths on what is still called the Hambleton Drove. Whereas they came across cows being driven down on a long journey from Scotland, I meet only small groups of walkers enjoying what is now part of the Cleveland Way National Trail. Long before I and the Wordsworths walked here, William the Conqueror took this path when returning to York after his Harrying of the North; it was subsequently used by monks, with paths snaking off to monastic settlements at Byland, Rievaulx, Newburgh, Mount Grace and Arden.[16] There are several lanes bounded by walls and twisted trees that meet the drove, some of which are not legally recorded. I stand at the entrance to the evocatively named Bad Lane (not a public right of way), looking down the track. A bale of barbed wire has been placed in the branches of a hawthorn, rusted to the point where it has become part of the plant.

Like the Wordsworths, I am making my way slowly up the hill. The land feels barren, with little tree cover. Bad Lane becomes Solomon's Lane. A collection of lumps and an isolated gatepost in a field bordering the path are all that remain of a

15 A cloud-streaked sunset seen on this spot inspired William Wordsworth's sonnet 'Composed After a Journey Across the Hambleton Hills, Yorkshire' in which the view evokes for him the 'Indian citadel, Temple of Greece'. Visions 'Of silent rapture; but we felt the while, We should forget them; they are of the sky, And from our earthly memory fade away'.

16 'Harrying' is a very bland word for what the historian William E. Kapelle, among others, has rightly termed genocide. William's scorched-earth tactics in the north left some communities so desolate that up to seventy-five per cent of people died or never returned.

large folly-cum-farmhouse built by Solomon Metcalf in 1812. The building, known as Solomon's Temple, was designed apparently to ape the Jerusalem original, and had images of the twelve Apostles and pinnacles depicting the sun, moon and stars. Today only one house stands here, a neat holiday cottage, a neighbour to the temple. It used to be a drovers' inn called Chequers, which remained in business up until the Second World War. On the wall of the house the original pub sign survives, now protected under glass. Beneath a painted chequerboard, it reads:

BE NOT IN HASTE
STEP IN AND TASTE
ALE TOMORROW
FOR NOTHING

Earlier in the day, a taxi driver had, upon hearing that I was walking the drive, mentioned that there is always 'breeze, draft or gale' up here, and it truly is a windswept spot. The Chequers would have been a welcome sight for tired drovers, with rich ale and a peat fire, which is said to have burned continuously in its hearth for 200 years. For a moment, I feel envious of the shelter of this old inn.

Leaving the short stretch of tarmacked road in front of the building, the path follows the edge of the escarpment with long sweeping views all the way across to the Pennines and Black Hambleton, which looms ahead. The drovers on this path were headed in the direction of York, about thirty miles south, where they would sell their cattle before returning to Scotland or press on to the rich grazing grounds of the south-east, fattening their animals for sale at Smithfield Market in London. If I were to follow their southern journey from York, the easiest way would be along the York–Selby greenway. But this route is a representation of the drovers' ultimate demise. For this fourteen-mile traffic-free cycleway follows the old East Coast Mainline railway line, the spread of which made the centuries-old tradition of droving obsolete. Some drovers tried to cling on to their way of life, insisting on accompanying their animals in the cattle cars of the trains. The last recorded great drover journey, bringing a flock of Welsh mountain ewes from Ceredigion to Harrow on the Hill, was in 1900. After that droving disappeared.

I've reached the top of Black Hambleton, on this vast long-distance route for animals and people, and the track is now edged by stone walls, a view of grass, heather and tree plantations directly below. As I look down into the low-slung Vale of Mowbray and across to the purple-brushed Cleveland moors, I give a small thanks to the drovers for using – and in a sense saving – this path.

3.   The Parish Road and Turnpike

Two birds swoop, spiral and dive across the Lancashire sky. For a brief moment they move in tandem, rising and falling, almost touching, before gracefully peeling apart. Looping in great arcs, these two 'wanton' lapwings, as Tennyson called them, are engaged in a nuptial dance.

Lapwings like to nest in open landscapes, away from a field boundary. They are historically associated with unproductive and scrubby ground, with common land, heaths, moors and lightly grazed wetland, inhabiting the areas collectively known as 'the waste'. The systematic enclosure of these lands in the eighteenth and nineteenth centuries, coupled with a Victorian taste for their eggs (Mrs Beeton praises the 'beautiful translucent bluish colour' of their whites after cooking and recommends serving them in a terrifying dish of aspic jelly, chilli and truffle), led to a sharp decline in their numbers and a shift in where they live. In Britain they are most commonly found across lowland areas of northern England and the Scottish borders, no longer of the waste but of farmlands and fields.

These two particular lapwings are flying over irregularly shaped spring-green fields. I'm watching them from a country lane which winds through a low, wide valley, a northern English agricultural landscape far from the waste. This valley lies just north of Carnforth, a small market town probably most famous for its railway station. The steam-enveloped platforms and iconic clock, the backdrop to Laura and Alec's chaste affair in *Brief*

Encounter.[1] The valley is formed on the east by a long band of high fells and crags (the names of which invoke a desire to climb and explore: Cragg Lot, Hutton Roof, Farleton Fell, Dalton Crags). On the other side, separating us from the coast and the treacherous mud flats of Morecambe Bay, the limestone cliffs of Warton Crag loom, a dark prominence in the west.

I look away from these distant rocks and the lapwings above to the Ordnance Survey map in my hand. On paper, the valley is rippling with a dizzying array of colour. Straight through its centre runs the bold blue of a motorway, the M6, accompanied by its vivid pink neighbour, the A6. The subtler blue of the Lancaster Canal snakes along contour lines to the eastern side of the valley crossed by the thick black line of the Settle to Carlisle railway. Weaving under and over is the yellow of the local road network and a scattering of green-dashed footpaths and bridleways. On closer inspection there are also the spindly lines and squares of pylons and power cables.[2]

One of my walking companions on this spring day, Brian Jones, a Rambler and local historian, talks of the significance of this constrained north–south corridor. Of how the earliest routes went through the extreme west and east of the valley to avoid the boggy impassable ground in the centre. How later engineering improvements enabled the building of new roads, canals and railways straight through the middle. But they all ultimately went through this valley, avoiding the hills to either side. The strokes on the map represent tangible lines of human communication on the ground that have been laid down over centuries through the valley, taking the path of least resistance.

1 David Lean had originally planned to direct these scenes at a London railway station, but this being early 1945 the Ministry of War moved production away from London and potential enemy attack and to avoid the blackout.
2 And, hidden from my Ordnance Survey view, gas lines underground.

Easily overlooked is the country lane I'm walking on with Brian and fellow volunteers Neil and Joy. On the map it is denoted by a pair of thin black lines on white, but it is not recorded as either a public road or a public right of way; this is a legal no man's land and an unprotected part of the history of communication and travel in this Lancashire valley. We meet for our walk where the lane connects with the canal, just outside the small village of Borwick. The village spreads from this meeting point of canal and road: older grey stone cottages line the way through the village and there's a scattering of 1970s canal-side houses. Above these homes peeps the crenellated top of Borwick Hall, the local manor house.[3]

Despite its current lack of legal recognition, the locals clearly know they have the right to use this route. People are parking up on the wide verges. Lumbering and jumping out of their cars, they chat while dogs scurry and bark in the grass and gravel. This is obviously a popular place to start a walk along the canal towpath or into the surrounding network of paths which branch off from this unrecorded lane. It is difficult to say exactly how many centuries of travellers have journeyed down this route; at the very least, we can trace its existence back to the birth of modern mapping in Lancashire in the eighteenth century.

If you look at some of the early maps of this county, you could believe that it had hardly any roads. Robert Morden's *The County Palatine of Lancaster*, published in 1695, shows settlements almost as islands, surrounded by small clusters of hills and groups of trees, all drawn in uniform style. Between these are

3 During the 1650s interregnum, this manor house was a flashpoint of religious strife. It was from the hall that, with the support of his royalist patron Sir Richard Bindloss, the local chaplain Richard Sherlock penned thunderous pamphlets against 'dangerous fanatics' and quakers. In the hall's chapel Sherlock preached the banned *Book of Common Prayer*, changing just enough words to avoid punishment from the Cromwellian authorities.

the occasional lake or river crossed with a few bridges, unattached to any visible road system. The map leaves us with little sense of topography or connection between communities and places.

But, in the mid-eighteenth century, a new generation of cartographers emerged who revolutionized the mapping of Britain, creating maps which started to reflect what the country truly looked like. Whereas earlier cartographers often merely 'improved' on previous maps by publishing their own editions (some could call that plagiarism), these cartographers set out with new instruments and techniques to measure the land itself. Among the modern mapmakers was William Yates, who turned his attention to Lancashire, publishing a map of the county in 1787.[4] Yates used the latest methods of triangulation, establishing the distance and position of points in the landscape by taking bearings from known locations. He set up triangulation points on natural features – now prime walking destinations, such as the Old Man of Coniston and Pendle Hill (the site of the famous seventeenth-century witch trials) – and on tall, man-made structures, such as churches in Manchester and Leigh, and windmills in Kirkham and Preesall.

The Yates map, published a century before the first Ordnance Survey map of the county, fills in many of the blanks, and a true road network emerges from the paper. The unrecorded lane we are walking down is clearly shown, demonstrating that it is at

4 Not much is known about Yates the master cartographer, though his will gives us some clues to his life and family. We know that he had six children – William, George, Joseph, Sarah, Hannah and Patty. He leaves land to his children, alongside bequeathing his surveying equipment to George and a camera obscura and silver teapot to Hannah. Joseph gets his ticket to the Lyceum and the Liverpool Library, Patty his harpsichord, and Sarah receives a liquor frame and bottles. William, by then a doctor working in the West Indies, gets the gold medal which Yates was presented with by the Society of Arts for his survey of Lancashire, and a share in the Liverpool Water Works.

least 230 years old. It runs north to south between Borwick and the hamlet of Capernwray. In both settlements the only marked building is the manor house, a good indication of the affluent audience that bought these maps. Compared to our crowded modern map of the area, the Yates map is still sparse. There is only one other route shown in the valley, marked out boldly a little to the west. This is the first of many major transport developments through this tight valley, and perhaps one of the reasons our unrecorded lane has been overlooked: a turnpike road. It was one stretch of a national system which saw travellers charged tolls that were collected to repair, maintain and create thousands of miles of road across Britain.

By examining how our roads in the pre-car age were maintained, a picture emerges of the changing face of travel over centuries, of who roads served and for what purposes. For much of the past 2,000 years, the maintenance of public lanes and roads was a local matter, a reflection of a time when most people didn't stray far from home. Local communities, the gentry and the church (in all its guises: the parish church, the bishops, abbeys and monasteries) maintained their local roads for their own use – farming, trading and communication. And beyond this collective self-interest was a motivation which may seem alien to us today: an imperative to contribute to the maintenance of roads, bridges, fords and ferries as an act of piety and charity.

In his fourteenth-century monumental narrative poem *Piers Plowman*, William Langland lists a raft of acts which the rich merchant should undertake to ease him along the path to salvation. Alongside giving food to the poor and the imprisoned, setting scholars to study and helping maidens to marry (or alternatively 'to make them nuns'), the merchant is implored to make profit in order to:

> . . . repair rotten roads · where plainly required;
> And to build up bridges · that were broken down.[5]

As was often the case in medieval religion, this duty could take on the flavour of a direct transaction. For example, when a bridge at Treverbyn, north of St Austell in Cornwall, needed work, an indulgence was issued in 1412 by 'Edmund, by Divine Mercy, Bishop of Exeter, to his beloved servants in Christ'. Indulgences were acts undertaken in order to reduce spiritual punishment for transgressions; in the case of Treverbyn, those who donated money for 'the construction, repair, or emendation' of the bridge would be granted a full forty days' penance from sin.[6]

A path or road meeting a river was always a potentially dangerous point in a journey, and it was in these places, at the

---

5 In the original Middle English, the section reads as follows:

> And wikkede weyes wightly amende,
> And do boote to brugges that tobroke were . . .

Piers Plowman has long been considered one of the finest works of English medieval literature, to be placed alongside *The Canterbury Tales* and *Sir Gawain and the Green Knight*. Composed in the shadow of the Black Death and the Peasants' Revolt, it tells of a man called William who, sitting above a field in the Malvern Hills, has a series of dreams or visions which show him (and the reader) how to live a true and Christian life. While clearly a moral poem, it is brilliantly funny, subversive and salacious.

6 We have records of many other similar indulgences, such as the one issued to those who financed the maintenance of the road and bridges between Billingham and Norton in County Durham. Elsewhere in the north-east of England a local landowner, Reginald de Rosels, allowed the Abbot of Whitby to build a bridge on his land in exchange for the absolution of 'all the ancestors of the same Reginald of all fault and transgression they may have committed against the church of Whiteby and have made them participant of all the good works, alms, and prayers of the church of Whiteby'. Which seems like a pretty good deal.

ford, ferry and bridge, that the medieval church collected tolls for maintenance (long before the turnpikes). Water crossings have a long history as places for quiet reflection, prayer and for making offerings to the divine. Objects ritually cast into the water have been found across prehistoric sites, and if you visit the Great North Museum: Hancock, in Newcastle, you can see two large pillars of stone on which are depicted a fish coiled around a trident and an anchor. These are shrines to the Roman gods Neptune and Oceanus placed under the Roman bridge across the Tyne.[7]

In the medieval period, bridge chapels were established, places where travellers could stop and pray for continued safety. Of course they were also expected to 'donate' some money. There were over 200 of these buildings (including those which sat next to ferries and fords). Many were destroyed in the eighteenth and nineteenth centuries, pulled down alongside the medieval bridges they flanked, as contemporary road transport required wider crossings. Some managed to survive, such as in Rochester, Derby and Rotherham. On the High Bridge in Lincoln, the chapel straddles the structure – the oldest surviving building-covered bridge.[8] In Wakefield the medieval bridge (now reserved for pedestrians and cyclists) lies only a few feet from a modern concrete counterpart over the River Calder.

7 The Latin name for this bridge was Pons Aelius, the 'Aelian Bridge'. Aelius was the family or clan name of Hadrian. In London, a statue of Hadrian was dredged up from the muddy Thames in the late nineteenth century, another ritual object associated with a river crossing.

8 Tolls were easily enforced on bridges where other options for crossing rivers, especially with large loads, were difficult. Tolls on the old London Bridge, charged for over 500 years, proved so successful that they not only paid for the maintenance of the bridge itself, but also enabled the construction of the Tower, Southwark and Blackfriars bridges.

The decision to build this later crossing saved the medieval bridge and chapel from destruction.[9]

Permission to charge tolls was also naturally in the gift of the monarch (it is the King's Highway after all). Towns and cities were granted the right of 'pavage' – tolls to repair and maintain urban streets and key roads out of town.[10] Beverley in East Yorkshire was the first to charge this toll and received the most grants of pavage of any town in Britain. These tolls were collected at the three great gateways set in the town walls at Newbegin Bar, Keldgate Bar and North Bar. All the gates over the roads into the town are now lost, victims to successive redevelopment, except for the crenellated tower of the North Bar. By looking at the records of the toll gates, we can see that, at least in 1420, this was the primary thoroughfare into town – the money collected here exceeded the combined total of the other gates. The North Bar was slated for destruction in the twentieth century as part of a plan to improve access for buses into the town, but was saved after a local bus company was commissioned to build double-deckers specially designed to squeeze under its pointed stone arch.

A spot, buried somewhere under London's Whittington Hospital (itself named after a famous traveller), was the site of another instance of early tolls. It was here, in the fourteenth century, that 'our well-beloved William Phelippe, the hermit',

9 Although the bridge chapel itself is not quite what it would have been on its construction in the fourteenth century. It was substantially rebuilt and altered by George Gilbert Scott in the nineteenth century, and in the late twentieth century the stonework was repaired with five new carved heads featuring, among others, the Bishop of Wakefield and a retired local Labour MP.

10 Alongside pavage were 'pontage' (for the maintenance of bridges), 'murage' (for walls), 'keyage' (for harbours and ports) and, evidently unique to Southampton in the fourteenth century, 'barbicanage' (for the repair of the barbican – a fortified gateway).

lived in his cell next to the Great North Road on the slopes of Highgate Hill. William upgraded the road, digging out gravel and laying it over the carriageway. An act that not only improved the surface for all those who travelled over it but also created a pond – a welcome station for horses to drink deeply after they came up the steep hill. William must have been an influential hermit, as Edward III soon came to know of his work in maintaining this important highway and granted him permission to collect tolls to maintain the 'Hollow Way' for 'our people passing ... between Heghgate and Smethfelde, in many places notoriously miry and deep'. William's way is preserved in the name of the London area Holloway.

Walking in Lancashire, the route ahead is clear. Grass banks up from the edge of the lane, merging into the bordering hedges. From these hedges reach trees, not yet in leaf, sentinels marking the course of the gentle drifts and curves of the lane. Soon our route turns into something else, more enclosed, and greener. The grey-flecked surface is replaced by grass, neatly divided into two rows showing the passage of people and tractor. Heads of stitchwort, bluebells and cowslips bob in small banks. When we spot puffs of white-flowered garlic mustard, sometimes known as Jack by the Hedge, I can't help but pose for a photo, stepping back into the dense thicket. Further along, Brian points out a detail which would have completely passed me by. The hedge has been laid in a distinctive Lancashire style – stakes on either side, with cut stems bent over at a forty-five-degree angle and woven expertly through the verticals. This is one of more than thirty hedge styles across Britain – carefully and gloriously documented by the National Hedgelaying Society. It's a small detail but one that ties this particular lane to its county.

Thanks to its appearance on the Yates map of Lancashire, we know that this lane dates to at least the eighteenth century. This puts it in a period when maintenance had shifted away from the hodgepodge of local arrangements and charity to one set down by central government. The change happened in the mid-1550s, a gloomy time in English history. Mary Tudor was in the middle of her brief five-year reign. Crucially, in the bizarre world of hereditary monarchy, Mary was childless, despite the hopes raised by a recent false pregnancy. The Catholic queen was attempting to reverse the Protestant Reformation in England and 1555 saw the first of the executions in what became known as the Marian persecutions, later earning the queen her sobriquet of 'Bloody Mary'.

Amid this dramatic religious strife, it is perhaps unsurprising that biographers of Mary Tudor tend to overlook a piece of legislation relating to everyday travel in her realm. The Highways Act passed in the bloody year of 1555 was the first piece of modern legislation related to our road network. By the time of Mary's reign, the Tudor dynasty was firmly established, the state was being centralized and the economy was growing steadily. A functional state with a flourishing commercial sector relies on an effective network of transport and communication, and the informal maintenance of roads was starting to break down (especially as one body which funded maintenance, the monasteries, had been swept aside by Mary's father, Henry VIII).

The Highways Act passed what it called the 'very noisome and tedious' burden of road maintenance on to local parishes. Each parish was to appoint 'two honest persons' who would act as the Surveyor of Highways, or 'way-warden', in the area. On the first Sunday after Easter the surveyors would announce to the parish, often from the church pulpit, what work was required and which four upcoming days the local inhabitants would devote to maintaining the roads, all of which would take place before 24 June (the feast day of John the Baptist). Landowners had to supply carts and wains and able-bodied men; those who didn't own property had to do the work themselves (or pay 12d for every day missed). Local law officials, the Justices of the Peace, were charged with keeping everyone in line.

As we walk further up the Lancashire lane, I gently knock some of its rough surface with my boot. A piece of loose gravel unexpectedly skids over earth clods and tarmac into the grass fringes, startling something living in the hedge which quickly rustles away. I think about the local parishioners repairing this road over the centuries, their hard work of scraping and levelling, filling holes and divots, perhaps clearing vegetation and larger rocks from the carriageway. In other places they may have wandered the fields collecting stones – even some prehistoric monuments and the ruins of dissolved monasteries were broken up to fill potholes. But in this valley, stores of road-repairing material were more easily to hand, though the large glacial deposits of gravel and sand would still require dragging to the road.[11] I wonder how much of these work parties' efforts remain somewhere far below, entombed under dozens of subsequent strata.

What the 1555 Act mandated was essentially a system of forced collective labour (more politely known as statute labour) overseen by the local worthies. If we could have walked past these groups of labourers repairing our Lancashire lane several hundred years ago, it would be entirely unsurprising to hear grumbles, complaints and general efforts to look busy while avoiding work. Not only was the labour hard, crucially it took the workers away from earning money for four days during one of the busiest times of the agricultural year. Removing them from the fields and workshops directly affected their ability to put bread on the table. These unhappy, unpaid workers became

11 These deposits have been worked out and turned into lakes which flank the M6; now they are places for holiday parks, sailing and recreational fishing.

known as the King's Loiterers, and one 1696 report unsympathetically warns that those working on the roads 'come and go at their Pleasure, and spend most of their time in standing still and prating'. Though it was not only the labourers who looked to avoid their legal responsibilities. In his work of the 1570s, the clergyman William Harrison describes the attitude of many landowners to their responsibilities under the Highways Act: 'the rich doo [sic] so cancel their portions'.

The Surveyor of Highways wasn't a particularly attractive job either. While they were spared the hard manual labour, they had to carefully survey the parish roads on a regular basis; keep track of spending and fines; and chide and cajole their neighbours into unwelcome work (which included denouncing them in church or reporting them to local courts if they skipped their duties). In the Cornish parish of Sennen, spiteful villagers elected John Ellis, a well-off yeoman and an early convert to Quakerism, as the Surveyor of Highways reportedly 'out of envy', laying the burden of this role on him as a passive-aggressive punishment for his religious beliefs (compounded by the requirement for the office holder to take an oath, an act antithetical to Quaker beliefs).[12]

The system of statute labour in parishes was deeply flawed; in the words of historian Joan Parkes, it failed to take 'heed of the frailty of human nature'. But the system remained, patched and tweaked, for the next several hundred years. In 1563, the number of days of enforced labour was raised to six and the Justice of the Peace was given additional powers to force parishes to maintain their paths (and fine those who failed to do so). In 1661, Charles II

---

12 John Ellis perhaps didn't help himself. One of his first acts as Surveyor of Highways, despite not having taken the oath, was to remove two ancient crosses, declaring them 'popish relics'. Ellis was eventually imprisoned for twenty weeks for failing to take the oath.

issued a proclamation to limit the weight of carts and wagons to reduce the wear on the country's ailing road network. The system was briefly abolished under Cromwell's Commonwealth but revived in 1662 with power for justices to charge a local tax to supplement the statute labour.

Even as the 1555 Highways Act was passed, the volume of cross-country (and indeed inter-country) travel was rapidly increasing as the Tudor economy grew (though it was punctuated by deep recessions). A key flaw in the system of statute labour was that it put the bulk of the burden of maintenance at a local level, while more and more roads were being used by those outside the parish. This increase in national traffic even led to a shift in how we name paths, a semantic change which emerged in the 1550s. For centuries the words 'street', 'way' and 'lane' (or perhaps more accurately 'strete', 'weye' and 'lane') described our paths. These words are associated with physicality in either their material links between places or in the tangible making of paths. The etymology of 'street', for example, can be traced back to the Latin *via strata*, which is related to the paving of the route. It's a word that has not only survived in English – it is a survivor across Europe: *straat* in Dutch, *straße* in German and *strada* in Spanish. In the 1550s, this word denoting place began to be replaced with one denoting movement, more in keeping with the beginnings of a modern network: 'road' (coming from the verb 'to ride').

Having left the solid definition of the enclosed lane and set out across a wide field, it isn't clear exactly where the path lies. Brian, Joy, Neil and I fan out slightly as the grass rises up ahead of us. Tracing our own momentary tracks over this rising green belly, we drift together at the field's gentle summit and walk alongside the River Keer. Facing us is a solid bridge formed of blocks of stone, each grey and lichen-swept at their edges with honey-hued centres. A steep flight of steps leads from the field to the bridge, a small door made of a battered and fraying piece of plywood at the top. The stair treads have a pillowy sag where thousands of feet have climbed up before us. At the top we look up the valley, a ripple of green slopes to the north, through which generations of transport have been weaved. Old tracks, the railways and canals, and tucked among these, a series of turnpike roads.

The name 'turnpike' is, on the face of it, a little odd. The earliest recorded mention of the word comes from a poetic account of the siege of Rouen in 1418:

> He made a dyche of grete coste,
> Pyght with stakys that wolde perysce,
> With turnepykys, and with many an hers . . .

Here the turnpike is one part of the defences of the town, its history rooted in war. A spiked barrier to stop the enemy, a form of the *cheval de frise*, used in medieval Europe through to the Second World War in the Pacific and in the streets of Cold War Berlin. Its domestic role on the roads of England and Wales, however, was to control traffic and collect tolls. Although much less obviously grisly in purpose, it must have been strange for people to first see these artefacts of war being erected in their landscape.

The roads which these barriers barred represented a revolution in transportation in England and Wales, and an acknowledgement that the parish system of maintenance wasn't working. It was a reaction to the increased traffic on the nation's roads, traffic which caused them to look, in the words of one commentator, 'more like a retreat of wild beasts and reptiles than the footsteps of man'. If a parish was unfortunate enough to have a heavily used route running through its boundaries, their maintenance work would be significantly higher than in its neighbour parishes. To combat this, stretches of ancient highway, on which people had long journeyed for free, were turned into toll roads with non-pedestrian travellers contributing to road repair and maintenance. Entirely new toll roads were also laid – a road-creation programme in Britain on a par with the Roman Empire's or the motorways of the 1960s.

It was on the Great North Road, that key artery into the capital (the same road which saw the hermit William Phelippe collect tolls), that the turnpikes began. Justices of the Peace in Hertfordshire, Cambridgeshire and Huntingdonshire asked Parliament for help with the maintenance of their sections of the 'ancient highway and post road leading from London to York, and so into Scotland'. The justices were concerned that the 'great trade of barley and malt' had led to the road being 'so ruinous and almost impassable that the ordinary course appointed by all former laws and statutes of this realm is not sufficient for the effectual repairing of the same' (a problem not helped by the hilly terrain over which the road ran). Parliament passed an Act to allow the law officers to levy tolls on the road. Thus the first official toll gate – or turnpike – was built at Wadesmill, a small hamlet clustered along this old road in an unassuming part of Hertfordshire.[13]

Following on from this legislative experiment on the Great North Road, thirteen similar schemes were established under the control of local justices (and therefore known as justice trusts) in the run-up to the beginning of the turnpike system proper in 1706. In this year a section of the old Roman Watling Street between Stony Stratford (now a suburb of Milton Keynes) and Fornhill in Buckinghamshire was turnpiked. A new model was

---

13 It was an ordinary road just outside Wadesmill that was the site of one man's Damascene conversion in the 1780s. A student called Thomas Clarkson was resting on the roadside approach to the hamlet when he received a revelation from God regarding the immorality of slavery. It was a moment which set him on his life's mission to campaign for the abolishment of the slave trade.

created which set the course of the turnpikes for the next 130 years. A board of trustees was established to appoint officers, collect the tolls, borrow capital and ultimately repair the road. The model called for independent trustees but, inevitably, the boards were stuffed with the prominent and the powerful, including many Members of Parliament, businessmen, doctors, clergy and a host of knights, viscounts and baronets.

Instead of the work, and money, involved in road maintenance being primarily the responsibility of local authorities, the upkeep of these key routes was now brought into the world of complex finance. The trusts became a vehicle of capital which took out large loans and mortgages (by the 1830s, the turnpike trusts of England and Wales had a mortgage debt of over £7 million), employed administrators and attracted investors who would expect to make money in dividends from the turnpikes' profits. Travellers were now charged a puzzling range of rates and tolls, depending on their mode of travel, the goods they travelled with and the road they took. A long period had begun when it was private enterprise rather than the state which held guardianship, and large parts of the King's Highway, along with the ancient rights of way, held in common by all men, were essentially privatized.

Turnpikes spread slowly at first, on routes from London or clustered networks around specific towns, typically in the southern half of England (places like Bristol, Worcester, Hereford and Tewkesbury). Other early turnpike schemes were associated with local industry and maintaining roads for commerce: textiles in Somerset, coal in Lancashire and Yorkshire, salt from Droitwich and the manufacturing associated with the bright burst of the 'industrial enlightenment' in the West Midlands. By the mid-eighteenth century 146 turnpike trusts managed around 3,400 miles of road, and over the next two decades another 417 trusts were formed and the total mileage managed quadrupled to some 15,000. At the height of the turn-pikes, in 1835, over 1,100 trusts were responsible for over 20,000 miles of roads (a quarter of the entire road network) and were collectively bringing in an income of £1,527,297 per annum (equivalent to around £100 million today).

Alongside these roads came new structures in the landscape. While certain key thoroughfares already had milestones (advertising the distance to the next town), from 1767 they became compulsory on all turnpike roads. These markers, made of stone or cast iron, can often be found hiding in the grass verges alongside our roads today. A neglected part of our heritage – hit by cars and battered by overenthusiastic council workers – many were removed in the Second World War, never to return. The Milestone Society estimates that there are 9,000 surviving in the UK (of which just under 3,000 are listed by Historic England).

Often found alongside the gates were toll houses, buildings from which the keeper of the tolls would emerge to assess and collect the fees required from travellers to continue onwards.[14] Across the country, some of these squat little buildings survive, many now private homes while others have been converted into cafes, visitor centres and, in one Derbyshire example, a fish and chip shop. The toll house at Abbey Sands, on the Torquay sea-front, went to its retirement as a gardener's cottage, later becoming a public toilet, and is now set to be converted into a bar.

Less honest travellers tried to bypass the gates by joining the turnpike at side roads, away from the eyes of the toll collectors. Trusts, in turn, frequently tried to plug any holes by moving gates, erecting new ones or locking non-turnpike gates (some of

14 Often keepers would have another trade to keep them occupied as they waited, such as the making and repairing of shoes. In 1859, Charles Dickens wrote of a 'turnpike-keeper' who 'unable to get a living out of the tolls, plied the trade of a cobbler. Not only that, but his wife sold ginger-beer'.

these measures can be found in modern place names such as Chain Bar Lane). From 1773, fines of up to £5 could be levied on those who tried to use the turnpikes but avoid the gates (and landowners who allowed people to cross their fields to bypass the gates could be fined £2).

Some sought to avoid the turnpike roads entirely, choosing another route free of tolls. Trusts fought back by persuading local officials and courts that these relief routes should be entirely closed to the public and the traffic funnelled back to the toll roads where money could be made. A game of cat and mouse, in which ordinary people were often the losers. While these roads may now be lost to public access, elsewhere increased traffic on the alternative routes helped ensure that they became, and remained, physical paths in the landscape. The passage of people over time on these routes had a hand in their status as public rights of way today.

Improvements by the turnpike trusts did, in some instances, contribute to enjoyable walking today. In Oxfordshire the turn-pike road to Wantage originally followed the ancient lanes between Grove and East Hanney, but in the late eighteenth century the turnpike was improved to cut straight across fields, avoiding the settlements. While the new route is now the A338, an unpleasant place for a country stroll, the turnpike improve-ment left the old lanes intact, and now quiet hedged paths arc and wind between the villages.

While the turnpike trusts restricted people's free movement at the time, the Acts which enabled their creation, alongside the trusts' carefully kept records, can help reclaim our access today. A forgotten, unrecorded path can be restored to our maps through evidence that it was once a turnpike road. Even paths which met the turnpike, perhaps where a side gate was thrown up, can be reclaimed – walkers, cyclists and horse riders welcomed back.

Brian explains how the age of the turnpike affected the

valley north of Carnforth and where the routes of these old
roads can be traced. The first turnpike here was laid down in
1751 and started from the ancient Lancastrian market town of
Garstang and went north, stopping just short of the village of
Burton-in-Kendal.[15] Subsequent turnpikes were established
through the valley – the Ulverston turnpike in 1818 and the
'New' turnpike in 1824. We can find traces of these successive
turnpikes, and where their routes were altered and tinkered
with, emerging from the overlapping lines of communication
in the valley. A milepost, rusting slightly in a nock of drystone
wall just outside Bolton-le-Sands; a concrete footbridge and
public footpath which follows the line of the turnpike road
over the M6; the surprising width of a country lane running in
the shadow of the motorway.

The turnpikes that Brian shows me were not isolated stretches
of road but part of a larger network which spidered across Lancashire and beyond. This new and improved network was crucial
in an area dominated by lumpy geology and crossed by many
rivers, brooks and streams. The growing industries of coal,
cotton and malt needed quick and safe passage, and – despite
their cost – turnpike roads *were* an improvement on the previous method of transporting goods on packhorses. One link in
this network of north-west turnpikes was the route from Austerlands, on the historical border of Lancashire and Yorkshire,
to Wakefield. This trust was established in 1758 to repair the
existing road. The twenty-seven-mile route, cutting across the

15 The latter end was at the seemingly inconsequential beck of Heron Syke,
which marks the border between Lancashire and the then county of Westmorland (two years later another turnpike was established to go north from
Heron Syke, which ran across the whole of Westmorland to Eamon Bridge
on the Cumberland border).

Pennines, was split into sections to be divided between separate contracts, one of which was won by a man who was just beginning to venture into civil engineering – a man who would become known as one of the 'Fathers of the Modern Road', alongside Thomas Telford and John Loudon McAdam (who gave us what became tarmac).

John Metcalf led a colourful and long life. Blind from the age of six due to an attack of smallpox (he was known as Blind Jack of Knaresborough), he was, at various times, a semi-professional violin and oboe player, horse trader, local guide, stagecoach driver and military recruiter, as well as an accomplished card player, cockfighter, swimmer and hunter. He also knew the slow-moving state of English roads. In 1737, at the age of twenty, he struck a wager with Colonel Liddell, the MP for Berwick-upon-Tweed, that he could walk faster on foot from Harrogate to London than the colonel could drive in his carriage. Jack won the bet, walking the 210-mile distance in five and a half days. It was his experience with the military in Scotland and working various stagecoach routes in northern England which led to his work in the making of roads. Jack prided himself on the quality of his roads – ensuring that they were all built on good foundations, with a smooth convex surface and drainage ditches – a thoroughly modern model we can see now across our road network. Following on from the improvements to his section of the Austerlands–Wakefield link, he went on to build over 180 miles of new road, many across difficult Pennine terrain, before retiring in 1792 and dying in 1810 at the age of ninety-two.

Many turnpike roads, such as those built by Metcalf, had a transformational effect on the quality of travel across the country. Daniel Defoe is full of praise for the innovation. In his *A Tour Thro' the Whole Island of Great Britain*, published in the mid-1720s, he highlights the impact of an early Essex example:

These roads were formerly deep, in time of floods dangerous, and at other times, in winter, scarce passable; they are now so firm, so safe, so easy to travellers, and carriages as well as cattle, that no road in England can yet be said to equal them; this was first done by the help of a turnpike, set up by Act of Parliament, about the year 1697, at a village near Ingerstone.

That isn't to say that the turnpikes were universally successful in improving travelling conditions. In *A Six Weeks' Tour through the Southern Counties of England and Wales*, the agriculturist Arthur Young documents the road network of the 1760s. He finds some of the turnpike roads in appalling condition. The stretch between Bury St Edmunds and Sudbury is pockmarked with 'pools of liquid dirt' and scattered with loose flints 'sufficient to lame every horse which moves near them', while between Cardiff and Newport the turnpike road features 'hugeous stones as big as one's horse'.[16]

Despite the difficulties encountered by Young, the new turnpikes had a demonstrable effect. Journey times for travellers tumbled as turnpikes spread. In 1700, it took an average of ninety hours to travel from London to Manchester (depending on overnight stops); by the 1780s this had fallen to twenty-four hours. The emerging business class benefited as the cost of freight halved in the 150 years of the age of the turnpike. Local landowners and farmers profited from these better roads, with

16 Young kept careful notes on each road he encountered, labelling each stretch in categories from 'Excellent' to 'Very bad, vile'. His assessment shows the disparity in quality on turnpike roads, while still recognizing that they were a general improvement. On his tour of northern roads in 1771, he found that 19.9 per cent of miles of turnpikes were 'Excellent' compared to just 3.7 per cent of other roads. He judged 18.8 per cent miles of turnpike to be 'Very bad, vile' but 32.8 per cent of other roads to be in this lowest category.

property income in parishes with turnpikes rising faster than in non-turnpiked communities, by about twenty per cent.

The transportation of passengers, and alongside it a growing postal system, expanded enormously during the age of the turnpike. Speed was important. Coaches were given evocative names: *Quicksilver*, *Greyhound*, *Comet* and the *Rocket*. Russell's Flying Wagons plied the route from Exeter to London, and the Flying Machine on Steel Springs was created to take post and passengers from Sheffield to the capital. The Flying Coach route, established in 1754, excitedly advertised, 'However incredible it may appear, this coach will actually (barring accidents) arrive in London in four days and a half after leaving Manchester.' Letters and people were now winging around the country on this speedy coach network.[17]

These were the letters and journeys of the comfortable middle class and the rich (Arthur Young had two godfathers – the Bishop of Rochester and the Speaker of the House of Commons; Daniel Defoe was the son of a prosperous businessman and freeman of the City of London). The landowners and businessmen were making money from the improvements in transportation, but for the general populace their rights to use ancient lanes and byways for free was being stripped. As Thomas Dunham Whitaker writes in his later history of Leeds:

17 For some this spreading of information and people was not a welcome development. An anonymous essayist in 1761 worried that the towns and cities of Britain were becoming 'little Londons' as 'the manners, fashions, amusements, vices and follies of the metropolis now make their way to the remotest corners of the land . . . along the turnpike road'. Twenty years later, the peer John Byng complains in his diaries that he meets 'milkmaids on the road, with the dress and looks of Strand misses' and wishes 'with all my heart that half the turnpike roads of the Kingdom were plough'd up'.

To intercept an ancient highway, to distrain upon a man for the purchase of a convenience which he does not desire, and to debar him from the use of his ancient accommodation, bad as it was, because he will not pay for a better, has certainly an arbitrary aspect, at which the rude and undisciplined rabble of the north would naturally revolt.

And as turnpikes spread, revolts did indeed break out in the north of England and beyond. Herefordshire, Gloucestershire and Somerset saw turnpike riots in the late 1720s. In 1734, 'the rabble' destroyed all the toll gates between Gloucester and Bristol. The punishments for destroying a turnpike gate or toll house escalated as Parliament responded to the growing violence, from public whipping and three months' imprisonment in 1727, to seven years' transportation from 1731, to the introduction of the death penalty 'without clergy' for anyone caught burning or destroying a toll gate in 1734. These threats did little to dissuade rioters. On a summer night in 1749, a group of shirtless men, some with their faces blackened, descended on the turnpike gates and houses at Don Cross just north of Bristol. They set about boring holes in the large posts that flanked the turnpike, into which they poured gunpowder and blew the barrier clean away.

In June of 1753 in West Yorkshire, crowds roamed the countryside, pulling down toll gates and destroying toll houses, chased by two troops of the dragoons sent from their garrison in York. The rioters had set their sights on the gate over Harewood Bridge outside Leeds on the land of Edwin Lascalles, the lord of the manor (and owner of a thousand West Indian slaves). Lascalles was also on the boards of both the Leeds to Harrogate and Otley to Tadcaster turnpike trusts, earning him a modest £48 a year but also, more importantly for this wealthy man, influence over where the turnpikes would physically run, which he used to shape grand landscape schemes in his manor. As 300 rioters, clutching clubs and swords, converged on the Harewood Bridge gate, Lascalles sent eighty of his armed tenants and servants to meet them. A battle broke out, leaving men wounded by the road, and ended with Lascalles and his men seizing thirty rioters as hostage.[18]

The wave of turnpike riots in the eighteenth century wasn't a one-off. A century later a series of uprisings, described by Hilaire Belloc as 'something like a little civil war', was to occur in Wales. On the edge of the small hamlet of Efailwen in Carmarthenshire stands a small roadside cafe. The building looks a little like a chapel, with pointed arched windows and corners cut off at an angle. It was, in fact, built to resemble a toll house, and the name of the cafe, Caffi Beca, gives a clue to why. It was a May evening in 1839 which secured its place in Welsh history.

The first indication that something was afoot came as night fell. Clattering and the murmur of excited voices came down the road, and a group of men emerged from the gloom intent on destroying the toll gate. Like earlier rioters they carried weapons and had blackened their faces with soot from the hearth, but it was the rest of their appearance which marked them out. Men dressed in petticoats with long tresses of ersatz hair, made from ferns and scraps of horsehair, on their heads. This was the first extraordinary sight of 'Rebecca', the collective name for the cross-dressing rioters who targeted the turnpikes. A possible allusion to a verse from Genesis: 'And they blessed Rebecca and

18 This wasn't to be the last of the battles over the turnpikes around Leeds. Later that month, a man was arrested for refusing to pay the toll and imprisoned at the King's Arms inn in the city. A group of 500 men assembled to rescue the man who was being held captive alongside prisoners accused of breaking down the turnpikes. The rioters smashed the windows of the pub and ripped up the pavement, to which the dragoons fired into the crowd, killing eight.

said unto her, Thou art our sister, be thou the mother of thousands of millions and let thy seed possess the gates of those
which hate them.' This performative act of resistance was carried out by men who were being forced to pay to use *their* roads
(in the case of the Efailwen, tolls that impacted the trade in lime
which they took from the coast).[19] It was an infringement of
their long-held liberties and another cost in the face of rising
poverty and unemployment in the area.

The action at Efailwen was just one crest of a wave which
became known as the Rebecca Riots, all undertaken by men
dressed as women. Another incident, reported in the *Northern
Star & Leeds General Advertiser* in 1843, gives us more detail of
these incredible scenes:

> On the night of Monday last, Rebecca recommenced opera-
> tions . . . and totally demolished the Cwm Glan Cross Lane and
> Rhnyador gates. On this occasion she is said to have been
> attended by about 200 of her daughters . . . mounted on a white
> horse, attired in a white dress, white hat, and white veil, and
> when the work of demolition was completed, she entered a car-
> riage drawn by four white horses, and, the toll keeper asserts,
> vanished into thin air.

Alongside the riots of the eighteenth and nineteenth centuries, opposition to the turnpikes continued in print.
Denunciations of the toll roads are infused with a sense of what
has been lost, a nostalgic longing for the old, slow and free paths
across England and Wales, a sentiment expressed by a later
writer in *Punch*:

19 The rioters at Efailwen were successful. The gate destroyed in May 1839
was rebuilt but torn down again in June. Another gate was erected further up
the turnpike at Llanboidy, but this too was destroyed. Eventually the turnpike trust gave up and agreed not to re-erect the gates.

Ah! the old, old roads – they are deader now than Adam,
And we fling the years behind us on a shining tar-macadam,
But the old, old roads, let's be glad that once we had 'em,
For we'll never see their equal any more.

At the forefront of the contemporary criticism was the great agricultural reformer, scourge of political hypocrisy and radical William Cobbett. Cobbett was a defender of local ways of life and of rights held in common, both of which he saw as being threatened by the turnpikes. In one of his series of *Rural Rides* across the south and Midlands, Cobbett was setting out from London to Uphusband (now known as Hurstbourne Tarrant) in Hampshire:

> It is very true that I could have gone to Uphusband by travelling only about 66 miles, and in the space of about eight hours. But my object was not to see inns and turnpike-roads, but to see the country; to see the farmers at home, and to see the labourers in the fields; and to do this you must go either on foot or on horse-back. With a gig you cannot get about amongst bye-lanes and across fields, through bridle-ways and hunting-gates . . .

If Cobbett was unimpressed with the turnpikes of his day, he would be aghast at what some of them became. After continuing expansion in the early nineteenth century, the turnpike system was effectively ended by the Highways and Locomotives (Amendment) Act of 1878, which specified that all roads 'dis-turnpiked' after 1870 were to become main roads. The tolls were going and turnpikes became the core of our current road net-work. In our Lancashire valley, the later rerouting of the Garstang to Heron Skye turnpike is now the fast-moving A6, and to walk alongside it is to battle through scrubby saplings hemmed in behind a crash barrier.

Nowadays the records of turnpike roads have been turned to

a task that Cobbett would have approved of: the saving of the old ways for people to walk, cycle and ride upon. As we near the end of our walk, our unrecorded lane has become very much such a track; the hedge has encroached, and you could barely squeeze a cart down it. The lane stops in a quiet hidden place by the River Keer, flanked by an old mill building. We have come to an area of the valley where the different lines of communication meet. The two old ways of crossing the river are still here, a ford with cobbles laid on the riverbed and a narrow arched packhorse bridge rising four feet into the air. And towering above all, coming from a discordant angle, are the black, grey and red pillars of the railway viaduct.

It was the spread of economically more viable railway lines which put an end to the turnpike age. As the railways took to full steam, roads were falling to disturnpiking across the country, with many remaining turnpikes acting simply as feeders to the rail network. By 1881 there were just 184 turnpike trusts operating and the very last toll gate, on the Holyhead Road in Anglesey, closed for good in 1895. The move from turnpikes and carriages to rail and steam was a passing of epochs, a division between past and future. In 1860, when the writing was on the wall for the horse-powered turnpikes, William Makepeace Thackeray marked this transition:

> Do you remember Sir Somebody, the coachman of the Age, who took our half-crown so affably? It was only yesterday; but what a gulf between now and then! THEN was the old world. Stage-coaches, more or less swift, riding-horses, pack-horses, highwaymen, knights in armor, Norman invaders, Roman legions, Druids, Ancient Britons painted blue, and so forth – all these belong to the old period . . . But your railroad starts the new era, and we of a certain age belong to the new time and the old one.

4. Railway Mania

The earliest known print to feature a railway is beautiful and alive with colour. Dominating the bottom and right is the railway itself, a wagonway without a steam engine or horses, powered simply by gravity. The low wagons sit on their broad tracks with small groups of interested spectators clustered around. Well-to-do Georgian ladies wearing large hooped petticoat skirts. Gentlemen in knee-length coats, silk breeches and upturned tricorn hats. This railway was clearly a fashionable tourist attraction. One man gestures directly to the other central feature of the engraving, the glorious Prior Park, a Palladian mansion set in formal gardens, with winding paths bordered with trees, plump mounds of grass and neat bedding plants. The house is bathed in a shaft of sunlight, which streaks out of a break in the wispy light clouds above. The colour of the house matches the neat blocks sitting on the wagons; they are both built from the same material: Bath stone.

Prior Park was the home of Ralph Allen, the man who built the wagonway. Born in 1693 in Cornwall, Allen originally made his money and fame from contracts to deliver post – in the process, he revolutionized the postal system, saving the post office over £1.5 million over the course of his forty-year career. With his wealth Allen bought the Bath stone quarries at Combe Down and Bathampton Down, commissioning John Wood the Elder to build Prior Park in the 1730s as a giant advert for the beauty and advantages of the stone from his quarries. In 1728, Allen bid to provide the stone for Greenwich Hospital in London but lost out to suppliers of Portland stone who had deviously described

Allen's Bath stone as 'to a Cheshire Cheese, liable to breed Maggots that would soon Devour it'. Despite this setback, Prior Park, with its accompanying wagonway, was a declaration to the world that the solid honey-coloured Bath stone was the future for fashionable architecture. It was to be Ralph Allen's quarries which created the distinctive colour of the city of Bath, with its sweeping Georgian terraces and grand public buildings.

The Bath stone quarried by Allen caps the top of Combe Down, where Prior Park still sits (now a private school). Directly below this layer is a large deposit of Fuller's earth, a useful clay used for millennia in the washing and processing of cloth, in cat litter and cosmetics, for chemical decontamination, and blown through high-pressure hoses to create the tornado dust cloud in *The Wizard of Oz*. Deep below this are the Midford Sands, named after a village less than a mile south, which was laid down during the Jurassic. On a warm July day I'm walking through the centre of Combe Down, deep underground, these millennia-old layers stacked above me.

Passing through the portal of the Combe Down Tunnel begins an eerie walking experience. The lights are dim, every ten feet pointing down to illuminate slivers of brick wall and bouncing off rippled sections of rock, the yellow glow catching their undulated alien surfaces. Walking away from the light of the outside world, I look up and, for a moment, I register a deep black sky rather than the hundreds of feet of rock and stone above me. An experience of endless openness to enclosure and constriction in a matter of seconds. Venturing further into the tunnel, I reach a point where I can no longer see any glimmer of daylight behind me. The Combe Down Tunnel, snaking under the suburbs of Bath, is over a mile long – the longest walking (and cycling) tunnel in Britain – and I am far from seeing my way out. It isn't a straight tunnel and, in the distance, white light flickers quickly, its source hidden round a far-off gentle bend. I'm reminded of a story I read of police exploring the caves, tunnels and catacombs beneath Paris. They stumbled across a fully working cinema, showing fifties film noir and modern thrillers, the seats carved out of the Parisian limestone. My brief illusion is punctured as the light gets brighter and the flickering more intense, resolving itself into a cyclist whizzing past me.

My senses have been thrown off by walking through the tunnel. Outside, the day is warm and bright, but under this hill a dark chill runs north to south, cooling the sweat from my morning's walk. I touch one of the exposed sections of rock, the Midford Sands. It is rough and crumbly, leaving a wet sand residue on my hand.[1] A breeze gently rattled and batted the trees on the path I took to Combe Down, but walking into the tunnel brings cold silence. With no landmarks, it is difficult to judge distance. I've been walking for about ten minutes and think that I must be around halfway through, when I hear a very faint sound of instruments and music ahead of me. It's strange, slightly unsettling music: the low hum of a cello alongside a higher-pitched viola. Walking further on, the music envelops me, seeming to emanate from the damp stone itself. The sound moves with me, responding to my steps. It is designed to do so; the composition flexes and changes depending on the pace of whoever is passing. At one point a jogger is coming up behind me, their presence heralded by the speeding up of the viola, the tempo pushing forward and faster, sounds I hear long before the regular beat of the actual runner's shoes on tarmac. There are sixteen compositions which flow into each other, written by the

---

1 The geologist William 'Strata' Smith, the 'Father of English Geology', oversaw the quarrying of the rock in Combe Down. He tried unsuccessfully to promote the rough, sandy properties of Midford Sands as an aid to the cleaning of flagstone floors.

artist Mira Calix. The music emanates from metal discs surrounded by gently pulsating coloured lights set into niches in
the tunnel wall.[1] The discs are designed to mimic light refractors
set on the front of steam trains, a gesture to the Combe Down
Tunnel being part of a later development of the railways to
Allen's wagonway – the age of steam.

The arrival of steam-powered transport heralded a techno-
logical and societal revolution. The railways effectively shrank
the country, enabling quick connections to previously isolated
places and new types of journeys – for leisure and commerce.
The thousands of miles of tracks laid down over the course of a
century moulded the land and intruded on the traditional infrastructure of travel – a physical and emotional disruptor of the
walking and riding network. It was a force which altered,
destroyed, created and, inadvertently, helped to preserve paths.

On a dark night in the early 1780s, the local vicar of the parish
of Redruth in Cornwall was venturing out of his church on
clerical business. The gloom thickened as he walked down a
narrow, high-hedged path, leading from his church located about
a mile out of town. Suddenly a violent fizzing sound came from
down the path and out of the shadows emerged 'a fiery monster',
zigzagging rather erratically between the hedges, a vision of
what the vicar took to be 'the Evil One in propria persona'. Following behind, whooping and cheering, was William Murdoch,
a Scottish engineer, the monster's creator.

What the vicar had witnessed was one of the first trials of
steam-powered self-propelled vehicles. Murdoch's was a strange
little thing; three-wheeled and unmanned, it only stood a foot

1 The music and lights form the installation called *Sound Passage*, created by
United Visual Artists and commissioned by the charity Sustrans, now the
custodians of Combe Down.

high – more of a model. It was one of several early locomotives designed to run directly on the road rather than rails – spaces which hitherto had only ever seen horses, carts and people. Though Murdoch gave up on experimenting with vehicles (he later achieved his fame through being one of the first to develop gas lighting), the lanes of Cornwall hadn't seen their last devilish steam monster.

Richard Trevithick was a neighbour of Murdoch in Redruth. Known as the Cornish Giant, he came from a family deeply embedded in the local mining industries. Visiting his father's workplace at the Dolcoath Mine as a child, Richard used to wander away from the dull workings of the office to explore the site, becoming fascinated by the steam engines that pumped water up from the depths below. On Christmas Eve 1801, Trevithick tried out his 'Puffing Devil' (unlike Murdoch's invention, this was a fully sized vehicle carrying passengers) by running it through the streets of Cambourne. It was reported that when the 'steam carriage', driven by the inventor himself, reached a toll gate and asked what the toll should be, the keeper replied, 'Nothing for you, Mr Devil . . . if you only let me alone.' When Trevithick tried out a later engine, his 'London Steam Carriage', down Oxford Street in the capital, it was pelted with rotten eggs and discarded cabbage stalks by cabmen (perhaps fearing a threat to their trade), before it careened out of control and ripped through sixteen feet of iron railings.

The idea of steam-powered vehicles on the road was ultimately abandoned. These alien vehicles on the roads of England, terrifying at the time, never took off. Nearly fifty years later, the story of steam would be much different.

As the sun rose on a Sunday morning in late September 1825, the small community of West Auckland in County Durham was vibrating with excitement. A local holiday had been declared and traffic stretched for several miles outside the village. The *Morning Post* reported that 'Gentlemen's carriages, post-chaises, gigs, jaunting cars, waggons and carts' pulled up, accompanied by solo horse riders on 'spirited steeds . . . broken-down hacks and stupid donkies [sic]' and thousands on foot. They gathered next to the River Gaunless and at eight o'clock a cry of 'All ready' was heard.[2] This was the signal for the steam locomotive, *Locomotion* No. 1, to pull away from the makeshift station. It carried waggons of coal and flour but also pulled a carriage appropriately named *Experiment*, in which were packed excited local dignitaries. The Stockton and Darlington Railway line had opened as the first passenger steam service.

This venture was the creation of a father-and-son partnership – that of George Stephenson (the 'Father of Railways') and Robert Stephenson. George drove *Locomotion* No. 1 on that first day in September 1825, but Robert was absent, having travelled across the world to set up railways for South American mines. Back in Britain by 1827, he reunited with his father to work on their next big project, a railway from Liverpool to Manchester. The new line opened in 1830 to serve these two rapidly industrializing cities and was, in many ways, to be the model for future railways.[3] The line was twin-tracked, so services could easily operate both ways, was controlled by a signalling system and was fully steam-powered (the Stockton and Darlington had horses helping in places). There was also a proper timetable (initially departing three times a day at seven a.m., twelve p.m. and four p.m.),

2 The Gaunless is a wonderfully named river, which means 'useless' in Old Norse.
3 The scale of the growth of these cities is astounding. In 1760, Manchester had a population of 17,000 and Liverpool 25,000. By the time the Liverpool and Manchester Railway Company had formed in 1824, Manchester had a population of 150,000 and Liverpool 135,000.

differentiated classes (first and second and then, a decade later, third class) and, crucially, this was the first intercity service.

In the mid-1830s, the first railway in London opened, the London to Greenwich, a commuter line. As the investor prospectus states, the new line was built to link up 'the population of Deptford, Greenwich, Woolwich and their vicinities' (which the company regarded as 'equal that of a first-rate provincial town') with London Bridge, competing directly with busy ferry traffic on the Thames. The railway was the first to be entirely elevated and built through a densely populated area. Six million bricks were used to build over 800 arches, which supported a great long viaduct carving its way out of central London.[4]

This mammoth line not only helped to create a new class of railway commuter but brought a new path to the city, with a 'pedestrian boulevard' running alongside the tracks. Using this path, pushed high above the historic jumble of London roads, could save twenty-five minutes and a mile and half from a walker's journey in exchange for a penny toll. The boulevard foreshadowed how disused elevated lines are now being transformed into new paths, like the recently opened Castlefield Viaduct park in Manchester and the proposed Camden Highline in north London (both inspired by the widely popular, Instagram-friendly New York High Line). Unfortunately, the London to Greenwich boulevard didn't last long, replaced by a third railway track. Such paths along train lines didn't become standard in the growth of the railways. We missed an opportunity to create a whole new walking and riding network, to run

4 Having always lived in south-east London, I've passed under these glorious brick arches thousands of times – they are part of the fabric of my life. Many of these arches are now home to light industry, but originally the railway company had hoped to build and sell houses. Two six-room show homes were built under the railway line but, completely unsurprisingly, they proved too noisy for dwellings.

alongside rail, which could have connected our towns and cities across the country.

These early railways had some shaky economic periods, but ultimately they proved that railways could be commercially successful and demonstrated that there was both passenger and freight demand. They set the groundwork for a rapid growth in the coming decades – the birth of railway mania. In 1837, Britain had a railway network of only 500 miles, and in the next six years only another fifty miles were added. But in 1844 alone, 800 miles of track were authorized by Parliament by way of forty-eight separate private Acts of Parliament.[5] In 1845, 240 Bills were presented to Parliament, of which half were passed, representing another 2,816 miles (had all these been built, the £100 million of capital required would have represented more than one and a half times the gross national product for that year). And the Bills and Acts kept coming, with a further 3,350 miles authorized in 1846 in 263 Acts, and almost 2,000 further miles authorized in 1847 in 187 Acts. Over four short years an amazing 9,500 miles of railways were proposed with over 6,000 miles ultimately being built. A further mania followed with another 160 Acts passed in 1861, 251 in 1865 and 199 in 1866.

Behind each of the railway Bills and Acts are a set of detailed, beautiful records. On a hot summer's day I'm escorted down corridors and up flights of stairs in the Palace of Westminster to view some of these records in the Parliamentary Archives. I'm at the opposite end of the estate to the Elizabeth Tower and its famous bell, Big Ben. The archives take up most of the Victoria

5 From the 1820s Parliament allowed the creation of joint-stock companies which proved a useful vehicle for building railways. Railway companies could now be created through a private Act of Parliament. Parliamentarians not only passed the Acts; many were involved in the companies themselves. By 1847, one in eight members of the Commons held a position as a director of a railway company (rising to one in five by the 1860s).

Tower, next to a grassy park running along the Thames, a Rodin statue as its centrepiece. In the red-carpeted, book-lined reading room there is a trolley waiting for me, carrying an oversized, slightly battered folder. Inside are four bound books and three large bundles of paper, each like a long roll of wallpaper that's been squashed flat. These are the original plans for George and Robert Stephenson's London to Birmingham railway, which was enabled by an Act in 1833 and completed in 1838, becoming the first intercity service into the capital.

The main railway plan is a long linear map, showing the proposed railway's course across the country and each parcel of land it would affect. Through these records the public could inspect how the railways would impact their communities and upend their land.[6] Each parcel of property on the map has a number corresponding to an entry in the Book of Reference, which carefully records the nature of the property, owner, lessee and occupier. The document is so long I need to inspect it in unfolded sections. It's a strange way of looking at the country, a narrow slice through seven counties. Between and across parcels of land, roads are shown in a prominent orangey brown, among fields of varying age. The narrow strips of ancient pastures and larger square post-enclosure fields cut through with the confident, ever-present line of the proposed railway. Hovering my finger over the plan, I think about a recent railway journey of my own. As my train raced through the Hertfordshire countryside, I glimpsed Berkhamsted Castle, a golden beacon in the raking late-summer sun, a mere forty feet away. The crumbling ruin of a castle built

6 Similar records were produced for the building of the canals. Some of the new railways were built directly on top of where canals already ran. Before venturing into the Combe Down Tunnel, I walked parts of the Somerset Coal Canal. Sections of this canal were replaced by the later railway but I still found parts of the old towpath to walk and a set of locks marooned in a field.

to protect a strategic route in the eleventh century now stands shoulder to shoulder with the nineteenth-century railway.

Robert Stephenson, in a reflective mood while in conversation with friends in 1850, gives a flavour of the almost supernatural transformation that the railway building brought to the land:

> As I look back upon these stupendous undertakings, accomplished in so short a time, it seems as though we had realized in our generation the fabled powers of the magician's wand. Hills have been cut down and valleys filled up; and when these simple expedients have not sufficed, high and magnificent viaducts have been raised, and, if mountains stood in the way, tunnels of unexampled magnitude have pierced them through, bearing their triumphant attestation to the indomitable energy of the nation, and the unrivalled skill of our artisans.

The railway plans are a pen-and-ink representation of this physical upheaval. They show all these monumental structures of which Stephenson was so proud and the topography, the very shape of the earth, which was to be remoulded. This was a disruption not limited to rural England and Wales; in *Dombey and Son*, Dickens describes the chaos that the building of the railways brought to the city streets:

> The first shock of a great earthquake had, just at that period, rent the whole neighbourhood to its centre. Traces of its course were visible on every side. Houses were knocked down; streets broken through and stopped; deep pits and trenches dug in the ground; enormous heaps of earth and clay thrown up . . . Everywhere were bridges that led nowhere; thoroughfares that were wholly impassable . . . There were a hundred thousand shapes and substances of incompleteness, wildly mingled out of their places, upside down, burrowing in the earth, aspiring in the air, mouldering in the water, and unintelligible as any

dream ... Boiling water hissed and heaved within dilapidated walls; whence, also, the glare and roar of flames came issuing forth; and mounds of ashes blocked up rights of way, and wholly changed the law and custom of the neighbourhood.

Later in the book, Dickens describes a journey taken by Dombey on the railways, that 'power that forced itself upon its iron way . . . defiant of all paths and roads . . . piercing through the heart of every obstacle'. This defiant disruption of the railway lines on these traditional paths is clearly shown on the railway plans, which detail every public and private road, footpath, bridleway and track to be crossed by the 'iron way' – routes which would face a future of being diverted, channelled across, over or under the tracks, or simply lost entirely.

As each new railway line was proposed, and then built, across England and Wales, a familiar cry of outrage was to be heard about how they would affect the long-used paths taken by locals.[7] These missives often took the form of contrasts. The old ways were associated with cleanliness and health, and the railways brought disruption, dirt and decay. In Blackburn, a new train line closed a footpath which was 'the only, and . . . very healthy summer's walk for persons in this locality'. In Essex the Eastern Counties Railway Company were accused of destroying 'the old paths, which were healthy, airy, and convenient' with the scant compensation of a narrow-walled path 'in some places most disgusting'. Traditional and familiar patterns of

7 The last of the English counties to experience this upheaval was Cornwall. In 1850, Wilkie Collins had sought to discover the land beyond the railways in his book *Rambles Beyond Railway or Notes in Cornwall Taken A-Foot*. However, just a year later, in the second edition of the book, Collins acknowledges that the 'all-conquering railway had invaded Cornwall in the interval and had practically contradicted me on my own title-page'.

movement on foot and horseback were being usurped in favour of commerce and modernity – a sentiment captured by one writer in the newspaper *Bell's New Weekly Messenger* in 1838, who complained that the venerable footpaths which latticed the fields between towns and villages around London were being irrevocably lost for the benefit of 'the heartless [railway] speculator who expects every interest to give way to his'.

The new railway lines, thousands of miles long, could not stop all the paths they crossed. They couldn't be monolithic barriers; they had to be porous. England and Wales had a network of thousands of miles of path and road, so passages across the lines had to be created, with the construction of numerous bridges, underpasses and level crossings, to enable continued movement. It was the last of these which caused the most disruption to free movement for walkers and horse riders. Unlike at bridges and tunnels, level crossings required the public to wait until the trains passed, a source of much frustration.[8] The parish council of King's Norton in the West Midlands adopted a resolution opposing level crossings on any public roads and footpaths within their parish, because they would be both 'dangerous to the lives of Her Majesty's subjects' and 'annoying to the ratepayers'. The annoyance at waiting led the mayor of Northampton to lament, 'We were so extremely anxious to get the railways in the first instance . . . and have blamed ourselves ever since that we permitted it, and certainly should not do so again.'

From the early days of steam travel there was a drive to separate people from the tracks. Thousands of miles of fencing were

8 Although there were also complaints about the bridges. In south-west London, residents complained about the sub-standard wooden footbridge which had been built to carry the old church path over the railway line – the steps were too high and the absence of banisters and side boards was 'particularly unpleasant to ladies'.

installed along the lines, dotted with cast-iron no-trespassing signs, although this didn't stop some from using the new railways as additional paths – new routes to surreptitiously use on foot. The viaduct over the Solway Firth was a particularly popular ersatz footpath, used on Sundays by people crossing from Annan in Scotland (where the pubs were closed) to Bowness in England for a drink. Pedestrians crossing the early railways 'on the level', especially before a full plethora of safety devices, were a particular point of danger.[9] Thousands of stiles and gates were erected at both sides of the level crossings to slow travellers on foot – a clear indication that the railways took precedence. From 1839, where a public road met the railway, barriers were installed for road traffic, each operated by a 'good and proper person'. Today Network Rail, the company responsible for our rail infrastructure, seeks to manage the potential danger of level crossings with a whole host of modern devices – LED lights, automatic obstacle detection technology, safety cameras, audible warning devices and telephones at the path side for checking whether a train is coming. The railways remain one of the few spaces in which trespass is a criminal offence in England and Wales (other examples of where the criminal law, rather than civil, applies to tresspass include areas reserved for military training and sensitive sites such as the Palace of Westminster).

Even where diversions and crossings were created for paths, they were not all recorded as public rights of way when the definitive maps were drawn up in the 1950s and 60s. Many small fragments of the heritage of our paths – where they went over,

9 This danger was heightened in places where it wasn't clear what was a public right of way. In 1847, a forty-eight-year-old jeweller from Bristol was crossing the Great Western Railway line when he was hit and killed by a train. His widow and friends contended that the public had the right to use the 'Challow Crossing' over the tracks, and that therefore the railway company was negligent in not erecting clear barriers and signage.

under and along railway lines – were left unrecorded and unprotected. These are crucial links in our historic walking network; it is very hard to find another way round when a railway line is in the way. Volunteers take the same steps I did up the Victoria Tower, or else sift through their local records office to study these glorious railway plans, hunting for paths near and around our railways to help reclaim them for public access and put them back on the map.

In 2017, Network Rail sought to close or divert dozens of level crossings in Cambridgeshire, Essex, Hertfordshire and Suffolk as part of their Anglia Level Crossing Reduction Strategy. Volunteers from the Ramblers combed through the proposals and objected to the closure of forty-five crossings. The public was mobilized, with county, district and parish councils and Members of Parliament joining the fight to retain vital crossings, and ultimately thirty-four were saved. The inspectors' judgements at the public inquiries gave an insight into the value of our paths where they cross the railways – for individuals and communities. One path was used by hundreds of people a day to shop, walk to school and play football at the local ground. Proposed alternative routes would take pedestrians out of woodland and fields and force them on to busy and dangerous roads. A path was saved because its diversion would deprive the public of a spectacular view of Ely Cathedral and another where we would have lost a particularly fine panorama of the River Stour.

There are over 6,000 level crossings on the railways across Britain today and, as the East Anglian experience demonstrates, the paths they carry are under threat. Network Rail has closed over 1,200 level crossings in the past decade and has a stated desire to have no such crossings on the railways. Removing all level crossings, without satisfactory diversions or accessible bridges and tunnels, would have a dire and dramatic effect on our path network. Hundreds of miles of public paths would be severed or become so inconvenient that people would stop using them, depriving us of our historic passages through the landscape.

Having seen the light at the end of the tunnel, my eyes adjusting back to a summer's day walk, all is peaceful as I leave the Combe Down Tunnel.[10] This feat of engineering was created as part of the Somerset and Dorset Railway Company's extension into Bath, authorized by Parliament in August 1871.[11] When the Midland Railway Company built a station at Bath, the Somerset and Dorset company saw an opportunity to link their line between the English and Bristol Channels into the wider national network. Creating an extension from the isolated Evercreech Junction station to Bath would allow new markets for Somerset coal and other freight. It would also enable passengers to travel relatively easily to the burgeoning resort towns of Poole and Bournemouth.

The desire for the railways to connect to the coast demonstrates the role they played in a revolution of tourism and leisure. Along the lines now came the day trippers, the holidaymakers and the excursionists. Cheap fares enabled people to travel, enjoy a day out and come back before nightfall. Out of the railway stations poured groups of factory workers, schoolchildren

10 This is in stark contrast to the noise and strife of its construction with explosions of dynamite and the crack of hand tools. When in operation, the tunnel was a notoriously horrible place to run a train through. It was low-ceilinged, lacked ventilation shafts, and its steep gradient meant greater amounts of coal were needed. Train workers recalled the choking, suffocating atmosphere. According to John Sawyer, a fireman stoking the engines: 'The footplate through the tunnel was terrifying. I'll never forget the heat, the steam, the smoke.' When a BBC documentary crew investigated the then abandoned tunnel in the 1980s, they found inches of soot still caked to the inside.
11 The plan for the extension to Bath shows over 300 different paths, most of them public, being crossed by the proposed line. These include specific references to 13 turnpike roads, 147 footpaths and 63 public roads.

and temperance enthusiasts, off to explore the streets and alleys of towns and cities or promenade along the seafront. The new railway lines opened up parts of rural England and Wales previously unexplored by many. Trains brought the people to the paths and expanded where a new generation of walkers, strollers and ramblers could easily explore on foot. Those arriving by train could now be seen 'roaming about in the lanes and the fields' and day trippers described the joy of 'ramble[s] . . . listening to the music of the waves, and wondering that so short a time had elapsed since the din of the busy city had surrounded us'. By 1888, a quarter of a million third-class passengers a year were using the Cockermouth, Keswick and Penrith Railway to take in the spectacular vistas and visit the tourist towns of the Lake District. The railways had opened up the countryside to an urban working-class population and made it possible, in the words of one newspaper columnist, that:

In a very short space of time one can travel into the wildest parts of England, where houses are miles apart, and into the deep glades of the forest, where the stillness is only broken by the cheerful songs of the birds; or climb to the lofty mountain top and gaze upon the vast expanse of hills, moors, forests, plains, villages, and towns, spread like a panorama at one's feet.

Alongside the leisure seekers of the south coast, the Somerset and Dorset extension to Bath carried bricks from Burnham and Bridgwater, beer from Shepton Mallet, milk to London and the south-east (up to 500,000 churns a year in its heyday), Cheddar cheese from Glastonbury, and troops, tanks and munitions to embarkation sites for the D-Day landings. Facilitating commerce and pleasure, this line operated for a total of eighty-two years but ultimately, along with so many more, it fell to what became known as Beeching's axe.

★

The railways reached their zenith just before the First World War, when there were over 23,000 miles of line operating. Incremental closure of lines took place after this, and by the early 1960s, Britain had around 17,000 miles of track, with 7,000 stations open to rail traffic. Of these, 3,500 stations produced just 2 per cent of the passenger receipts and the most profitable 0.5 per cent of stations produced 26 per cent of total receipts – something needed to change (at least in the minds of some at the time). In 1961, Harold Macmillan's transport minister, Ernest Marples, appointed Richard Beeching to head the British Transport Commission and then later the British Railways Board, under which the railways were given more commercial freedom but, for the first time, were expected to run entirely on profit, without any consideration for the social good of the network.[12] Beeching threw himself into streamlining and 'eliminating the Railways deficit before 1970', with his transformational, destructive report 'The Reshaping of British Railways'. In this, Beeching sets 'a clear course for the railways', a direction which he confidently asserts 'must be right'. He recognized that 'changes of the magnitude of those proposed will inevitably give rise to many difficulties affecting railway staff, the travelling public, and industry', but he says that they are 'certainly not too drastic'.

Despite Beeching's attempt at reassuring words, for a great many the changes were simply too radical. The report recommended that 6,000 miles of line and over 2,000 stations be closed. Opposition was fierce, as across the country people protested the

12 It is interesting to look at Ernest Marples. Marples had made his fortune founding Marples, Ridgway & Partners, a civil engineering firm which specialized in road building. As reported by the *Guardian*: 'the M1 was very much the darling of Ernest Marples . . . although the company didn't officially build the M1, it certainly had a finger in the pie.' Though he sold most of his company shares on becoming a minister, he reserved the right to buy them back. Perhaps it isn't surprising that Marples favoured roads over rail . . .

closure of their rural railway lines, especially as these were often their only form of public transport.[13] In most places the fight was futile. Of the 7,000 stations at the start of the decade, only 3,000 survived into the 1970s. The miles of line fell by a third.

Rail passengers travelling for leisure to rural destinations today spend an average of £83 per trip, with rail having a wider economic, social and environmental benefit to rural areas of £490 million.[14] In an echo of the Victorian newspaper reports about the potential for discovery by railway, in 2005 Parliament's Transport Committee noted that 'a healthy and effective rail system can attract visitors to areas they might otherwise have missed'. The Beeching cuts, so focused on eliminating stopping services and branch lines, made accessing our rural landscapes much harder. Communities are now cut off from public transport, their paths much more inaccessible to those without a car. But the cuts did lead, however unintentionally, to the creation of new paths.

On Saturday, 5 March 1966, station staff at Evercreech Junction on the Somerset and Dorset Line were dressed in mourning clothes as they loaded a symbolic coffin to the strains of 'John Brown's Body'. The final scheduled departure for Bath left the station to the sound of detonators exploding as the railway line was dismantled behind. For years the line was abandoned, with railway structures adrift in the landscape.[15] Nearly forty years

13 The government response was that buses would replace the lost rail services. It's a promise that hasn't aged well, with the decimation of rural buses since deregulation in the 1980s. In the last decade alone, 3,000 bus routes have either been reduced, altered or withdrawn, many in rural areas.
14 Figures from the Rail Delivery Group's 2021 report 'More Than a Journey'.
15 The empty Combe Down Tunnel developed a reputation as a perfect spot for young couples to get some 'private time' and there were also reports of a prankster who took to leaving recordings of steam trains in the abandoned tunnel, which, understandably, 'scared the pants off everyone in there'.

later, in 2005, work began to establish the Two Tunnels Greenway, and the Combe Down Tunnel reopened in 2016. A four-mile walking and cycling path was created from a remnant of this lost railway line. This new path was just one of many formed from the infrastructure that the railway cuts left behind; railway history can now be walked and cycled.

At Plessy in Northumberland, a section of one of the earliest wagonways, constructed at the end of the seventeenth century to take coal from the inland pits to the coast, is now a tarmacked bridleway bounded by vibrant scrubby hedgerows. About thirty miles away, a third of the Stephensons' Stockton and Darlington Line is accessible for walkers and cyclists. There are hundreds of disused railway paths across England and Wales – over 3,000 miles in total – along which can be seen the defunct artefacts of the railways, the memento mori of the age of steam. The old marker posts erected to display crucial information to train drivers are now swallowed by verdant vegetation, and the dormant signal boxes and empty station buildings, the platforms that have seen their last passengers, are now viewed at an incongruous angle by those walking past on the ripped-up trackbed. These are paths such as the twenty-four-mile Consett and Sunderland Railway Path, which follows the line of the former Stanhope and Tyne line; the Cinder Track running through the North York Moors, and the Phoenix Trail crossing the Buckinghamshire–Oxfordshire border, risen from the ashes of the old Wycombe Railway.

Former railway lines are naturally suited for conversion into paths. They are already defined physical features, strips of wide, flat land many miles long with solid pre-existing infrastructure which glides over rivers, valleys and boggy ground. Disused railway paths act as passages for plants as well as people. This process started on the operational railways. Species such as the bright yellow Oxford ragwort, an escapee from the city's botanical gardens, have made their way to the far corners of England; the purple heads of buddleia, now a familiar sight thriving on sidings and embankments; and tomato plants growing between the railway sleepers – the result of undigested seeds being disgorged from train toilets. The disused railways are still havens and natural corridors for wildlife, and welcome green corridors in towns and cities. The Wildlife Trusts operate nearly thirty ex-railway sites as reserves, such as the Teifi Marshes in west Wales and the Green Line in Nottinghamshire, which supports twenty species of birds and eleven species of butterflies and moths. The Parkland Walk between Alexandra Palace and Finsbury Park, now forming part of the Capital Ring, is London's longest nature reserve and here you might come across foxes skulking along the old railway line or see the snuffle holes and burrows of furtive badgers.

There was no grand plan to repurpose defunct railways as walking and cycling routes. A few lines were simply donated to local councils for use as paths, while some authorities bought old lines with, ultimately unfulfilled, intentions to create new roads. In other places councils have successfully negotiated with the private owners of the old lines to open them up for the public to use. However, the majority of our old railway lines have been lost entirely to public access; they've been sold off in parcels, firmly returned to private ownership with fences and no-trespassing signs. Even where paths for people have been created, most are not legally recorded as public rights of way. While they are well maintained and incredibly popular with the public, their status is not protected in perpetuity.[16] These paths deserve protection and care so people can continue to walk and cycle where steam and diesel once charged through our cities, towns and countryside.

16 Although lines owned by charities such as Sustrans and Railway Paths can be certain of long-lasting protection.

5. From the Ground

Cornwall is very nearly an island, cut off from mainland Britain by the Tamar. A river which starts less than four miles from the north coast, in the parish of Morwenstow, running south for a full sixty miles into Plymouth Sound and the Channel. Crossing the Tamar, by one of its twenty-two bridges, fords and ferries, is to journey from Devon into a county infused – to outsiders – with images of the strange and the other; a place at the edge of the land, a brew of witch stories, smuggling and of the wildness of moors and cliffs.

The Cornish landscape is littered with the pits, hills, heads, shake holes, chimneys and paths of one particular industry – mining. They are fragmented remains, which to Daphne du Maurier are 'memorials to daring and to courage, to the spirit of the miner himself, undefeated in adversity and loss, braving the centuries past, the centuries to come'. The mining heritage of Cornwall contributes to its picture of deep romance, its distinctive impression part of the modern conception of this ancient county. A legacy from prehistory to the Industrial Revolution which is worn with pride.[1]

Celia Fiennes, the traveller and writer who rode, as the title

1 A legacy now preserved and sanctified in UNESCO World Heritage Site status, which has spread far beyond the county itself. In the late nineteenth century, miners from Cornwall travelled to work in the world's mines (a fifth of the Cornish male population left between 1861 and 1901). The miners formed a large part of a Cornish diaspora. One remarkable example is in Real del Monte in the Mexican province of Hidalgo, where Cornish surnames still continue and Cornish pasties (or *paste*) are a popular local dish.

of her memoirs describes, *Through England on a Side Saddle in the Time of William and Mary*, depicts journeying through Cornish mining country in the seventeenth century, one of its heydays:

> I went a mile farther on ye hills and soe Came where they were digging in the tinn mines, there was at Least 20 mines all in sight wch employs a Great many people at work almost night and day, but Constantly all and Every day including the Lords day . . . Thence I went to 6 miles good way, and passed by 100 mines some on which they were at work, others that were lost by ye waters overwhelming them.

The exploitation of the ground in Cornwall leaves a physical and cultural trace, outlasting the industry itself. Mining is an industry intimately tied to singular places. Factories, hotels, supermarkets, data centres – each can, theoretically, be established anywhere. Most agricultural products can be produced every-where, given enough technology and investment (and disregard for the environment). But minerals cannot be moved without rip-ping and scraping them from the ground first. Mines and quarries are therefore the places they belong, but are often difficult to reach. Paths are required to take workers and equipment to the mines and quarries, and to transport the fruits of their labour away for processing and sale. Many of these tracks, through roughly used post-industrial landscapes, can still be walked today.

Over 600 mines dot the coast of Cornwall, and the millions of people walking the South West Coast Path pass some of Cornish mining's most iconic images. On the Penwith peninsula (the 'headland at the end') the engine sheds of the Botallack Mine, with their monumental chimneys, stand as giant waymarkers clinging to the cliff side. Standing stones of previous industries. The pits themselves extend a mile from the shore, hidden under the Celtic Sea. The paths of the miners are still here, deviating from the National Trail. These are dead-end paths where no surface is quite horizontal and careful steps are required. Where tourists now tread nimbly to explore, miners and their mules travelled back and forth throughout the day, 'trotting down tracks that the pedestrian stranger trembles to pass'.[2]

Forty miles along the coast path is Cligga Head, outside the village of Perranporth, where strange blocks and circles of concrete can be found. The battered vestiges of walls, a decaying modern temple. This is what is left of an industrial complex on the exposed beauty of this cliff top – the remains of a tin and wolframite mine (from which tungsten is extracted for munitions) and an explosives factory run by the Nobel company (which bought out the previous owners of the factory, the British and Colonial Explosives Company). Much of the headland is criss-crossed by the tracks of the mines and miners, leaving what was once described by a parish councillor in the 1970s as a 'Spaghetti Junction of roadways'. The area is now designated as open-access land – and the public are free to roam using these strange tracks across the promontory. It is a freedom that was not afforded to previous generations. When the mines and factories of Cligga Head were still busy with industrial activity, they physically blocked the old ways, and their operations curtailed the public's opportunity to walk along the cliffs here. In the late nineteenth century, the *Cornubian and Redruth Times* reported that they had made it 'impossible to go from Perranporth to St. Agnes', a 'chasm' on the network had opened up, marooning 'hundreds of tracks'. The paths that disappeared under the mining and industry of Cligga Head were nonetheless still shown in guidebooks. One unlucky tourist, dutifully following his guidebook in 1899, wandered into the site and was prosecuted and fined £1.

Further inland, other patterns on the earth have been left by

2 Cyrus Redding, *Illustrated Itinerary of the County of Cornwall*, 1842.

Cornish mining. Around the moors, mining for tin was carried out on a smaller scale through a system of 'setts', where so-called 'mineral lords' would issue leases to individual miners or groups called 'adventurers'. Independent tin miners, working modest plots, mean that these areas are unusually thick with a byzantine network of country lanes enabling access to each sett.[3] These are quiet inland lanes often overlooked by tourists seeking the spectacular beauty of the Cornish coast.

At St Austell, in the south of the county, aerial photography shows the impact of a different kind of mining, which has obliterated paths rather than creating them. Here there is a mass of swirling lines and acres of smooth land beside the usual patchwork of green fields and the fine filigree of hedgerow lines. Turquoise lakes shine – clustered circles, like giant paint pots in delicate pastel shades: vats for settling and storing china clay sludge. Since the discovery of this clay here, otherwise known as kaolin ('white gold'), its removal from the ground has shaped a new landscape. Giant mountains of spoil, dubbed the 'Cornish Alps' in 'Clay Country', now rise, with heather browning their lower reaches and snowy-white clay peaks. The Ordnance Survey map from 1906 shows an industry which hasn't reached its end in colonizing the terrain. In the subsequent 117 years, the quarries expanded, swallowing fields and farmhouses along with whole host of footpaths and country lanes.

Alongside the tin, clay and tungsten mined in Cornwall, we can also add arsenic, coal, copper, feldspar, flint, fluorspar, gold, granite, gypsum, lead, limestone, lithium, manganese, peat,

---

3 These arrangements, and, in fact, all criminal and civil law, was governed under the Stannary Parliaments and courts (from the Latin for tin, *stannum*). It was a unique legal system which issued some of the oldest laws in English history, predating Magna Carta. The last Stannary Parliament in Cornwall was convened in 1752.

perlite, potash, sand, shale, silver and numerous others to the list of minerals, materials and metals dug out of the English and Welsh soil over thousands of years. The nature of these mining and quarrying operations has varied, and continues to, according to topography, geology and history. As in Cornwall, they all leave their own distinct echoes across the land and in their effect on our paths. The old maps show us what has been lost, places to walk which are gone for ever. But elsewhere we can experience the routes that this industry created, walk in the deep footsteps of the miners and quarrymen.

The Pennines are the backbone of England. Their valleys, peaks and fields, which are now associated with farming and tourism, gave us the first of our National Trails (the Pennine Way). But for generations this land was exploited for what lay underground. Livings, and occasionally fortunes, have been made on the minerals found here – from albite to zircon.[4] In the North Pennines in particular, workers have pursued precious deposits and veins of ores of galena and, to a lesser extent, cerussite. From the Roman Empire to the Victorian age, at least 4 million tonnes of these ores have been hauled out of the ground for the extraction of lead. It's a versatile product that has been used in a myriad of industrial processes, such as pottery glazes, lead crystal, paints and roofing, and even as an additive to wine, cider and beer.[5]

The process of getting lead from the Pennines was not easy. Under the hills was a complex system of shafts, tunnels, tracks and caverns. Miners picked their way down ladders or stemples (cross bars driven into the sides of the shafts) to reach the site of the ore veins themselves. The work was dangerous and

4 The full list is glorious, taking in, among many others, Bowlingite, Cinnabar, Labradorite, Schulenbergite, Ullmannite and Wroewolfeite.
5 Lead salts were used as a sweetener, a cheap alternative to sugar.

unpleasant. Miners – sweating and covered in dust – preferred to work upwards, using picks and hammers. Even though the dust and stone would fall directly on them, this was better than having to bend and scrape it out of pits below.[6] Gunpowder was deployed where the ore was laid in harder deposits. Tunnels were reused by successive generations of miners as improvements in systems to remove the foetid air made it possible to go deeper and deeper. Terrifying names were given by the miners to the effect of carbon monoxide and other gases, such as 'chokedamp' or 'blackdamp'. Transportation of the ore started below with the miners required to haul it in barrows to rails of oak or cast iron that were laid through vast tunnels called levels (which could be as deep as 600 feet below ground and extend for up to two miles) on which horses would pull their cargo.

Much of the extraction work of lead mining in the Pennines remains hidden below ground, shut away. Tunnels and shafts are blocked up, inaccessible to all but the bravest of underground explorer. Signs of caution are now posted – 'WARNING . . . Mine Shafts . . . Danger of Death . . . Keep to Footpaths'. Some ghostly remains can be found in the fresh air – a smattering of neat stone structures and occasionally equipment, discarded when the mines closed for good. Above ground, the impression of the mines is largest in the paths created. Once the ore emerged it went through a series of processes, each with an assigned location. First it would be 'dressed' (separated from the worthless minerals known as 'gangue'), perhaps not far from the mine itself and then went on to be smelted at a mill further away, before the extracted lead was sent onwards for shipping and sale.

6 The lead miners' job extended beyond working the veins of ore. They were also responsible for selecting and placing the wooden struts that held up the tunnels and dealing with the ever-present issue of flooding in the mines.

The traffic was not just one way; tools, ropes and fuel all needed to be transported in.

Horses were crucial to lead mining for much of its history – Galloways (favoured for their 'speed, stoutness and sure-footedness over a rugged and mountainous country') were bred locally and worked in packs of up to twenty. Each horse would carry about 100 kilograms of ore in panniers strapped to their sides. There was no preexisting network of road which served the mines; there was no other reason for anyone to build them and little cause for anyone to visit these remote lead-mining spots; the horses therefore travelled on tracks specifically created for the transportation of the lead – precise tracks for a single purpose.

The trains of horses passed over packhorse bridges, distinctive for their arched humps and low parapets which enabled the panniers to cross freely. The miners themselves would use these paths, carrying their week's provisions in bags, leading to their nickname: 'pillow baggers'. The horses (and the men that drove them) were known as 'jaggers', a term which lives on in the name of roads such as Jagger Lane, an as-yet-unrecorded path leading to the old mines at Hartforth on the edge of the Pennines in North Yorkshire.

Paths were often created as zigzags, to better negotiate the steep, marshy, rocky ground. One mining company in the mid-eighteenth century described the lead-mining area of Alston Moor as in 'such a part of the world that they are seldome [sic] without rains . . . Mountainous and Rotten that it would be with difficulty that a man could walk upon the mosses in many places'. The conditions meant that many lead-mining tracks were part of a shifting network; they had to be abandoned and remade nearby as they washed away or became dug out by hooves.

The complexity of the lead paths etched into the countryside can be contrasted with one quarrying industry which – uniquely – created its finished product on site. Millions of fully formed units were shipped off across the country and the world from the slate industry of north Wales.

The village of Llanberis sits in a place of water and rock, sandwiched between the mountain of Moel Eilio (Eilio's hill) and the two-mile-long slither of Llyn Padarn, one of the largest lakes in Wales (*llyn* is Welsh for lake; Padarn was a sixth-century saint with a church dedicated to him in the village). Llanberis bristles with activity, the high street lined with cafes, hostels and outdoor stores. What mainly brings people to Llanberis is its reputation, in the words of the tourist information leaflet I pick up, as 'Snowdon's Village'. It is from the village that the Llanberis Path starts, the longest – and easiest – track to the summit of Wales's highest mountain.

Some of the earliest accounts of ascending Yr Wyddfa (the Welsh name for Snowdon, which I will continue to use, as well as Eryri for Snowdonia, in line with a recent change by the National Park), are from those visitors who came for science – to collect plants, to test out early barometers and to measure the height of the mountain itself. Local guides, and usually accompanying translators, were required to negotiate paths which scaled difficult terrain through the blanketing cloud – terror is a common theme. Thomas Johnson, in what is often said to be the first account of the ascent in August 1639, describes his party's narrow path through thick mist and writes of the group being 'horror stricken by the rough rocky precipices on either hand and the Stygian marshes, both on this side and that, the greatest of which is called "Abode of the Devil" by the inhabitants'. Over a century later, in 1769, an anonymous writer tells of being 'inveloped in darkness, and night seemed to have regained her ebon throne. Neither house nor tree was near to afford us protection, but all was one vast continued waste'.

The 600,000 people who walk the 'busiest mountain in

Britain' each year are following in the footsteps of many generations. There are now several main established routes up Yr
Wyddfa, converging from all sides of the mountain. The original
tourist's path closely follows the Snowdon Mountain Railway
that was built in the mid-1890s, but each reveals a particular history.[7] In addition to the Llanberis Path, there is a route via Crib
Goch (a perilous walk along an arête, the narrow ridge of land
between two valleys), the Pyg Track (the shortest), the Snowdon
Ranger Path (named after a Victorian mountain guide, John
Morton, who took to calling himself the 'Snowdon Ranger'),
the Watkin Path (after Liberal MP Sir Edward Watkin, who after
creating this path invited the then eighty-three-year-old prime
minister Gladstone to open it in 1892) and the Rhyd Ddu Path
(walked in the first official ascent of the mountain in 1639, now
the quietest route). Rounding off these is the Miners' Track, a
path used by the copper miners from the mine on the shores of
Llyn Llydaw, a lake nestled just below the summit of Yr Wyddfa.

In the nineteenth century, Llanberis not only functioned as a
jumping-off point for Yr Wyddfa but also as a place of hard work,
specifically for the quarrying of slate, the major industry in this
Welsh valley. Slate had been quarried across Eryri and north Wales
for centuries, probably as far back as the Romans. On the slopes of
Elidir Fawr, a mountain directly opposite Yr Wyddfa, lie the ruins
of the Dinorwic Quarry, which was first established in the late
eighteenth century and which, at its height, was the second-largest
slate quarry in the world. This was one of a string of slate sites

7 Early tourist excursions up Yr Wyddfa were made easier by access to ponies
and guides to complete the ascent, and refreshments and a hotel (and even
tents) being available at the summit. Many contemporary commentators
detested the arrival of the railway there. For instance, mountain climber
Henry Salt bemoaned the 'refreshment-rooms, cigar-ends, urinals, hoards of
trippers, to whom the mountain means no more than the pier at Margate or
the Terrace at Windsor'.

across north Wales, including significant quarries in the Nantlle Valley and mines near Blaenau Ffestiniog, each chipping away at the mountains of Eryri.[8] In the 1870s, over 3,000 men were employed at Dinorwic Quarry (and several hundred more at smaller quarries clustered around Llanberis), blasting and levering great slabs from the side of the mountain. In open-sided sheds machines cut the slate into blocks, which were then skilfully split by hand into individual roofing tiles using a mallet and chisel. These would be dressed into standard sizes, with names such as Empress, Duchess, Marchioness, Wide Lady and Broad Lady.

The quarry of Dinorwic lies to the north-east of Llanberis, its silent terraces inscribed across the mountain. To walk the paths up and through the quarry, I turn away from the Yr Wyddfa trekkers, crossing over the land bridge and out of the village which separates Llyn Padarn from its neighbouring lake of Llyn Peris. An extraordinary solitary path zigzags and creeps up the side of the mountain, running through a scattering of trees. The path is narrow and bound by neat, high walls of slate on both sides – they come up to my neck. It resembles a tunnel where branches hang over its course, a meeting of the man-made and the natural. Peeking over the wall I look down at the lakes below, glazed inland seas at the valley bottom. Ahead, one of the long winding walls has caved in, the path buried and preserved in a rock tumble. The public right of way is diverted along a new route with stainless-steel steps to negotiate the tricky terrain. Further up, as the path rejoins the old route, there is no drop on the other side of the wall, as the tide of spoil (the cast-offs of the quarry) comes right to its top. It reminds me of the artist Richard Wilson's installation *20:50*, where a narrow path juts into a room filled with slick oil perfectly reflecting the

8 The works near Blaenau Ffestiniog are rare, in that they are slate mines, as opposed to quarries.

space above. The Llanberis version is rougher, the high vertical slate walls are surrounded by a flat horizontal plateau of greyish slate mirroring the overcast Welsh sky.

Many quarrymen trekked to work along this route; in its enclosed intimacy it feels like a personal space, a contrast to the wide, grand vista seen over the top of the slate wall. Even when the path opens out at the top a sense of solitude lingers. Moss flourishes everywhere, softening the tops of boulders, hanging from stunted lichen-blotched trees and collecting in cumulous drifts on the ground. To the right of this glade, a further path has been blasted through the rocks, a grand entrance way to an area of flat ground on which stand two rows of abandoned buildings. These empty, windowless, roofless shells are what remain of the barracks for the quarry workers, and were condemned in 1937 as unfit for human habitation. Many of the early quarrymen at Dinorwic lived locally, but as the quarry grew workers came from further away and would stay here, with no electricity or running water, for the working week.[9] These buildings were called Dre Newydd or the Anglesey Barracks, a reference to where their inhabitants travelled from.[10] On a Monday morning the quarrymen would leave their Anglesey homes at three a.m., walk across the island to catch the ferry to the mainland and travel to the quarry train before walking the path I have just taken. A full day's work was still ahead of them at this point.

This path wasn't just for the beginning and end of the working week. I imagine quarrymen walking up and down, squeezing past each other, as they made trips to Llanberis for provisions and to visit

9 Electricity was introduced to the quarry in 1905 but the owners didn't deem it necessary to extend this to their workers' accommodation.
10 Many of the quarrymen who travelled also farmed smallholdings on Anglesey and brought their own produce to the barracks, leading to the nickname given by other quarrymen of *moch Môn* or Anglesey pigs.

the pubs and chapels. Socializing during the working day took place at the Caban, the workplace canteen, which was a place to hear the newspapers being read, to discuss local, national and world events, share song and poetry, and agitate for reform.[11] In the mid-1880s debate and unrest, stirred up in the Caban, led to a walkout of the workers that was supported by the North Wales Quarrymen's Union. Their grievances were many: general pay and conditions and favouritism displayed by managers. After five weeks the quarrymen of Dinorwic returned, having won most of their demands.[12] Workers' grievances at Dinorwic were exacerbated by the cultural divide between the English owners and managers and the predominantly Welsh-speaking workers.[13] There was a distinct colonial attitude displayed by the bosses to their native workers (it's notable that the workshops at Dinorwic were modelled after a British Empire fort). A pamphlet and song sheet published by the striking workers called for solidarity:

11 The events and rhythms of national and world politics shaped the fortunes of the slate industry. The railway manias of the mid-nineteenth century led to a spike in demand for Welsh slate to roof the stations, engine sheds and new settlements clustered around the tracks and stations. The American Civil War saw new speculators in slate, businessmen who were turning away from their Lancashire cotton factories due to the interruption in supply caused by the war.

12 A report from the *Liverpool Daily Post* about the strike talks of the distress of the local populace and the apparently bizarre reaction of the owner of the quarry, G. D. W. Assheton Smith, who 'in order to alleviate the suffering . . . last night opened a series of amateur dramatic entertainments' at the ballroom of his mansion.

13 Dr David Gwyn describes the slate quarries as 'the most Welsh of Welsh industries, the only major industry that throughout its history has been conducted in a language other than English in the British Isles'. Eryri is still a bastion of the Welsh language. The 2021 census recorded that almost seventy per cent of Llanberis aged over three speak Welsh (although this dropped from seventy-five per cent in the 2011 census).

We appeal for help to all mankind to assist us, and prevent a class of Welsh workmen being trodden upon as mere slaves. We are not a band of agitators; we seek nothing more from our employer than to be ruled and treated as men, and as MEN – as subjects of the British Empire in the nineteenth century.

The empire and slate were bound together. The wealth of Richard Pennant, the owner of the neighbouring quarry at Penrhyn, came primarily from his four sugar plantations and a thousand enslaved workers in Jamaica (there is still a village on that island called Pennants, and Pennant remains a common surname, handed down from when it was imposed on the islanders' ancestors). In addition, the staunchly pro-slavery Pennant was MP for Liverpool in the 1770s and 1780s, one of the largest ports for slave trading, as well as chairman of the West India Committee, which argued against the abolition of the slave trade and, when abolition later came, for the compensation of slave owners.[14]

The owners of slate quarries profited from Britain's imperial project. One of the major export areas was Australia, to which 5,500 tons was exported in 1882, alongside 114 tons to the West Indies (which probably includes slates to roof the colonial buildings of Pennant's plantations) and 290 tons to British South Africa in the same year. The money that Pennant made from slavery enabled the expansion of his Penrhyn operations. These funds were crucial to Pennant creating new roads in the area, and improving existing ones, reducing his transportation costs from 27p to 20p per ton. The importance of industry investing in new, more efficient paths is highlighted by less well-financed

14 Richard Pennant died just after the 1807 Act which abolished the slave trade in the British Empire. His second cousin, George Hay Dawkins-Pennant, inherited his slate quarry and Jamaican plantations and later received £14,683 17s 2d compensation for the 764 enslaved people he owned under the Slavery Abolition Act of 1833 (equivalent to £1.3 million today).

operations which were unable to transport economically the finished slates; at Yr Wyddfa's Arddu quarry, a small-scale venture failed so spectacularly that the slates remain neatly stacked there to this day. In addition to roads, railway lines associated with both the Penrhyn and Dinorwic Quarries were built. New ports were even created on the coast, such as Port Penrhyn and Port Dinorwic (now known as Y Felinheli).

Quarrying at Dinorwic slowly declined in the first half of the twentieth century, with operations ceasing in 1969. I'm walking through the dead quarry; the terraces on which slate was once extracted are now platforms for new paths running through the site. A single tree grows dozens of feet above me on a solid outcrop of slate, tentatively identifiable as a rowan from this distance. Pillars of solid slate, the underlying mountain, backdrop the terraces like impenetrable battlements that have wearily survived a war. Some bear the visible marks of quarrying: cuts, scrapes and ledges. Part of Elidir Fawr has gone for ever. While fragments can be found piled alongside these Welsh paths, much of this mountain sits passively on buildings across the world: Abuja, Melbourne, Kingston and Copenhagen. The introductory video at the National Slate Museum (located in the workshops of Dinorwic) is entitled 'To Steal a Mountain'. The deafening chaos and scale of this 'theft' was described by one late-nineteenth-century observer:

> The summit of Elidir Fawr lies back, serene and quiet, amid the clouds. Nothing is visible here, however, but its lacerated shoulder, rising to a prodigious height in jagged terraces laid bare by half a century's ceaseless work. It seems as if puny man were determined to expose the very entrails of this great mountain, and one might well fancy it groaning in its agony, for all the ceaseless and horrid din, the rattle of trucks, the shout of countless men, who swarm like ants along the giddy heights, the crash

of falling rocks, the creaking of machinery, the roar of blasting, and when a brief interval of silence admits it, the dull splash of some avalanche of loosened debris toppling into the lake.[15]

It's early in the morning and for a brief moment I am alone in this quiet field of shattered rock, a tidal flow of slate frozen mid-slip. The empty tracks from funicular railways stride through the site, and strange buildings, their use lost to me, scatter the view. These structures give the impression that the slate is self-organizing, and jumped from the endless mess of spoil to temporarily arrange itself into neat walls.

A band of orange and pink heather creeps up the flat surface of one of the inclines, a broad stroke of colour on a grey canvas. Except the further I move into the quarry, the clearer it becomes that there is no such thing as slate grey. The slate shimmers with petrol hues – purple, dusty pink, sage and steel blue. Moving through the site, the colours change, especially as I edge towards the end of the quarry, where the rock promises to give way to green fields. Here there are no buildings at all, the narrow path has been cut through pure spoil. I glance down and spot a single parsley fern growing through the slates, thriving in the acidic soil buried somewhere under the slopes. From one angle this great mound looks almost pure white, catching the emerging morning sun, but in a few slate-crunching paces it becomes a pixelated field of light heather.

The Dinorwic Quarry has been transformed from a place of work to one of recreation, although, below my feet, industry lives on. There is now a power station known as Electric Mountain buried deep within Elidir Fawr – ten miles of tunnels replacing 12 million tonnes of rock. Just before I arrived at Dinorwic the slate mines of north Wales were granted

---

15 In A. G. Bradley's *Highways and Byways in North Wales* (1898).

UNESCO World Heritage status, an indication that this is something of the past. On my walk back through the site I pass climbers who have hopped the fence round the path and are now scaling the vertical sides of the exposed mountain. Dog walkers and day trippers emerge, wandering the wide plateaus to a viewpoint across the valley. The quarry at Dinorwic was alive for a brief period in the history of this mountain, though the legacy of those 200 years is likely to remain for ever.

Dinorwic contends still with a crucial question: what to do when the machines are turned off, when the din of mining and quarrying has subsided, and when the workers have moved on. There are challenges – these operations leave innately dangerous landscapes as they scraped, pitted and burrowed into the earth; chemical contamination often lingers in the soil. But creative solutions have been found for these post-industrial landscapes.

A hundred miles away, in the south Wales valley of Sirhowy, a country park has been formed from the hulking mass of a former coal tip. Green grass and sweeping, smooth paths have replaced the black spoil. The heritage of this land is celebrated in one of the largest earth sculptures in the country – a 650-foot bank shaped into 'Sultan the Pit Pony'. Where once miners worked, the public is now flocking. This new green space, with new places to walk, proved so popular during the pandemic that a visitor centre is now being built and additional bus routes laid on.

The story is repeated elsewhere. In Cornwall, life has now returned to some of its scarred mining and quarrying lands. Through the old China clay quarries, dozens of permissive paths have been laid down, miles of new clay trails for walking, cycling and horse riding. They weave through a slightly eerie land, the old signs of industry (drying chimneys and lakes coloured turquoise by the mica suspended in the water) next to the ephemera of modern leisure: the picnic areas, toilets and car parks.[16]

On the slopes of Dinorwic, as in Cornwall and the Pennines and at hundreds of other former mining and quarrying sites across England and Wales, there are opportunities to remake and create paths for the future, new routes through these revived and repurposed landscapes. These places give us opportunity for connection to our industrial past, to walk in the footsteps of the miners and quarrymen, and new places to explore along the pathways.

16 An extraordinary natural revival and survival has taken place at two mines in Cornwall, where the Cornish path-moss (*Ditrichum cornubicum*) has been discovered on the spoil heaps. This moss has only been found in one other place in the world and the total world population covers 0.16 square metres (just bigger than a sheet of A3 paper).

6. Enclosure

The village of Seething, in the Norfolk flat lands, is not living up to its name. All is quiet and bathed in an early blue light on this Saturday morning. As I walk the length of the village, along its central thoroughfare, I pass footpaths which occasionally dart between the curtained-shut houses. Rural alleys open out on to large damp fields rutted with claggy peaks of November mud. Grass and crests of earth glisten with the daybreak moisture, water pooling in ghostly footprints. Looping back around and returning to the heart of the community, past the rusting pumps of a long-closed petrol station and a weeping willow reflected in the village pond, this main road forks in two, creating a triangle of land, a meadow covering its lower portion. A path runs through the grass, faintly traced by previous feet on the ground. Autumn leaf litter has collected, marking the course of the path with a dull brown smear. I am clutching a slightly crumpled printout from the Norfolk County Council website. On it is a tiny drawing of a church viewed from the side. The building is in three distinct sections: a tower, a boxy nave and a smaller chancel on the end. Looking up, I can see the very same church: St Margaret and St Remigius. Two ash trees obscure the furthest ends, but advancing up the path, these part like curtains at the edge of a stage. I see the accuracy of the drawing in my hand. There is the tower (in real life I can see the flints neatly arranged in rows up its barrelled form with a cap of red bricks – a Victorian repair job), and to the right the same nave and chancel (although the drawing doesn't show their different roofs of thatch and slate).

This Norfolk church is depicted on a map from the early nineteenth century, produced as part of a plainly bureaucratic process. It's a fact which makes the inclusion of the carefully drawn church in miniature even more charming. It was drawn up by government-appointed commissioners in the process of enclosure (sometimes also 'inclosure'), which saw drastic transformations in the use of land and the removal of traditional rights held in common. Across swathes of England and Wales, the very character and form of the land we now walk is a direct result of the process of enclosure, the rationale and effect of which have long been contested. For some it was a simple process of rationalization, a way of making agriculture more efficient and providing food for all. Many others simply view it as a disaster and a travesty; historian E. P. Thompson thought it 'a plain enough case of class robbery', which entailed the 'destruction of the traditional elements in English peasant society'.

To explain what enclosure was and why it is such a fundamental part of the working-class struggle (or at least the modern concept of the history of struggle), we need to consider what it replaced. This is a tricky subject and generalizations are fraught with danger. The details, form and material effects of enclosure in England and Wales were varied. The landscapes it left behind were different in character and shape depending on the traditions and customs it replaced and local natural conditions. But most were disruptive. Pre-enclosure, large areas (particularly in the Midlands) were farmed in an 'open-field' system. Not all such systems worked the same but there are commonalities. I picture myself walking through the pre-enclosure open-field landscape. Setting out across massive fields (there may have been just three or four very large fields per manor), which are sparsely hedged or fenced, or even, as the name of the system suggests, completely open. The large field I'm walking through would be worked by individuals and families in scattered strips, parcels unconnected to others, a distribution which, in theory, encouraged cooperation – fields farmed in common with collective decision-making. Perhaps I come across a whole tract of land that has been left fallow, a pause to allow the earth to regenerate, and I might wander past a roaming animal, eating the stubble and fertilizing the ground. On my pre-enclosure walk I don't pass many scattered outlying houses, instead I need to head to the focus of settlement, where the farmers have collected together, living side by side at the heart of the village with paths branching out to the surrounding countryside.

Crucial to pre-enclosure life was land, nearly always owned by someone (often the lord of the manor) but over which commoners had rights. While sometimes called wastes, these were not necessarily barren lands as the usual commoners' rights attest. They provided the non-landowning population access to life-sustaining resources. On these lands there was often the right to graze domesticated animals; hunt and trap fish and other wild animals; collect wood, turf and peat for fuel; forage for berries and wild plants; and to take minerals or soil. These vital rights are vividly described by the Dorset poet William Holloway in his poem 'The Peasants' Fate':

> The common, clad with vegetative gold,
> Whose well-dried stores allay the wintry cold;
> Whence ev'ry family its portion claims,
> To fence the hovel or recruit the flames.

Enclosure was the commercialization, privatization and, to me, the outright theft of the land. The land was 'rationalized', the open fields replaced with compact, enclosed parcels surrounded by barriers – the sort of fields we are familiar with today. The shape of where people lived changed as well; the core village dispersed, with farmers coming to live in outlying houses next to their own fields. Some of these new homes can be identified by their being named after events contemporary with enclosure – for instance, in Norfolk alone there are four Waterloo Farms (plus, across the country can be found farms with names such as Victoria, Canada and Wellington). Initially these enclosures were done by local agreement, a process which in theory could benefit all who farmed the open field – everyone would still be able to farm a roughly equivalent piece of land. But in practice the deck was stacked against the poorest tenant farmers and cottagers and they often were left with the least desirable, and least productive, land. The real boom and doom of enclosure came in the eighteenth to the nineteenth centuries, though, when changes came with parliamentary approval.

As enclosure came under the auspices of Parliament, it became more formalized. Landowners could apply to have their enclosure ratified by an Act of Parliament, following which officials were appointed to survey, remap and reallocate the land, roads and paths of the area. From 1801, General Inclosure Acts were passed which brought even more uniformity to the process, setting out standards. Over four thousand private and general Acts of Parliament enclosed more than seven million acres of land (more than four times the size of modern Lincolnshire, England's second-biggest county). While there was a requirement to advertise changes and established mechanisms for appeals, the system was still very much in favour of the larger landowners. As historian Christopher Hill points out: 'the poorest cottager was always free to oppose a parliamentary enclosure Bill. All they needed to do was learn to read, hire an expensive lawyer, spend a few weeks in London and be prepared to face the wrath of the powerful men in his village'.

Many wealthy landowners used enclosure as an opportunity to exclude people from the land and to curtail public access to paths. People were now cast as trespassers on land they had once freely roamed, on paths they had long walked. In the very last years of the eighteenth century, a request was made by the Earl of Coventry to the commissioners in the Cotswolds area of Chipping Campden. He wanted a private drive to his house set out in the enclosure, with the public having to take the long way round. He was talking to a receptive audience. Despite the commissioners being obliged to be 'disinterested persons' and having to take an oath of impartiality, as the Chipping Campden Historical Society have documented, all three of them were either land agents or lawyers for the biggest landowners in the areas (the same landowners who prompted the enclosure in the first place). So neither disinterested nor impartial. The influence on and subversion of rights-of-way processes by the gentry is not confined to the eighteenth and nineteenth centuries. One Ramblers volunteer tells the story of a village hall meeting in the late 1970s that had been called to discuss a review of the definitive map in the area. The village land was almost entirely in the control of a local duke. The meeting was chaired by the duke's land agent, who after welcoming those present and explaining the purpose of the gathering, pronounced: 'I rule that there are no public rights of way within the parish . . . Meeting closed.'

Enclosure should be seen as part of a wider and longer history of major landowners removing public paths with little formal opposition. Roads and paths were diverted, along with whole villages being swept away, to facilitate more economical farming practices or to create fashionable landscaped grounds and parks for large country houses: a rural idyll without the rural people. A feudal, exploitative capitalism. As expressed by Oliver Goldsmith in his 1770 poem 'The Deserted Village':

> And rich men flock from all the world around.
> Yet count our gains. This wealth is but a name

That leaves our useful products still the same.
Not so the loss. The man of wealth and pride
Takes up a space that many poor supplied;
Space for his lake, his park's extended bounds,
Space for his horses, equipage, and hounds.

Removal of long-used paths entailed the destruction of rural working-class history and memory; to George Orwell the perpetrators were 'land-grabbers . . . taking the heritage of their own countrymen, upon no sort of pretext except that they had the power to do so.'[1]

Not only were rights removed – rights of way and commoners' rights – but enclosure helped form the visual aesthetic of whole tracts of our landscape today. It was a process of uniformity and simplification. In many enclosures of common land, untidiness was replaced with a 'cleansed' landscape. Scrub, rough grass, marsh, mixed trees, bracken and gorse were removed, to be replaced by neat fields of enclosed grass. From biodiversity to monoculture and a process of nature depletion which we still feel today. In Hardy's Blackmore Vale, behind the Dorsetshire Gap, where the valley was once filled with trees, the woodland was removed and the land subdivided into geometric fields.

To enclose the land meant blockading the countryside, the barriers of choice dependent on the landscape and what resources were locally available. The most common way to enclose these new parcels of land was through that ubiquitous

---

1 In her incisive uncovering of the darker aspects of countryside history, *Green Unpleasant Land*, Corinne Fowler details the connections between colonial wealth and enclosure (a subject also addressed by Nick Hayes in *The Book of Trespass* and Guy Shrubsole in *Who Owns England?*). Money from slavery and colonial enterprises financed the enclosure of English land and the removal of paths.

feature in the countryside: hedges. In his classic *The History of the Countryside*, Oliver Rackham details some of these new elaborate planting schemes. An enclosure hedge created in 1718 on the border of the parishes of Snailwell and Chippenham in Cambridgeshire involved the planting of 36,000 hawthorns alongside 5,000 crab apples and 280 elm saplings. Between 1750 and 1850, in the height of parliamentary enclosure, over 200,000 miles of hedges were planted. Rackham has calculated that this length of hedge would have required a billion individual plants. Other barriers included fences and, as we will see in a later chapter, ditches. While the art and application of drystone walling stretches back millennia, enclosure in the uplands of northern England led to a marked proliferation. When I was at university in Nottingham, I remember going out into the Peak District properly for the first time and encountering an almost alien landscape. Neat lines of stone walls carved up the valleys and hills, each new enclosure of land defined by these threads of grey stone.

Paths continued to exist in the enclosed land and that meant that people needed to cross these newly erected barriers. The number of gates, and in particular stiles, grew significantly. Stiles are a ubiquitous element of our countryside, part of the paraphernalia of paths and movement easily overlooked (also in this category, I would add stepping stones across rivers, horse-mounting blocks and the numerous styles of gate seen on our paths).[2] The form that stiles take varies according to available materials and local tradition; they are distinctive countryside

2 The stile is not overlooked by all, though. There is a passionate Twitter community that appreciates and celebrates the humble stile, led by @LakesStiles, who organizes an annual '#StileCup' competition. For members of this community there is a cult book, a definitive guide to the wonderful variety of stiles found on our paths: Michael Roberts's *Gates and Stiles: The History and Design of British Gates and Stiles*. In addition to the stiles I mention above, Roberts

vernacular forms. They can be beautifully simple; the 'step' stile is the one you will probably first picture in your mind, a couple of wooden steps in a line of a hedge or fence. Where walls block the way, the wooden steps are replaced with stone (sometimes coming directly from the wall itself) or there may be a squeeze stile, two upright pieces of stone which sheep can't get through but people can, just about, manage. Stile design can get complicated, though; an encounter with what is known as a 'clapper' or 'tumbledown' stile is described in the *Mid Sussex Times* in 1907: 'a gentleman came to what at first might appear to be a five-barred gate, over which he attempted to climb. To his surprise the whole of one side collapsed, and him down to the ground somewhat ungracefully. However, as soon as he released his hold the gate resumed its former shape'.

In *Nature Near London* (1883), Richard Jefferies urges us to always climb a stile if one presents itself, to find out what lies beyond. The stile in this context is, in the words of the Chiltern Society, 'more than a section of a field fence with a step in it'; it is 'a symbol of a right of way for public access to the countryside'.[3] The presence of a stile, seen nestled or buried in a wall or hedge, can be a first clue to an unrecorded right of way, of a path which deserves to go back on the map. But the role of the stile in a modern Britain is rightly contested. The old stone stile, worn down by centuries of steps, is a material part of our heritage, but all stiles are barriers to a more accessible countryside. Teams of volunteers across the country are removing stiles (although

---

includes other categories, including the 'ladder', the 'staircase', the 'grid', the 'slab', the 'vee', the 'zig-zag' and the 'turnstile'.

3 From a 1970 leaflet uncovered by Dr Abbi Flint as part of the In All Our Footsteps project. When there is a stile or gate on a public right of way, the responsibility for maintenance lies with the landowner. If they fail to adequately maintain it, the council can undertake repairs themselves and send the bill to the landowner.

focusing on the wooden ones with little intrinsic value) and replacing them with gates or simply leaving gaps for people to walk through.[4] National Trails lead the way in these efforts. Offa's Dyke National Trail, which runs for 177 miles near the length of the England/Wales border, had over 900 stiles when it first opened in 1971; today there are fewer than 250. The Yorkshire Wolds Way (79 miles) and the Thames Path (184 miles) are now stile-free. On the Thames Path, near Cricklade in Wiltshire, they have dealt with the heritage versus accessibility problem rather well; here an old slab stile has been left in place, with the path simply skirting around it. We need to get rid of the idea of the wooden stile being a fundamental part of the beauty of the countryside. They all need sweeping away to enable millions more people to use our paths and access nature.

As well as setting out new systems of agriculture, tenancy and ownership and destroying traditional paths, from enclosure new paths were born. Paths ran around and through these newly enclosed parcels of land, over which stiles and gates spanned. The enclosure maps and awards created whole networks of paths with an array of names (some of which have largely disappeared from our lexicon): public carriage roads, private carriage roads, halter paths, bridleways and footpaths. Looking at these new paths in individual enclosure records may give the impression that the process was a positive one for our network, but ultimately in many parts of England and Wales we lost more than we gained. Sometimes the old paths were retained (often called 'the ancient lanes' in the enclosure records) but usually it

---

4 Many of these are Ramblers teams, such as the one on the Isle of Wight who have just installed their 250th gate. The removal of stiles (and gates) is supported by government guidance, which details that they should only be in place where necessary for land-management purposes.

was a destructive process with customary pre-enclosure paths obliterated.

This world turned upside down is most beautifully and gut-wrenchingly described by the poet of enclosure, John Clare. His verses are a cry against the uprooting of his beloved rural North-amptonshire life. He writes lovingly of 'the lonely nooks in the fields & woods . . . before enclosure destroyed them'. These are poems which meet George Eliot's maxim that 'if Art does not enlarge men's sympathies, it does nothing morally'. He speaks of the loss of nature, of untidiness and of the paths he once knew. In 'The Village Minstrel' he writes:

> Here once were lanes in nature's freedom dropt,
> There once were lanes that every valley wound –
> Inclosure came, and every path was stopt;
> Each tyrant fixed his sign where paths were found,
> To hint a trespass now who cross'd the ground.

The result of enclosure was largely a new uniformity in our paths. The commons and the waste were often the places of narrow, rough and meandering tracks, where people followed natural desire lines.[5] In *Rural Rides*, William Cobbett describes what it was like to travel in these open landscapes on horseback; riding great distances on and off paths, his course is only corrected by stopping occasionally to receive directions from local people (often shepherds). The new enclosure roads attempted to bring 'rationality' to ancient landscapes, so the new roads were straighter (often the old roads were straightened) and wider.

---

5 Desire lines or paths are those created by the feet of people where they naturally want to go, which isn't always where we think it is. On one university campus in America they used these wanderings of people to decide where to put their paths. Leaving the ground unpaved for a season, they let their students roam and then paved the tracks they created.

Many enclosure Acts prescribed generous widths, open, expansive roads to replace the paths of before, whose extents were set by limits of where people naturally wandered. For instance, when the commons outside Oxford were closed, the university students complained. Not only were they deprived of the easy ability to learn natural history on the ground and walk and ride freely in the fresh air, but 'the former pretty winding trackways were replaced by dull and dusty footpaths along the newly made, formally direct roads'.[6]

Looking away from the church of St Margaret and St Remigius and across the enclosure map of Seething and the surrounding area, I examine the paths drawn confidently on these old maps. There is a network of named roads painted in a light brown, most of which are marked as for the public. These roads directly map on to the public network today, although some names have become more pedestrian with the passage of two hundred years. Biggott's Lane is now Grange Road, Wheelwright's Lane has become Woodton Road. Hag Lane is now recorded as a footpath, officially known today as Mundham Footpath 10. I see footpaths that continue along the same alignment today, such as the path I took to approach the church, but the map also details many more pre-enclosure paths which were removed – paths whose public use was built up over many years but were swept away with the stroke of the enclosure commissioner's pen. Between the roads shown on the enclosure map is a patchwork of land, all divided into plots and labelled with the names of their owners. There isn't exactly a great variety, with the wealth and power of the land concentrated in a handful of people. The same names appear again and again: Charles Kerrison, Robert

6 As detailed by the historian Gordon Mingay in *Parliamentary Enclosure in England: An Introduction to its Causes, Incidence and Impact, 1750–1850*.

Grimer, William Smith and most often, Thomas Kett Esq. The surname 'Kett' on this map jumps out, a name which recalls one of the earliest and most explosive fights against enclosure.

In the winter of 1548 and into 1549 much of eastern and southern England was in a state of disruption and dissent, with uprisings known as the Commotion Time. Edward VI had acceded to the throne two years earlier, but the country was being ruled by a Lord Protector, the Duke of Somerset. Edward, then only eleven years old (and ultimately never to reach maturity as a king, as he died aged fifteen), was the first monarch to be raised as a Protestant. The Commotion Time grievances were a varied and localized mix of the religious and economic, with a dose of personal animus. Uprisings took place in Buckinghamshire, Hampshire, Oxfordshire and Sussex in support of a Catholic revival, and there were broadly pro-Protestant revolts in East Anglia. One non-religious thread throughout was an opposition to enclosure and Robert Kett, a distant ancestor of the Thomas who is found all over the Seething enclosure map, was at the forefront of one of the biggest.

Robert Kett was no poor rural labourer; like his descendant Thomas, he was a significant landowner. But when disturbances broke out in Norfolk, he joined the anti-enclosure crowd, even pulling down his own fences. The rebels set up a camp at Mousehold Heath, just outside Norwich. The city was then the second biggest in England and the ranks of the rebels were swelled by urban artisans and workers. A proto-democracy was established on the heath with villages sending representatives to a council headed by Robert Kett. The council petitioned the king and Lord Protector with a list of twenty-nine demands focused on land and church reform (although only one explicitly mentions enclosure). Following a short truce between the rebels and Crown, Kett's men attacked Norwich in order to ensure a steady supply of provisions. The king sent several armies to Norwich

and after a battle outside the city on 27 August 1549, the rebellion was crushed (and Robert Kett, along with his brother
William, was hanged).[7]

Our view of political radicalism in Britain is perhaps coloured by the experience of the past three centuries: a trade
union and labour movement which is primarily associated
with industry and with towns and cities. The steel and coal
workers of south Wales fomenting the Merthyr Rising, Manchester's Peterloo Massacre and the fascists chased out of east
London's Cable Street by trade unionists, socialists, commu-
nists and British Jews. Before the Industrial Revolution,
radicalism and actual revolution often came from the countryside. The belief in resources held in common and opposition
to enclosure was one of the primary sources of discontent over
generations. Sometimes this opposition took an extraordinary
form, such as the practice of skimmington: cross-dressing as a
way of opposing the state and enclosure, a foreshadowing of
the later Rebecca Riots.[8]

While we will never get back the specific paths that enclosure
destroyed, I don't think it is too much to ask that we should at

---

7 Kett's rebellion is now commemorated with an eighteen-mile trail starting
from the outskirts of Norwich, launched by Norfolk County Council in
2022.

8 Skimmington was a practice that had various uses and forms. Perhaps the
most commonly cited is when a community came together to shame the
transgressor in a married couple (perhaps an adulterer, domestic abuser or a
'nag') in a ritual parade with the banging of pots, clattering of animal bones
and ringing of bells (in this context synonymous with the term 'rough music').
The ritualized shaming was turned against authority in protesting the enclosures, most often in the south-west of England, with men dressing as 'Lady
Skimmington' and women sometimes donning male clothes. This upturning
of gender norms can be seen as a symbol of disorder, a way of reinforcing the
protestors' outrage against the enclosure of their common land.

least have the new ones it created. The enclosures, backed by the authority of Parliament, should have been followed and the ways they set out should now be on our legally recorded maps of public paths. But paths have been missed off, whether by accident or appropriation.

On the other side of Norfolk, on my way to a lost enclosure path, my boots tread a sandy track through an expansive autumn-coated woodland. Oaks grow closest to the path, with tall pines looming behind. The branching paths are straight avenues fringed with bronzed leaves. Groups of people are gathering around cars, dog walkers and fungi hunters setting out into the woods. This is Breckland, a mosaic of heathland, forests, inland sand dunes and grassland that straddles Norfolk and Suffolk, the part of Britain which gets the most extreme temperatures. The woods here are not ancient; they are planted and imposed – a response to post-First World War panic about England's reserves of timber. The Forestry Commission created Thetford Forest, the largest planting in interwar Britain, complete with the biggest tree nursery in the country, a network of smallholdings of foresters and summer camps where 500 men could be trained for 'agricultural work in overseas Dominions'.

Afforestation, the planting of seventy-three square miles of trees, was not the first effort to mould and change Breckland. A map produced by the cartographer William Faden in 1797 shows an extensive patchwork across Norfolk of common land, heaths and warrens (areas for the breeding of rabbits for fur and meat). In the eighteenth and nineteenth centuries, enclosure had chipped away at the traditional Breckland scenery, at places shown on the Faden map: Rodney Warren, Thompson Heath and Methwold Common. Pre-enclosure and pre-afforestation impressions of the area by those travelling through are overwhelmingly negative, impressions which yearned to bring order to the wild land. The schoolmaster, priest and writer William

Gilpin came through here in the 1760s. Gilpin was a man in pursuit of the picturesque (a term he helped popularize), and he didn't care how artificial these scenes were. He describes Breckland as having the 'appearance of a beaten sea-coast; but without the beauties . . . a piece of absolute desert almost in the heart of England'. These were not unusual eighteenth-century sentiments regarding the commons and the waste. Defoe describes an area of heathland in Surrey as 'a vast tract of land . . . horrid and frightful to look on, not only good for little, but good for nothing'.

This turning away from the wild deserts, and the 'civilizing' influence of enclosure, is captured in a guide to the railways of Norfolk and Cambridgeshire published in 1847. Breckland, as seen from the train, is described in glowing terms:

> From the top of the bridge, there is a wide and extensive view . . . where the country, formerly a barren common, now presents innumerable fields and inclosures, interspersed with houses, and forming a most agreeable landscape.

As the trees thin out, I emerge into the world shaped by enclosure, walking on uncommon ground. A red-brick-lined bridge over the River Thet seems to mark the transition as the last gasp of the tree planting is extinguished. The pines have been replaced by a pastoral world of fields and boundaries. Gilpin would approve. Crossing the road, I begin on another path, which runs through a tunnel of trees – these are not part of a wider wood, but make up the field boundaries which flank the way. A twin track of grass leads the way forward, the end of the path out of sight. The sand of the Thetford Forest track has been replaced by sticky mud concealed under a layer of gently rotting yellow, orange and brown leaves.

This path is not legally recorded, although people come this way. I place my feet in the boot and hoof prints of those who have been here before. Recording this path will add to a sparse record of rights of way in Breckland – the result of enclosure, afforestation, influence and subversion of paths by the gentry and the massive military site of the Stanford Training Area means that this part of Norfolk has the lowest density of public paths in East Anglia.[9] The further I venture, the more the path itself feels enclosed: the end is not in sight, the destination hidden round a curve. This path, on the outskirts of the small Breckland village of Bridgham, was subject to enclosure in 1804. The enclosure map sets out its public roads and path network in a lurid mustard yellow. Much of the network is recognizable and accessible today. You could take this map from two hundred years ago and let it guide you round the parish's paths. But the track I'm walking now, called the 'West Harling Road' on the enclosure map, is missing from our modern record of rights of way. The bureaucratic language of the enclosure award describes the walk I have just done:

> Public Carriage Road or Highway . . . called the West Harling Road branching out of the Thetford Road at Micklemere Pit aforesaid and proceeding in its present Course on the East Side of the Field to the Drove Way thence on the West Side of the said Drove Way and in its present Course to the Bridge where it enters the Parish of West Harling.

9 The Stanford Training Area has had an extraordinary impact. The parish of Tottington is the largest unpopulated community in the country, according to the 2011 census. Alongside it is the parish of Sturston, the only parish in Norfolk to be completely devoid of access. Eighty miles of paths and roads were closed to the public when the military moved in, and it is now a land without a single public footpath, bridleway, byway or road. The impact of these processes on the rights of way of Breckland are detailed in the paper *Mapping a Changing Landscape: Breckland c.1750–1920* by Jon Gregory and Sarah Spooner.

A public path, as clear as day, missed off our maps. Since this enclosure, like so many, happened with parliamentary approval it gives this path clear legal standing; it has been created but it needs recording. This has now been applied for by a Ramblers volunteer, Ian Mitchell. In a Breckland landscape where traditional paths have been swept away in the tidying of the land and enclosure, a path will be going back on the map – marked, legal, long-lasting and open for all.

Life and Death

7.   In Work and Poverty

I'm following the path of dancing yellow men. The footway ahead is emblazoned with wonkily painted figures, their upturned feet and legs splayed at jaunty angles. They lead me past a collection of low buildings, single-storeyed with bricks of a fleshy pink. The path is bordered by gravel and a bed of neatly trimmed shrubs – buttery spikes of mahonia and fluffy pampas grass. Specimens redolent of car parks and of workplaces – robust institutional planting.

These bright figures are plotting my course through a hospital in the Northamptonshire town of Kettering. The buildings which make up St Mary's Hospital were not originally constructed as a place of health and recovery but to house 'inmates' – places where the poor could be separated from society and put to labour. The fabric of this sprawling hospital complex was built in the late 1830s, to a design of the celebrated architect George Gilbert Scott – created as the Kettering Union workhouse.[1] This institution was one of many across England and Wales, operated by hundreds of 'Unions' and overseen by the 'Guardians of the Poor'. They were part of a national system, products of the 'New Poor Law' of 1834

1 George Gilbert Scott was the architect who designed the St Pancras Hotel, the Albert Memorial, St Mary's Cathedral in Glasgow and the Foreign and Commonwealth Office on Whitehall. He was one in a remarkable family of architects. One son (George Gilbert Scott Jr) designed churches, Oxbridge college buildings and the Dulwich Picture Gallery, and the other (John Oldrid Scott) designed dozens of churches as well. His grandson, Giles Gilbert Scott, designed Battersea Power Station, Liverpool Cathedral, and the iconic red telephone box, and his great niece, Elisabeth Scott, was the architect of the Shakespeare Memorial Theatre at Stratford upon Avon.

(officially the Poor Law Amendment Act), a system predicated on the belief that poverty was a moral failing. And one which only offered meagre alleviation from deprivation while instituting a dehumanizing regime to those who required the support of society and the state. A system which aimed, in the words of one official, to establish 'a discipline so severe and repulsive as to make them a terror to the poor and prevent them from entering'.[2]

The Kettering workhouse was built to accommodate 250 inmates, people from the surrounding district – the elderly, unmarried mothers, the infirm and the destitute. Children were also housed here: the 1881 census shows the youngest resident was just one month old. These were a generally settled population with some residents being in the workhouse for decades. The unsettled homeless, those unconnected to the area, were initially not part of the New Poor Law's workhouse system. The Guardians of the Poor Unions often saw the subject of 'vagrancy' as a matter for the police rather than the poor law, to be dealt with by criminal legislation. A key tool for this criminalization of the homeless – for the state coercion of the poor – was the Vagrancy Act of 1824, legislation passed in a climate of rising homelessness brought about by an economic slowdown and demobilization of soldiers following the end of the Napoleonic Wars. Under its broad remit, the Vagrancy Act persecuted gypsies, poachers, unlicensed pedlars, prostitutes and fortune tellers, and set harsh punishments (up to three

---

2 The cruelty of this new law was eloquently expressed in the resignation letter, printed in the *Northampton Mercury* in December 1839, of the Chairman of the Board of Guardians for the Kettering Union, George Robinson. He rails against a system which forces into the workhouse those who have been 'left destitute through the wickedness of their natural protectors' and the agricultural labourers who have lost their jobs, through no fault of their own. A system which had turned him from 'a guardian . . . contrary to my will, into an oppressor'.

months' hard labour) for anyone begging or sleeping in out-buildings and those 'wandering abroad'.[3]

In 1837, following a change in regulations, the workhouse was not only required to offer relief to the settled poor of their area but anyone who presented themselves at the workhouse gates in need of support out of 'sudden or urgent necessity'. Alongside the accommodation for long-term inmates of the workhouse, new 'casual wards' were created for those who did not live within the boundaries of the Union's jurisdiction, wards which became known as 'the spike'.[4] I've come to Northamptonshire to tentatively retrace the footsteps of those who came for only brief spells at the spike. A class of people whose lives, for ninety years, were governed by the twin laws of the New Poor Law and the Vagrancy Act: the 'tramp'.

The word 'tramp' has a long history and a problematic present. Often thrown as an insult – directed at the homeless, scruffy, or

3 The Victorians also used the law to punish other activities, not necessarily concerned with those on the move, such as the display of 'obscene' material in shop windows and, most notably, homosexuality (a use which went on well into the twentieth century, with gay men being charged with 'loitering with intent'). This act has been used in a myriad of different ways over its nearly 200-year history: to charge or prosecute a fraudulent Scottish Spiritualist (alongside the Witchcraft Act of 1735), streakers at sporting events and people taking leftover food from supermarket bins. Its provisions were repeatedly used to stop and search, primarily black men, in the 1970s and 1980s (the so called 'sus laws'). As I write, the legislation to finally repeal this cruel Act in England and Wales (it was scrapped in Scotland in the 1980s) has passed into law but not yet been enacted.
4 The etymology of the word 'spike' to describe the casual ward is uncertain. Peter Higginbotham, the leading historian of the workhouse, proposes a number of possibilities including the spike on which the tramp's admission tickets were pinned, the finial which could often be seen on the workhouse roof or the uncomfortable, spiky beds found in the casual ward.

sexually promiscuous.[5] But its etymology is born from walking, from tramping the paths and streets. Originally it was applied to skilled workers, walking between job sites, often supported by trade unions and craft guilds. But by the mid-nineteenth century, it became commonly associated with those without work at all, the homeless and the penniless. For centuries, those seeking work and shelter were a common sight on the paths of England and Wales, joined by millions more who walked to and from work, a daily movement through the landscape. The tramps, and the wider working class on foot, were seen as a perennial concern to the British state. The 1824 Vagrancy Act and the New Poor Law should be seen as part of a long legacy, stretching back to the fourteenth century, which sought to control the homeless and the poor.[6] When these groups were on the move, they represented a threat to the established order, harder to regulate and harder to control.

Despite the contemporary aversion to the destitute on the move, travelling from place to place was built into the system. The tramps who availed themselves of the spike could only be detained for two nights, with a day's hard labour in between (if the tramp was unlucky enough to be detained on a Saturday, then an extra night was required in the spike, as no work was done on a Sunday). The temporary inmates housed in the spikes could be put to work on piles of old rope, unpicking them into their constituent fibres (hence 'money for old rope'), or the

5 These associations, the use of 'tramp' as an insult, make me stop for a second every time I write the word in this chapter.
6 Earlier laws included the fourteenth-century Ordinance of Labourers, the fifteenth-century Vagabonds and Beggars Act and the late sixteenth-century Act for the Repression of Vagrancy. This Act, like the nineteenth-century Vagrancy Act, targeted a wide range of society, including minstrels, discharged prisoners and shipwrecked seamen (along with the usual 'vagabonds' and beggars).

breaking up of large rocks – the resulting chips often ending up as hardcore or gravel on the very roads the tramps were destined to wander (elsewhere in the workhouse complex could be found the treadmill – a tool for performative, exhausting and pointless walking). After their two nights, the tramp would be turned out, not allowed to return to the same spike for the next thirty days. These rules inadvertently created the 'tramping circuit' – informal routes across Britain, as tramps walked between a chain of spikes in search of shelter and subsistence.[7]

While we know, for instance from newspapers reports, of the existence of these well-walked routes used by the tramping fraternity, it is harder for us to ascertain the exact paths they trod. The routes of these informal circuits were passed orally from tramp to tramp – their movements represent a hidden map of the country. Not only are the exact ways they took lost, like today's homeless and poor, their direct experiences are often overlooked or barely recorded.

The story of these tramps is one that is largely second hand or pieced together through fragmentary documentation. There is a sadness in the mark that the tramps make in our official records and the newspapers of the day, their movements pieced together from their brief stays as inmates in the casual ward, from where they often fell foul of the law, or when their lives ended. I first became aware of these hidden histories when my YouTube algorithm threw up a talk delivered be Professor Nicholas Crowson at the University of Birmingham. He tells, with deep humanity, the story of a man called Robert, born in Cambridgeshire in 1845 to a family of agricultural labourers. Robert served in the army but left after an accident that made him, essentially,

7 The regular routes further institutionalized by, in later decades, the issuing of 'bread tickets'. These would be redeemed along the way to the next workhouse, ensuring that the tramps were kept to a predetermined path.

unemployable. Following this turning point in his life, he appears in the records charged with numerous offences, which often occur in the casual workhouse itself (such as destroying his own clothes in the Melton Mowbray spike in 1891).[8] From these records we can see his mobility, charged with offences in Yorkshire, Lincolnshire, Warwickshire, Nottinghamshire, Leicestershire, Bedfordshire, Hampshire, Kent and Cambridge-shire. Robert died in 1897, barely into his fifties.

In the late 1920s, a correspondent for the *Western Gazette*, in a series of articles on tramps, wrote of the regular and tragic suicides among their number. In conversation with a sympathetic porter in the casual ward he hears that not talking or engaging with the banter of the spike is seen as the 'first symptom of madness'. The porter recounts that 'there are men who will work all day in the wood-shed and never speak a word, and if you speak to them they do not answer. They talk to themselves sometimes, then in a few weeks you will hear of a suicide, an unknown man, and perhaps he is traced to some ward, and you know he has been in yours.' The newspapers provide other perfunctory reports of deaths, in the spike and at the path side. Joe found in a hayloft (*South Wales Daily News*, 1907); Andrew, aged fifty-nine, run over by a car (*Leeds Mercury*, 1913), an unknown seventy-year-old veteran of wars in the Crimea and China, who died walking alongside another tramp in the woods of Jerry's Hill in south-west London (*Portsmouth Evening News*, 1903).

These records tell us little about how the tramps felt, what they thought about their lives, and their feelings about the society that had brought them to walking the country. The closest picture we often get is refracted through the telling of outsiders. In place of the words of the tramps themselves and faced with a

8 We also know from the records about his tattoos, including an anchor and a Union Jack, and that he is described as 'eccentric'.

scant official record, we must turn to the accounts of those who chose to walk alongside the tramps, who briefly lived their lifestyle – the commentators, essayists and journalists who went undercover to expose the social ills of the workhouse, the spike and of life on the road. While usually sympathetic, these accounts were not made for the tramps but were usually written for the middle class by the middle class. Accounts which range from the visceral to the sentimental – often veering into what we might now call 'poverty porn' – give us the most vivid surviving picture of the tramping life.

Victorian and Edwardian imposters into the workhouse included James Greenwood, a journalist who went undercover in the Lambeth spike in 1866 to discover that he was to be lodged in a flimsy shed and encountered a bath 'containing a liquid . . . disgustingly like weak mutton broth'; and the American novelist Jack London, who met men who had been forced into destitution through workplace accidents or from having contracted smallpox (as he says of one former fish seller: 'he put his back under too great a load of fish, and his chance for happiness in life was crossed off the books'). The social reformer Mary Higgins describes the punishing life tramping the workhouse circuit in the early twentieth century; she was forced, at one point, to push a crawling companion up a hill so they could make it to the next spike. Like Greenwood forty years earlier, Higgins finds dirt and degradation – exposed wire mattresses, filthy straw pillows and an 'ocean of nauseous food'. Higgins gives us a rare glimpse into the life of a female tramp (women represented about ten per cent of the tramping population at the time – generally women entered the long-term workhouse while men tramped seeking work). She tells us of humiliation and danger, of the broken and unfrosted windows which allow the men to peer into the women's sleeping quarters, and gives an account of one spike which includes this chilling passage:

Suddenly a door at the end of the room was unlocked, and a *man* put his head in! He only asked, 'How many?' and when we answered 'Three,' he locked us in speedily. I could not, however, get to sleep for a long time after finding that a man had the key of our room, especially as our elderly friend had told us of another workhouse where the portress left the care of the female tramps to a man almost entirely, and she added that 'He did what he liked with them.'

Perhaps the most celebrated accounts from these fleeting outsiders come from the 1930s, towards the end of the quasi-formal tramping system – Laurie Lee's *As I Walked Out One Midsummer Morning* and George Orwell's *Down and Out in Paris and London.*[9] Laurie Lee's account is interesting in that he didn't set out specifically to ape the lives of the tramps but walks alongside them in his trek from his Cotswolds home to, eventually, the south coast of Spain. Lee brings more life to what it was like to walk the tramp's paths. The dusty feet from endless trekking and the exhaustion which leads him to collapse into sleep at the field's edge under a drizzling sky. He walks the old country roads which faithfully follow the line of ancient cart tracks and packhorse routes and observes the increasing domination of the motor car which has begun to 'cut the landscape to pieces, through which the hunched-up traveller races at gutter height, seeing less than a dog in a ditch'.

Joining Orwell and Lee on the 1930s tramping circuit was the Reverend Frank Jennings, who styled himself as 'The Tramp Parson'. Like Greenwood, Higgins and London, Jennings had started off by visiting the London workhouses, shadowing the

9 It is Orwell perhaps who defined 'the tramp' for a general audience: 'a native English species' with four distinguishing characteristics: 'he has no money, he is dressed in rags, he walks about twenty kilometres a day and never sleeps two nights together in the same place'.

poor and unemployed of the capital, but he then set off across the country to follow the tramping circuit. He walks alongside the tramps, who he calls 'the knights of the lone grey road', on a route which takes him from London through Hertfordshire, Bedfordshire, Northamptonshire, Nottinghamshire, Cambridgeshire, Essex and then back to the capital, a 400-mile trip that was completed almost wholly on foot. He writes that, 'save for two lifts by passing motorists, I managed to footslog the journey throughout' (one wonders how many of the actual tramps were offered lifts).

In his account of this journey, *Tramping With Tramps*, Jennings is seeking to know the tramps 'in their raw state . . . eager to study them from first-hand knowledge, to experience with them that heart-to-heart throb that denotes contact and partnership'. While there are certainly elements of sentiment in his account (for instance, he describes the tramps as 'picturesque folk'), he also squarely attacks the system which has led so many to be tramping the roads as 'injurious, uneconomic and unchristian'. For others the romanticism of a nomadic lifestyle leads to accounts which are simply shocking in their casual disregard for the lived experience of the tramps. Middle-class romantics appropriated the tramp's lifestyle, seeing a supposed 'freedom' in their endless walking across the country while seemingly ignoring the social, political and economic conditions that had forced these men and women into wandering homelessness. In his 1926 book *The Gentle Art of Tramping*, Stephen Graham urges the reader to set out walking, to escape from being a 'voter, taxpayer . . . to cease to be identified by one's salary or by one's golf handicap'. This is tramping as performance; we are advised to ditch our 'West-End tie, jewelled tie-pin . . . silver topped cane [or] visiting cards' (although Graham instructs his reader to always keep a collar and tie in the knapsack should they need to enter a bank or post office). Graham steals the very word 'tramp' and applies it to the middle-class leisure walker. His tramps are the 'true Bohemian, pilgrims, explorers afoot, walking tourists' and not those who walked between the spikes in poverty and homelessness. To him these are simply 'enemies of society – won't works and parasites of the charitable'.

It was Frank Jennings' account that had brought me to the Kettering workhouse. He writes of entering the Kettering spike accompanied by a tramp called Tim, a man who 'knows every twist and turning on the great main thoroughfares', having been 'so long on the road that he has become part of the landscape'. I set out into this landscape with a sense of unease, knowing that walking between the sites of the former workhouses of Kettering and Wellingborough will not bring true revelation to what it was like to walk these paths as a tramp. I'm much further away from these experiences than even the tramping interlopers of the nineteenth and twentieth centuries. I walk simply seeking clues to continuity and change on the path network over the course of ninety years.

I head out of Kettering, trying to track Frank Jennings' way, weaving through suburban streets and road works. I'm shortly sidetracked, stopping to peer through the gates and railings of Wicksteed Park. On this October Thursday morning the rides of this amusement ground are quiet, and nothing moves along the miniature railway track, installed just before Jennings' Northamptonshire walk. The park was created in 1921, by Charles Wicksteed, who could often be seen driving around the roads of Kettering in his open-topped brown car, his little terrier Jerry beside him occupying the only other seat. Charles had originally intended to create a garden suburb, a place for working-class housing at below-market rents. But after the 1919 Act which gave responsibility to local authorities to create public housing, Wicksteed decided instead to use the land to give 'healthful recreation to the working classes' (although some land was sold for private development, including the evocatively named Paradise Lane). I imagine Jennings treading the same pavement alongside the park, perhaps mixing with streams of people coming here to enjoy a day out. What they would have found was freedom – there was an absence of 'Keep off the Grass' signs at Wicksteed Park, and children and their parents were allowed to roam free over these 147 acres. The playgrounds and various amusements were not tucked away but placed front and centre in the landscape – a place of joy.[10]

I arrive at a stop on my walk, Burton Latimer, a small town which has seen the fortunes of industries ebb and flow. For much of its history Burton Latimer was a small agricultural village, where people went out into the fields for work – everyday working walks in the morning and evening. Mills would have dotted the outskirts of the town, focusing on the processing of crops (corn, mustard, and wheat) and cloth (silk, cotton, and wool). As with many similar towns, the arrival of the railway changed the world of work. Here, a heritage of milling cloths turned into wider manufacturing. Lace-making and clothing factories opened and the boot and shoe industry flourished (as it did across the whole of Northamptonshire); the railways also stimulated the quarrying of ironstone in the area [11]

When Frank Jennings and the tramps came through here in the 1930s, they would have seen a town sprinkled with light industry. The tramps might have picked up casual, one-off jobs

---

10 Charles Wicksteed was also a pioneer in the design of playground furniture, to be installed all over the park. What was claimed to be the 'world's oldest swing' was uncovered in a former house of his and has now been installed back in the park. The Wicksteed company remains a major manufacturer of playground equipment to this day.

11 In the 1950s there were still over forty factories in Kettering manufacturing shoes, with over 5,000 workers making over 5 million pairs a year.

at the fringes of these industries and the economy they supported: minor maintenance, hedge cutting, waiting tables, sandwich-board holding and street singing (in the week this meant songs, now largely forgotten, like 'Annie Laurie' and 'I Wanna Be Someone's Baby', and hymns at the weekend). The tramps engaged in small enterprise, buying cheap goods in bulk or damaged items, such as camphor balls, shirt studs, postcards, safety pins and stockings, and selling them on in the street.[12] One tramp regularly purchased damaged boxes of pills from the chemist to repackage and sell on (although not particularly carefully; we are told that 'Some of 'em get headache pills for a weak spine and liver pills for heartburn').

Looking at the interwar Ordnance Survey map, from the time when Jennings would have been tramping through Northamptonshire, I discern a route he may have taken. A footpath is shown running from Kettering to the outskirts of Burton Latimer. An old path, skirting a deserted medieval village, in the 1930s it presented a natural and direct route. Now, though, it has been diverted and tunnels round the buildings and scrappy places of modern commerce and industry. Liminal spaces bridging the rural and the urban. Away from a busy road, the rush and drone of traffic fades as I walk a thin, passage-like path. Directly in front is a monolithic white wall, unbroken by windows – the side of the Morrisons supermarket distribution centre. A place, along with its twin site in nearby Corby, which covers 1.2 million square feet of ground. Behind these anonymous walls, 1,100 workers receive 5,500 pallets of goods a day. There is no scent of grass, decay, or manure on the breeze. On the road behind is the

12 Frank Jennings recounts the patter of one stocking seller: 'There's lovely stockings for you. I can say this, that if any of you gents present your lady friends with stockings like these, there'll be trouble in the Divorce Court. See how nice my hand looks in these! But supposing it was a lady's leg instead . . .'

headquarters and main factory for what is now Weetabix, its production perfuming the whole of this industrial area – a pleasant smell, malty and sweet with a note of sourness.[13]

At the southern end of Burton Latimer, a small estate of new-build houses, the arms of wind turbines waving over a gentle slope behind, marks the end of the town. I now walk the hedge-fringed roadside through some scant copses and alongside cows in flat Northamptonshire fields. While the spike would have been the usual destination, the tramps also camped out in similarly rural settings. This may have been out of necessity – perhaps they couldn't return to the spike having contravened one of its many rules or the next spike was simply too far away for weary legs. For many tramps a night outside, especially in the summer months, would be out of preference.[14] Frank Jennings tells us that 'better anything than to be the spike' was the 'oft-repeated cry of the nomad on the King's highway'. Tramps could walk long distances to find some semblance of shelter, away from the spike (Jennings even tramped through the night in the summer months). They 'dossed down' along the paths, in secluded woodlands, tucked in the lee of a hedge or in outhouses, cowsheds and haystacks. Orwell notes a popular sleeping place just outside London, 'a regular caravanserai of tramps – one could tell it by the worn grass and the sodden newspaper and

13 When the Tramp Parson walked here the factory was newly established, the company then known as British and African Cereal Co. Ltd having bought one of the abandoned flour mills of the district.

14 Other options for tramping accommodation were cheap boarding houses and a number of private refuges and institutions. The latter included those administered by the Salvation Army and the Homeless Poor Society, and the Rowton Houses – hostels established by Disraeli's private secretary, Lord Rowton. Jack London and Orwell both stayed at a Rowton House as did Joseph Stalin while attending the Fifth Congress of the Russian Social Democratic Labour Party in 1907.

rusty cans that they had left behind'. Abandoned and demolished buildings were places in which they could often sleep undisturbed. Laurie Lee, when working as a labourer, took to sleeping (along with his girlfriend and her whole family) 'in the remaining fragment of a ballroom'.

The houses of Burton Latimer are behind; I'm on a flat-field-edged country lane. The first indication that I'm approaching a place of industry, marooned in the countryside, comes from having to step back on to the narrow verge as trucks sweep speedily past, threatening to knock me off my feet. The ground starts to get scruffier with dusty and sundried fly-tipped waste dumped by the roadside – craggy piles of sheared paving slabs and crumbling breeze blocks. The road leads through an industrial estate, sandwiched between a railway line and the River Ise. An eclectic range of modern businesses cluster along the roadside. Manufacturers of fencing and holiday homes. A classic-car dealership and a self-storage warehouse. A kennels and dog groomers. Towards the end of the estate, I look into a yard, where giant towers of pallets are being shifted around by a forklift, a sea of ever-changing wooden monuments reaching high into the sky. The attached buildings are somewhat out of place, visibly older than the metal-sided sheds and squat one-storey office buildings.

These outbuildings are part of the site's long industrial history, first the Finedon Iron Works and later a wagon works (there was also pottery elsewhere on the site). The iron workings only operated for a few decades but were an important source of employment for the area, as the *Northampton Chronicle and Echo* put it on their closure in 1891: 'trade is so bad that Finedon Furnaces have been blown out after being in blast for something like thirty years . . . this will have a serious effect on labour in the district'. The closure of whole industries, and a plethora of jobs where only short-term work was available, swelled the number of people tramping the paths seeking employment.[15] The trades who walked were numerous – the 1920s Member of Parliament Henry Broadhurst, himself a stone mason, writes in his autobiography of going great distances from one job site to the next in the mid-nineteenth century, walking alongside bricklayers, tanners and engineers. Eight years later, Laurie Lee meets carpenters and clerks who 'have been on the road for months . . . the treadmill of the mid-thirties'. To this we can add bookbinders, coopers, farm labourers, smiths, steam engine makers and tailors as some of the many trades which plied the roads from one job opportunity to the next.[16]

Except for an isolated row of houses, the 'Furnace Cottages', there are no other dwellings immediately around the iron-works.[17] Paths and roads run from the site, over and through fields, to the communities around: Finedon and Wellingbor-ough to the south and east, Isham and Burton Latimer to the north. All these places are over a mile away – walking these rural paths would have bookended the working day.

15 In the 1930s, Northamptonshire was also host to a different kind of walk for work. The Jarrow March (or Jarrow Crusade) came through here in 1936: 200 men who had already walked 205 miles and had another 86 to go to London so that they could present their petition to Parliament railing against the unemployment in their town.

16 From the early Victorian period, for many of these occupations, the tramping was sustained by trade unions who created regional and national networks of 'houses of call', public houses where workers from particular trades could find out about job opportunities or receive small amounts of money from the union's funds.

17 Cottages which were at risk of being destroyed in the late 1990s by the building of the Isham bypass. The residents took to their roofs to daub six-foot-high anti-bypass slogans across the row of homes.

Today only about seven per cent of people commute on foot, and it is easy to forget how much of a necessity walking to work was for the Victorians and Edwardians (especially in the countryside). Many simply didn't have access to a horse or wagon, having to rely on foot power alone, what was wryly coined as going by 'Shanks's Pony'. We also forget quite how far people used to walk to their jobs. A government report from 1867 found that children (some as young as ten) and women working in agriculture would walk between four and ten miles a day to and from work.[18] In the 1880s, a carpenter in rural Gloucestershire was recorded as walking fourteen miles a day *each way* for work, six days a week (that's at least forty hours of walking over the working week). The practicalities of walking these distances every day are rather mind-boggling. Waking up at dawn to walk on frost-crunched paths, on ways gummed with mud or along dusty roads. The weariness of starting a day of physical labour after a four-hour walk (and facing the same at the end of the day). The peril of a morning rainstorm, having to spend the rest of the working day in sodden, cold clothes.

In his novel *Greene Ferne Farm*, Richard Jefferies writes of the 'wearyful women [coming] homeward from the gleaning and the labour of the field'. They walk past a country house on 'such paths used by the workers, and going right through the grounds of the house . . . where the ancient usage has not yet succumbed to modern privacy, and were once the general custom'. There are thousands of such paths across England and Wales, forged by working people trekking from the home to the field, the workshop, and the factory. Paths which are

18 For one local vicar from Sussex, quoted in the report, this couldn't be an issue as 'agricultural children are not gentlemen's children, and they must begin young to work and walk'.

created, defined and solidified through millions of repeated, everyday journeys.

Twenty minutes' walk from the ironworks I reach the outskirts of Wellingborough on an old bridleway through a field where half a dozen informal paths wind down to the riverside, squeezed through bushes and pushing aside long grass. The bridleway tunnels into a chute-like passage as it runs alongside the railway line. Crossing the tracks in the 1930s would have brought a view of more fields before reaching the streets, houses, shops, and factories of Wellingborough. There is a small piece of no man's land – the path used to run for another half a mile, a slightly meandering line through the fields, but now my way goes right through another industrial estate. The wide gates of a large high-brick-walled yard are open, revealing a crisp mountain of plastic. The white frames of thousands of UPVC windows, ready for recycling, the arm of a digger rising from behind and picking through. As at Burton Latimer, the enduring memory here is of smell. The smell of unknown industrial processes, glue or maybe solvent, coming from anonymous buildings. Further on, there is the surprising scent of cardamom and some other spices I can't quite place. I look up the businesses later, spotting a manufacturer of hand-cooked gourmet Indian snacks: chevda, gathia and Bombay mix.

Through the centre of Wellingborough, I arrive at my journey's end – the town's workhouse, sprawling along the Irthlingborough Road, protected by a long wall topped with overflowing greenery. The view of the surrounding area from the highest workhouse window would have seemed similar to that which greeted the inmates 100 years ago. The layout of the park opposite, Castle Fields, has barely changed. Across neatly clipped stretches of grass there is a straight lattice of tarmacked paths on the same alignment as the park in the 1930s. The stone bandstand, erected in 1913 and refurbished ten years ago, provides further continuity over the past century. While the form of the park is little changed, the function of the workhouse buildings which face it have undergone a dramatic transformation. Much of the incongruously Italianate architecture of the Wellingborough workhouse – high rows of arched windows topped with an elaborate finial and weathervane – has now been converted into flats, people sleeping much more comfortably than the building's previous residents.[19]

In 1938, Pathé made a short newsreel about the tramps. The film focused on the signs that the tramps would supposedly chalk outside the homes they passed. Symbols for their fellow wanderers – marks on the farmhouse step or garden gatepost which denoted whether the homeowner would be receptive to a request for food or money. Like other newsreel films of the tramps, it is sentimental (the voiceover on a later Pathé film, from 1947, speaks of the tramp, in an echo of Stephen Graham, as the 'happy pauper who counts his riches by what he hasn't got: the worry of catching a train to work, standing in a queue, filling in forms for this and that, of making ends meet'). Towards the end of the 1938 film, the tramp in his battered hat and with a scruffy beard meets a fresh-faced young female hiker on a path outside a rural house. They exchange pleasantries, a meeting of two people, using the path network for very different purposes. A sharing of the paths which Jennings described: 'To the holiday-seeker, bound up in his pleasure, the road is a godly pal;

19 Wellingborough isn't the only place where former workhouse buildings have been repurposed for residential living. A workhouse in central London, which is said to have inspired Dickens' *Oliver Twist*, has recently been developed into thirteen luxury homes, with a thousand bodies being exhumed from the paupers' graveyard on the same land.

to the homeless and penniless roadster, wanted by none and spurned by the many, she is more often than not a wearisome, unheeding and cruel companion.'

The film is an early symbol of a transition of how we use, and how we conceive of, our paths. We have a picture of the walking network now, especially in rural Britain, that is firmly rooted in leisure – our paths are conduits for enjoying and connecting with nature, spaces for health and rejuvenation. Easily overlooked is the practical function the whole network played, routes for finding and sustaining employment or to seek shelter and relief. Standing on the pavement outside of the old Wellingborough workhouse, I reflect on the people who may have walked the paths before me. Men and women trekking across the country to find a job to sustain them and their families, the Finedon iron workers taking the paths on their daily commute and the tramps on their seemingly endless circuits to the next spike. I think about the men and women that Jennings walked beside on the roads: the wounded soldier, invalided due to a gas attack in the First World War, with six medals pinned to his chest; the former South African diamond merchant who had lost all his money and had taken to picking through refuse tips to resell scrap metal; the thin and sunburned sixty-five-year-old woman making rugs and kettle-holders from old clothes as she walked across the country. Some of the many ghosts who linger on our paths.

8.   The Church, Death and Taxes

At the tail end of the Humber estuary, where it meets the Rivers Ouse and Trent, next to a sloping path wending down to the water, there is a design cut shallowly but distinctly into the turf. A curled labyrinth, called Julian's Bower, is forty-four feet across but when walked, forms its own path of a quarter of a mile in length. The origins of this labyrinth, which has lain here with regular maintenance for at least 325 years, are cloaked in mystery and speculation.[1] Perhaps it was created for fun – for centuries the labyrinth was the focus for joyous games held in the village on the night before May Day. Another origin story sees it constructed to commemorate the restoration of the Stuart monarchy after the Interregnum. While for many the return of the king was a quasi-religious event, other theories place Julian's Bower as having a more straightforwardly spiritual purpose. It may have been created as an act of transcendental penitence by a conspirator in the twelfth-century murder of Thomas Becket. In this function, Julian's Bower would be walked in prayer, a moral maze for contemplation and reflection. The labyrinth is a maze in which only one path can be taken – a symbol of a singular journey towards God. It's an image repeated in Christian iconography, in further

---

1 Julian's Bower may be one of the oldest extant labyrinths in the country. There is a competing claim for St Catherine's Hill in Winchester. Local legend says it was created by the boys of Winchester College boarding school, a demonstration of their knowledge of classical maze design.

labyrinths outside in stone and turf, or carved on rocks and gravestones and laid out on the floor of churches.[2]

The use of a path as a tool for attempting to achieve salvation is unsurprising. The Bible tells us that to commit to and obey the word of God is to 'walk in love', 'walk in my law' and to 'walk in faith'. Believers are instructed to 'walk in my statutes, and keep my commandments, and do them'. Jeremiah rebukes the people of Judah for their apostasy with the words, 'Thus saith the Lord, Stand ye in the ways, and see, and ask for the old paths, where is the good way, and walk therein, and ye shall find rest for your souls'. Allegorical paths continue within the church building. Alongside labyrinths are the more familiar Stations of the Cross: images which form interior processional routes, mirroring the Via Dolorosa in the Old City of Jerusalem. The holy city path is barely a third of a mile long, walked by thousands of pilgrims a year (some with an accompanying cross), itself a replica of the way taken by Jesus to his crucifixion, burial and resurrection.

The church as path makers and followers extends well beyond labyrinths and the Stations of the Cross and past the strictly spiritual and allegorical. A few short steps (but hundreds of

---

2 Probably the most famous of these interior labyrinths is to be found within the Notre-Dame de Chartres, created in the early thirteenth century (which became somewhat of a template for labyrinths to follow – with its rounded design and eleven snaking rings). A dozen or so labyrinthine designs can be found in England, such as at Ely Cathedral, St Helena and St Mary's Church in Bourn, Cambridgeshire, and in the porch of Alkborough Church, a few hundred feet from Julian's Bower.

There seems to be a modern trend for the creation of labyrinths. In the past two decades they have been installed in Boxgrove Priory in Sussex, Chislehurst Methodist Church in south-east London, Mill Hill Chapel in Leeds and Wakefield Cathedral, as well as in public parks, religious study centres, private gardens and adventure parks. One, outside Bath, was made by protesters against road building in the 1990s and is maintained to this day.

years back) from Julian's Bower once stood a Benedictine Priory, whose monks are other speculated creators of the labyrinth. A small community, comprising a handful of monks and a chaplain, lived here by the Humber mud-flats from the eleventh to the thirteenth centuries. This community was dependent on another priory at Spalding, sixty-five miles away on the other side of Lincolnshire (itself an offshoot of Crowland Abbey, another eight miles south again). Monasteries, nunneries and priories were institutions very much *in* the world, whose power came from the temporal as well as the spiritual. The distance between these religious communities in Lincolnshire indicates the necessity for paths – the need for movement, for material connections – which leaves a legacy today.

At the very edge of Wales, there is a place where I've experienced a profound peace and a heart-seizing joy – a truly wonderful path which meanders through thick woods. In places, the trees seem to part for the path; the woodland and track are one. In others, this path diverts around trunks and over jutting, rising roots. Occasionally there are uplifting, centring views out of the woods, into the steep valley of the River Wye below and across to answering, reflected woodland. After a few miles the route starts to dip down from its lofty course, and the light fades as it plunges into the earth in a deep holloway. Leaving the woodland and passing through fields and around scattered houses, the path emerges in front of something very special indeed. Revealed is Tintern Abbey, a magnificent and haunting ruin, a place that has long attracted poets, artists, tourists and romantics.

The abbey at Tintern was built in this tucked-away valley by a monastic order that had journeyed from their birth in the marshlands of eastern France in the eleventh century: the Cistercians. These monks regarded themselves as a more perfect version of the Benedictines from whom they emerged. The Cistercians sought a return to piety, achieved through principles of austerity and hard work – sleeping on wooden boards in simple, unadorned cells, living in quiet prayer, they were the 'White Monks' clothed in habits of plain, undyed wool. In 1128, twelve Cistercian monks from France landed on the shores of Britain, establishing their first abbey at Waverley in Surrey. Within a few years they had come to the Wye Valley to form a community and to erect their first buildings in Wales, simple wooden structures in which to live and worship.

The key to the success of the Cistercians across Britain was their land, donated by wealthy benefactors (for instance, the establishment of Waverley Abbey was made possible with the support, and land, of the Bishop of Winchester). Often they were associated with the taming of wild lands, of bringing into cultivation previously unproductive ground – all in the spirit of hard work. They were never passive occupiers but powerful landowners who shaped and worked their extensive properties. The Cistercians were among the first major sheep farmers in Wales (important in and of itself in a nation which now has almost 9 million sheep) and they rose to become one of the largest traders of wool across Britain.[3] Their economic exploits didn't stop at sheep; they also kept arable farms, trapped fish and mined coal, iron, lead and silver.

At Tintern the Cistercians were endowed their first land by a local lord, Walter de Clare, and successive lords of Chepstow continued this support with further grants of territory. But these lands weren't wild, and the monks at Tintern found

---

3 Their riches were partly gained through two very helpful circumstances. Utilizing unpaid lay brothers meant that they avoided paying wages (although they did have to provide them with accommodation and food) and they were exempt from paying tax on the wool they exported.

themselves with well-managed and fertile ground. Like elsewhere, they organized their land into monastic farms (called granges), with much of the actual labour being undertaken by lay brothers. From behind the great abbey windows (the buildings we see in ruins today were constructed from 1269 onwards), the monks wielded and managed these productive lands to become powerful players in the regional economy. Tax records from 1291, when they were near the height of their power, show that they owned somewhere in the region of 3,000 acres of ploughable estate, plus grazing land for 3,000 sheep and cattle, horses and pigs.[4] These vast lands were ultimately managed by a very small number of monks – roughly twenty at the abbey's height.

The Cistercians were by no means alone in the ranks of powerful monastic landowners. At the time of their dissolution in the sixteenth century, it is thought that somewhere between fifteen and thirty-three per cent of all land in England (and perhaps up to fifty-five per cent in counties such as Kent) was owned by the monasteries. With land came wealth – the *Valor Ecclesiasticus*, a survey of religious property in England and Wales conducted in 1535 at the behest of Henry VIII (as a key part of his mission to wrest religious control from the Catholic church) details the monasteries bringing in £143,000 a year – more than £125 million in today's money.

The control and operation of such large landholdings required an extensive network of communication and trade. The monastic granges organized and owned by Tintern Abbey used pre-existing routes supplemented by the laying and improvement of new ways by the monks' army of lay brothers. Paths connected the granges – to move produce, to take animals to pasture – and to the wider world and the market. Paths which

4 These tax records are just for the land the Tintern monks owned in Wales.

still exist today, partially recorded and preserved, a shadow of a dense network that fractures out from the abbey's farmsteads over the wider landscape. Deep holloways, ridgeway tracks, bridleways, footpaths and thin, lonely ways carved up the mountainside, barely visible from the valleys, called 'rhiws' (rhiws were often used to take sheep to pasture and to connect the steep topography, but some had more specific uses, such as Rhiw Pyscod, the 'fish hill track', which was used to transport live fish to the monks' ponds).

Further north, in the Cambrian Mountains (known as the 'Green Desert of Wales' for its lack of people), a separate band of Cistercians founded an abbey at Strata Florida (Ystrad Fflur, the valley of the flowers). The travel writer Jan Morris tells us of the significance of this abbey and of those who lie within its grounds. It was the final destination for a long line of Welsh chieftains, 'buried in pride beneath the Cistercian blessing', and for the poet Dafydd ap Gwilym, whose resting place lies under that great tree of the British churchyard, the sacred and holy yew.[5]

Strata Florida didn't stand alone; it was connected with two other abbeys: Cwmhir elsewhere in the Cambrian Mountains and Strata Marcella. Here, as at Tintern, paths were created to join the abbeys and their granges. The wealth of the monks and the sweat of the lay brothers were directed to cut away at the sides of mountains and hills, shifting vast amounts of earth to create a flat path, in places paved or metalled, for the swift running of hooves and feet. It was a building project every bit as impressive as the creation of any modern bypass or motorway.

5 Yew trees have a long-held association with death. It has been suggested that the presence of yew trees in churchyards dates to the conversion of pagan sites into early Christian places of worship. The symbolism of the yew, whose red berries signify the blood of Christ, may be a back-formation.

Suddenly the twenty-four-mile journey between Strata Florida and Cwmhir could be ridden on horseback in a single day. These abbeys were as much economic entities as the operations from Tintern in the Wye Valley, if not more so. This path was a link across the landscape over which goods and animals could pass and along which the business of the abbeys, both spiritual and material, could flow.

The monastic paths exist today in fragmentary form, used for a multitude of purposes in the movement of dozens of subsequent generations. Many have been overlayed by our modern roads, connections to their past use frayed, but others are still there, not too far removed from how they would have looked to the monks. A path called the Monks' Trod in the Cambrian Mountains is one of these redoubtable survivors.[6] Its use as a major thoroughfare fell away before it could be tarmacked by later generations, perhaps due to its remoteness and its use and value being ripped away by Henry VIII's dissolution. By 1882 it was an antiquarian peculiarity, to be seen in scraps, a guidebook from that year telling its readers of a 'curious dilapidated bridge . . . the old monks' road across the hills . . . scarcely accessible now to wheels.'[7] The long path through the Green Desert of

6 A trod is an alternative name for a path, often but not exclusively paved in some way. They are now most associated with monastic use but can be found in other contexts. Many of the non-monastic trods were found in North Yorkshire. For instance, in Middlesbrough there was a small network of Sailors' Trods (used by river crews alongside the Tees), in Beverley there was the Gilly Croft trod (presumedly connected to the town's Hospital of St Giles), and in Kirkby a Pannierman's Trod (for packhorses).

7 However, this is not to say that the peace of this remote mountain walk is not under threat from modern vehicles. For several decades the use of four-by-fours and motorbikes on this unpaved and untarmacked track was banned, but this was lifted in 2021. Since then these vehicles have churned up this venerable route.

Wales between these great abbeys, on which abbots and monks walked and rode, along which religion and power were communicated, still lives on after more than half a millennium.

The survival of the monks' routes between the great abbeys of England and Wales is just one aspect of a forgotten network forged through centuries of Christianity. Monastic footsteps are joined by parishioners walking journeys of everyday belief and singular ritual. The most enigmatic and poignant of these are the paths over which the dead were taken for burial: the corpse roads.

On pretty much any walk, at some point I will want a place to sit. A place to slump and yield. To stretch out my toes and arch my feet, to feel calves push and pull. Somewhere I can enjoy moments of stillness, staring at a single point after hours of movement and a constantly changing view. When I want to rest I walk distractedly, consciously scouting out a good location. Sometimes a plateau of soft grass or vaguely horizontal log will suffice, but coming across a bench is perfect. Settling down with the knowledge that someone has made a choice to place a seat at this exact spot. As with graves in a churchyard, my eyes and thoughts often linger on a memorial bench's plaque. The few short words which try to set out a person's life and perhaps their connection to where 'their bench' now stands. Short statements which seek to describe the importance of these singular individuals for people who may never have known them at all.

It was a rain-filled day in the Lake District in 2017. In the tourist town of Ambleside, people clustered in groups, leaping puddles and dodging between shops and cafes. I walked past the seventeenth-century Bridge House over Stock Ghyll Beck, a famous building in this part of the Lakes. Harriet Martineau, the powerhouse Victorian journalist, travel writer and sociologist, once described it as 'the most curious relic of the olden time', a scene which 'every artist sketches as he passes by'. Little changes, and between rain showers, amateur photographers politely dance round each other to best photograph this tiny two-roomed building standing on a perfect arch of grey slate.

In the country outside Ambleside, the world is reduced to a palette of white, grey, black and green. A pall of mist has been drawn over the tops of hills, leaving only their very lower reaches visible. Despite the Lake District being one of the most popular walking destinations in Britain, I hadn't spent much time rambling here and this path is new ground for me. Looking upwards, all is hidden. Perhaps behind the grey are sodden, gently pastural slopes, or there could be dramatic masses of rock and mountain. The roadside pavement and drystone walls are wetted black from a distance, a thin silver sheen when close. Sodden fields are speckled with sodden sheep. Rydal Water is a solid matt grey, interrupted by an island of trees, the green of their leaves blunted at this distance by the drizzle. Stepping off a hard surface, the earth seems to invite my feet to come down, my boots sinking into the new mud.

Departing from the main road, I follow a more minor lane, tarmacked across the side of a hill in a sheltered tunnel of trees. I am now itching to sit, and to rest. I see a wide, flat stone, its base fringed with grass and backdropped by ferns. Placed right next to the road, behind a thin yellow line and under an umbrella of a tree, it resembles a throne. The perfect place to stop. As I sit, I don't pay any attention to the small white sign half hidden towards the back of the stone. I stay for ten minutes, staring at the rain and the trees opposite. As I stand up again, my rucksack scrapes against the sign; across the top are written the words 'Coffin Stone, or Resting Stone'. Sitting alone in this damp lane, I consider that I am not the first to settle here. I've been walking a path on which the dead were carried, with this stone a place to rest a coffin, allowing weary pallbearers a short respite.

There are many names for these deathly ways. While 'corpse

roads' are perhaps the most common, to our path lexicon we can add 'coffin path', 'bier road' (named after the 'bier', a stretcher or stand to hold a coffin) and 'lych way' (from the Old English 'lich', meaning corpse). Forming part of our present rights of way network, these also constituted paths for the living, for journeys to the regular services, to pray and to marry (another name for them is simply 'church path'). Nonetheless, it is their association with death and grief that makes these paths some of our most enigmatic, carrying not just bodies but layers of superstition and myth.

The corpse roads were formed by the practicalities of burial in early medieval England and Wales. This period saw a boom in church building, as churches were serving smaller, more dispersed communities. These smaller places of worship were fine for a parish's usual weekly service, but the 'main' churches, with all their pomp and importance, insisted on maintaining their hold over the burial of parishioners – not to mention taking the tidy sums which went with burials. It was quickly established, therefore, that rather than interments taking place at local 'daughter' churches, bodies would be carried for burial at the 'mother' church.

The daughter/mother church structure meant that corpse roads often crossed rough, forbidding and isolated ground in areas that were historically (and often are still) sparsely populated. The Ambleside to Grasmere corpse road that I stumbled across isn't a solitary occurrence in the Lake District; Cumbria is alive with a network of corpse roads, with over a dozen similar routes spread across the county, such as the one linking Wasdale to Eskdale, a six-mile walk over tough fells, or that of St John's in the Vale, where bodies were strapped to a horse or pulled on a sledge to navigate the bare, trackless terrain.

In less forbidding and remote ground can be found the Irton Hall Estate in West Cumbria. Here, routes to the local church of

St Paul's were almost lost – paths used by parishioners for centuries to take themselves and their dead to the church. Having been in the hands of the Irton family for generations, the hall was purchased by Sir Thomas Brocklebank in 1897; he disputed the public nature of these paths, believing their use was a privilege rather than a right. The locals were not happy to see their paths taken away; as the *Spectator* commented at the time, 'the Cumbrian . . . is . . . stubborn in defending his rights if he thinks those rights are trampled upon'. The local Bootle Parish Council sided with the villagers, and in 1899 a dispute broke out. It was a long-running argument which brought corpse roads to national attention.

During the lengthy legal proceedings of the Irton footpaths case, the court spoke to hundreds of witnesses. The newspaper accounts of the proceedings suggest that everyone was having a rather jolly time, as successive locals came to the stand to testify. When one witness said he used the path from both ends, Sir Edward Clarke (the QC and Member of Parliament, no less, instructed by Brocklebank) shot back with, 'Well, not at the same time'. This was followed by much laughter in the courtroom. A local pub landlord, asked if he had read a notice that had supposedly been pinned to one of the paths, simply said, 'I never read it, my dear Sir Edward, don't try it on again.' The court not only heard from many locals but also turned to the historical record of the area.[8] The clerk of Irton Parish Council presented a map to the court, seeking to demonstrate that this showed the public paths running through waste ground on Brocklebank's estate. The *West Cumberland Times* records the legal exchange in examining this potentially crucial document:

8 Just as volunteers do today when applying for public rights of way to be definitively recorded.

The Learned Judge experienced some difficulty in finding the Waste on the map, and Sir Edward Clarke remarked that it was almost too small to find.

The Learned Judge: Oh, I've got it. (Laughter.)

Sir Edward Clark: That's what all this litigation is about. (Laughter.)

Mr Shee [the counsel instructed by Bootle Parish Council]: That's what they've spent all the money on, and what they're spending more money on. (Laughter.)

The map that the judge had such difficulty reading was the Tithe Commutation Plan of 1840, part of a set of records which illustrate the intimate connection between the land and the church.

The word 'tithe' etymologically comes from 'a tenth', this being the proportion of agricultural produce – wheat, sheep/ wool, milk, corn, etc. – which would go from the harvest to sustain the local church.[9] There is no formal date for the beginning of tithing in England and Wales; King Æthelwulf of Wessex granted his churches the right to tithe in 855 and the much later Statute of Westminster of 1285 guaranteed its status (across England at least). As long as there have been tithes there have been disputes, anger and legal wranglings about their collection. In many places, agreements of varying formality were negotiated to avoid produce piling up in tithe barns, or to set a fairer nominal payment in cash. Tithes were sold, often to non-clergy, entrenching a feudal relationship between the peasantry and the landlord. The situation became worse with the dissolution of the monasteries, when many clergy and landlords

9 It's a system with biblical foundations: 'Then shall the Lord be my God: And this stone which I have set for a pillar shall be God's house: and of all that thou shalt give me, I will surely give the tenth unto thee.' It has parallels in earlier Jewish customs and the later Islamic Zakat tradition (and there has been a resurgence in modern American evangelical Christianity).

gave up collecting what they were formally due to avoid lengthy litigation and local anger. As the Reverend John Thirkens noted in 1828, 'If I collected the tithes in kind the land occupiers would harass me to death' (a real danger – in 1806 the Worcestershire village of Oddingley saw a grisly double murder over tithe collection, one of the victims being the local rector).

Ultimately it was agricultural developments and the march of the Industrial Revolution which exposed the unjust nature of tithes. New crops were being grown (such as potatoes from the Americas) and native crops were becoming more widespread (such as turnips and sainfoins), produce which had seldom been tithed, leading to arguments over whether they should be tithable at all.[10] Society had tilted away from being primarily agrarian, and producing tithable perishable goods, to an industrial one, producing non-tithable manufactured goods. Why should a rural community be taxed on their output when growing industrial towns weren't (and how could the clergy of these factory towns be sustained)?

The clamour for reform rose throughout the late eighteenth and early nineteenth centuries and in 1836 the Tithe Commutation Act was passed. Instead of getting rid of this contribution to the church entirely, the tithes were commuted and converted to a cash payment. To do this, local officials needed to work out what land everyone owned – and this meant maps. Almost eighty per cent of England and Wales was mapped. The first truly systematic attempt to show what these lands looked like in detail (in some places a full generation before the Ordnance Survey arrived). Tithe commissioners were appointed who travelled across the country, ratifying existing local agreements and

10 Sainfoin is a crop used for animal forage, the word coming from the French for 'healthy hay'. The scientific name *Onobrychis* translates as 'devoured by donkeys'.

creating new ones. The maps these commissioners produced varied significantly in quality and form, ranging from one-foot square to a whopping hundred-foot square. But they were in pursuit of the singular cause of taxation, splitting and evaluating the country according to who owned what and which parcels of land were tithable or not. Productive land came under the new tax, but barren wastes and Crown land didn't. Public land was also excluded, including public highways. It is the exclusion of these highways from the maps which is now used to reclaim, for the public, these paths. Bureaucratic documents produced at the beginning of the end of a centuries-old system, where the church had a direct stake and income from as much as two thirds of the land across the country, are repurposed to help prove public rights today and save paths to be used for generations to come.[11]

In Irton the evidence presented from the historical record and personal testimony proved successful. After years of legal battles (it was said at the time that this was the longest-running case in the history of the Carlisle courts), over 250 witness testimonies, hundreds of column inches in the press and thousands of pounds spent on lawyers' fees, Mr Justice Joyce finally confirmed the Irton paths as having 'been used as a right for as long back as living memory extended'. Everyone seemed thoroughly worn out by the case, so much so that there were cries for reform in how these vital paths, across the whole country, would be recorded and protected. Once again the *Spectator* lamented the bureaucracy and cost, calling for a

11 The system carried on (with the cash payment) until the Tithe Act of 1936, and tithes were abolished entirely by the Finance Act of 1977. The 1936 Act followed a resurgence of protest against tithes, when farmers blockaded roads and railways lines, poured mud on an auctioneer who was selling goods seized to pay the tax, and left a dead sheep on the car of a man sent to collect the tax. A few years earlier, the black-shirted British Union of Fascists jumped on the bandwagon, travelling from London to Suffolk to assist farmers who were resisting the tithe tax.

better way of settling such issues: 'these footpaths are so vital to the nation's well-being that some process ought to be devised by which the rights of private ownership or public enjoyment ought to be ascertainable and jealously safeguarded if encroached upon'. Fifty years later, a process was indeed brought into effect with the National Parks and Access to the Countryside Act, under which most corpse roads or church paths – including those at Irton – would be recorded in perpetuity.[12]

Whether they're recorded or not, the Irton footpath case demonstrates how the use of paths evolves over time. The Irton paths were established over decades for a primarily religious use but were repurposed as spaces for the movement of everyday life. A local tenant farmer recalls, with beautiful specificity, seeing 'butchers, doctors and strangers' walking the paths, while another recounted specifically directing tourists along them. Other witnesses talk of using the paths to go shopping, to go play in a cricket match, to fetch brewery yeast, visit relatives, to go to the post office or simply to venture out for a nice walk (in the words of one newspaper report: 'those who called at a certain public-house in the neighbourhood felt that after refreshing the inner man, a stroll over the Irton footpaths refreshed the soul as well.'). Which is not to say the original purpose of our corpse paths was ever completely forgotten – those of a superstitious nature continued to believe that to step foot on a corpse road should be avoided at all possible costs, unless one was carrying the dead.

Buried away in the 1871 volume of the rather obscure *The Collections Historical & Archaeological Relating to Montgomeryshire* are

---

12 This isn't to say that all of them have survived to be recorded on their original course. In his book *Spirit Roads: An Exploration of Otherworldly Routes*, Paul Devereux details the history of one old church path in Leicestershire. A section of this path is now lost, entombed under a modern housing estate.

details of the convoluted lengths to which a community in Wales went to keep the path of the dead separate from everyday life. Llansantffraid-ym-Mechain is a large, bustling village in Powys, close to the border with England.[13] The village and its parish church are named after St Ffraid (alternatively known as St Bride or St Bridget), who was said to have floated over to Wales from Ireland on a clod of turf. It is just below the little parish church that a strange burial custom took place in 'Corpse Field', a plot of land sloping down from the building, which became a processional ground for the dead. Instead of being carried on the usual path to the church, a coffin would follow a zigzag route across the field, the pallbearers drawing with their feet the profile of a man's head and shoulder. This temporary path, known as the corpse's shoulder (*ysgwydd y corph*), would be recreated every time a body was brought to the church. 'Though it might happen that a crop of hay was, at that moment, knee-deep, it was nonetheless deemed essential to carry the corpse through it, along the same path over which its predecessors had for ages gone to their long home'. The end of the corpse's shoulder would take the funeral party to a specific gate in the churchyard wall, the corpse gate (*llidiart y cyrph*), watched over by a sycamore tree. From this gate ran a straight path to the church door, a stretch known as the corpse's hundred yards (*can-llath y corph*). The origin of this convoluted route with its special entrance to the churchyard is not known, but it seems that there

---

13 The spelling of the village's name is a matter of some controversy; the inclusion of a 't' being seen as an anglicization of a Welsh name. The 't' was dropped for a while but reinstated after a local vote and with the approval of Powys County Council. However, that wasn't the end of the matter, as in 2018 someone took a blowtorch to the new road signs, blasting away the 't' and leading a local councillor to lament, 'It is so frustrating. We have just formed a committee to look at entering the village of the year competition next year and now this happens.'

was a dual superstition at play: the desire to never accidently recreate the path on which bodies were carried and the wish to send bodies along the special path for fear of who knows what. While the account of the superstitions linger, the consequences are perhaps destined to remain lost. The last burial to follow this route was in 1852 and the bottom of Corpse Field is now a new housing estate with a new road, a cul-de-sac called St Bride's Way. A public footpath runs from this road, across the field, resolutely *not* drawing the corpse's shoulder pattern.[14]

The nineteenth-century Yorkshire barrister turned antiquarian Norrisson Scatcherd explored the superstitious paths between the village of Walton, on the outskirts of Wakefield, and the mother church in neighbouring Sandal. For everyday business, people took the main highway, a slightly circuitous route round the field edges. Like the villagers of Llansantffraid-ym-Mechain, though, locals refused to take their dead along this route. Instead, they insisted on 'going through the grass, because the way through the field is the "corpse gate", the safer road to heaven'. In many places, corpse roads specifically avoided fertile ground in the belief that the carrying of a body would sterilize the earth beneath. A superstition also arose that, where a corpse road ran through a field, the line of the path should not be ploughed for fear of bad luck.

But the myth which lingered longest throughout the centuries,

14 In their *Encyclopaedia of Superstitions*, Edwin and Mona Augusta Radford tell of another superstition from an unnamed Norfolk churchyard. Here a woman's body was exhumed, to the consternation of the locals who believed that this would surely bring bad luck. The unfortunate woman's grave flanked the churchyard path and for many years the congregants would assiduously avoid walking past the spot, leaving the path to take a twelve-foot diversion (apparently in honour of the twelve apostles). Eventually the parish priest had a new path constructed, which followed this walked diversion.

in many different parts of the country, was that the very act of carrying a dead body across private land would create a public right of way. To avoid this, some funeral processions would pay a nominal 'toll' in the form of metal pins, which would be stuck in a gatepost to make it clear that the body was being allowed to pass here as a private, paid-for right. In some cases money was actually exchanged – the Swan Brewery in Leatherhead charged a penny for funerals to cross its yard.

The myths attached to corpse processions were long held and were repeated in newspaper stories well into the early twentieth century. As recently as 1977 it was noted, in a letter to the editor of the journal *Folklore*, that a wooden sign stood at the entrance to Palace Road in Brixton, south London, which read:

Private Road
Heavy Traffic
Funerals & Hawkers
Prohibited

If to walk a corpse road when not part of a funeral procession was unwise according to superstition, the converse was equally true. In 1940, the *Newcastle Chronicle* reported the tale of 'an old dame' who insisted that, upon her death, her body was to be taken along the corpse road. 'If ye de'ant,' the dame warned, 'I'll come again'. The corpse road in question, located in the North York Moors and known as the 'Old Hell Way', was the path, according to a local man writing in 1953, 'that the inhabitants of the two Fryups [referring to the hamlets at Great Fryup and Little Fryup] carried their dead from the times of the early Danish settlers'.[15]

15 With their typical proficiency for generating headlines, PETA, People for the Ethical Treatment of Animals, called for these villages to be renamed 'Vegan Fryup' to celebrate World Vegan Day in 2014.

It seems that the pallbearers had good reason to mind the dame's warning, as she was known to be a wise woman, or seer, who would undertake the practice of 'sitting up', a fascinating and long-lived custom. A 'church-watcher' would remain awake outside the building or on a nearby path on the eve of St Mark's feast day, 25 April. They would sit until the small hours of the morning, looking out for shadowy apparitions – the ghostly figures of those who would be buried in the church in the coming year. As the seer that undertook the vigil of St Mark's Eve, it is unsurprising that the pallbearers followed the wishes of the 'old dame' and dutifully carried her body, despite the waist-high snow, up Old Hell Way to burial.

If she had returned, the 'old dame' of Fryup wouldn't be the only spectral figure to stalk the corpse roads of England and Wales. The Ivelet Bridge, over which the Swaledale corpse road passes in the Yorkshire Dales, was said to be haunted by a headless black dog, seen constantly throwing itself in the stream. In Wales, a *toeli* or 'phantom funeral' was reported on several occasions, a spectral procession seen travelling along the corpse road at night. The eighteenth and nineteenth centuries saw dozens of reports of floating lights which would follow the corpse road and fly in straight lines across the countryside, irrespective of topography. These 'corpse candles' (in Welsh, *canhwyllau cyrff*) were said to be omens of imminent death (in reality these strange phenomena were probably caused by a discharge of static electricity, lightning strikes or perhaps the light from the setting sun glancing off rocks or water).[16] For as Shakespeare's Puck warns in *A Midsummer Night's Dream*:

16 Corpse roads have themselves become symbols of darkness and death in contemporary music and writing. Examples include 'The Long and Winding

Now it is the time of night
That the graves all gaping wide,
Every one lets forth his sprite,
In the church-way paths to glide . . .

Ghosts also ventured beyond the corpse roads. A field path in Lancashire was said to be visited every night by the figure of a lady, described as either dressed in rustling black silk or a free-flowing white gown. She would glide along ahead on the path before suddenly disappearing into thin air. On a footpath in Derbyshire, a different sort of trace was said to linger. A spot on the way between Dronfield and Stubley (the latter then an out-lying hamlet but now swallowed up by the town), was said to have been forever perfumed with thyme following the murder, by her lover, of a young woman who was carrying the sweet-smelling herb at the time.[17]

To add to the melancholy inevitability of death was everyday folklore connected to the paths so central to village life. Super-stitions swirled around the stiles found on the paths. It was regarded as bad luck to place them in a spot overlooking the sea, or to say goodbye over a stile, or to use a stile when a gate was available nearby, and a nail driven into a stile was said to cure a fever. The network of local paths were also sites of love, places for romantic trysts, perhaps inevitably given their ubiquity in the landscape. In his *Every Day Book* of 1827, the writer and pub-lisher William Hone floridly describes the romance of, and on, the English path:[18]

Bier Road' by death-metal band Carcass, and crime fiction and ghost tales with titles such as *Coffin Road*, *Corpse Road* and *The Coffin Path*.

17 One of many accounts of male violence against women which pepper our folklore in songs, poems and stories.

18 The fact that his series of books dealing with miscellany and antiquarian subjects (*Every Day Book* was followed by the *Table Book* and the *Year Book*)

It is along the footpath in secluded fields – upon the stile in the embowered lane – where the wild-rose and the honey-suckle are lavishing their beauty and their fragrance, that we delight to picture to ourselves rural lovers, breathing in the dewy sweetness of a summer evening vows still sweeter. How many scenes of frolic and merry confusion have I seen at a clumsy stile! What exclamations, and charming blushes, and fine eventual vaulting on the part of the ladies, and what an opportunity does it afford to beaux of exhibiting a variety of gallant and delicate attentions. I consider a rude stile as any thing but an impediment in the course of a rural courtship.

The gate – or stile – where couples met had particular significance as a threshold to new love. The wooden or stone steps of the stile were a sort of rural proxy for the staircase in the grand house, which functioned as a prime place for courting couples to gather at society balls. A gallery's worth of Victorian and Edwardian paintings portray lovers at a stile or gate, snatching moments of privacy or meeting to set off arm in arm down the footpath.[19] Sentimental and romantic paintings such as *Early*

---

were the most popular of Hone's output, hides the radical nature of his life. He was a reformist who championed many causes, including the abolition of the poor rate and the improvement of insane asylum conditions, and a fighter against state repression and miscarriages of justice. He was also a staunch defender of free speech, and was himself charged with blasphemy and sedition in 1817 (and found not guilty by the jury – Hone was also a strong defender of trial by jury of a defendant's peers).

19 Another spot on the rural paths, the kissing gate, has rather understandably been associated with young love. Some believe the etymology of this term to be entirely romantic, supposedly due to one person passing through and seeking a kiss in order to enable their companion to follow. But one etymological suggestion is that these gates are associated with death rather than love and that it is a corruption of 'kisting gate' – the gate to the churchyard at which the coffin would be laid down before entering (although quite

Lovers by Frederick Smallfield, *Before Marriage* by Arthur Howes Weigall, *Two at a Stile* by Kate Greenaway and Marcus Stone's *Lovers Embracing by Moonlight* demonstrate the role that paths played for new couples to be away from prying eyes, to flirt and to court (and possibly more).

Such romantic meetings and wanderings were a favourite subject of many writers of the nineteenth century and featured in the novels of authors such as Austen and Trollope. In Thomas Hardy's 'The Distracted Preacher', a story of smuggling by night and love by day on the lanes, footpaths and turnpike roads of Wessex, the eponymous preacher Mr Stockdale resolves to propose to the mysterious and fascinating Lizzy Newberry:

> With this end in view, he suggested to her . . . that they should take a walk together just before dark, the latter part of the proposition being introduced that they might return home unseen. She consented to go; and away they went over a stile, to a shrouded footpath suited for the occasion.

It is often easy to forget that in all the tales of superstitious corpse roads and young lovers meeting at the stile, these simple paths are expressions of real people living with the land – 'ordinary' lives informed by the religious and the material. Lives which were played out on seemingly unremarkable paths which nonetheless remain in folklore and literature and, as much as the churchyard or the memorial bench, in our individual and collective memories. These paths, at once ordinary and extraordinary, that I've found it easy to fall in love with.

---

how a coffin could be manoeuvred through a kissing gate, I don't know). There may also be a more simple and prosaic explanation: that the main part of the gate 'kisses' at two points when in operation.

9. Pilgrims' Paths

A small quiet corner of north Devon may be one of the most photographed places in Britain that you have never heard of. For seventeen years James Ravilious undertook an inward exploration, a labyrinthine journey on which he took tens of thousands of photographs in the land between the Rivers Taw and Torridge. He had been commissioned to show 'North Devon people to themselves' and over 10,000 photos and 79,000 negatives of his are now preserved in an archive in the small village of Beaford. Nearly all the photographs were taken within ten miles of this village in a period which spanned much of the 1970s and all the 1980s. They are photographs that lovingly document pancake races, village hall wedding receptions and morning prayers. They show the people of north Devon eating breakfast, hauling salmon nets and dancing in the streets, as well as tourists picnicking in fields and the village doctor making house calls.

James was the son of two artists: Tirzah Garwood, whose paintings, engravings and illustrations span a great range of subjects, with many giving an enclosed, richly textured view of rural and suburban life; and Eric Ravilious, the war artist and great documenter of the Sussex Downs. Eric was an artist of the paths, lanes and tracks which loop over folded hills and slopes, so it is therefore perhaps unsurprising that James connected with the landscape of north Devon when he came here in the 1970s. It's a land of rippling, gentle hills and lanes which plunge low, creating private, hidden spaces. James captured solitary and communal life in these lanes and roads. A group of suited men march round a corner under the banner of the Iddesleigh

Friendly Society, women out in front clutching trays laden with food. A man called Ivor Brock, a regular subject and neighbour of James, dressed all in black walks under an arch of trees down a lane. A flock of sheep, seemingly mid-squeeze and shove, follow their shepherd, Jean Pickard, filling the lane up to the untidy hedges. A book of James's photographs, published posthumously, takes as its title the last line from a Ted Hughes poem, written when in west Devon, 'Down the Deep Lanes'.

These lanes have a comforting familiarity. I have snatched memories of being driven down them as a child on a visit to the land where my grandad grew up before coming to London. The last time I was in north Devon, I was walking along the coast on my journey from Land's End to John O'Groats. From the tip of Cornwall I carried a perfectly smooth pebble, a constant small shape in my pocket, to be placed on his grave in the parish church in Fremington, just outside Barnstaple. It's to these deep Devonian lanes that I've now returned, but away from the sea, nine miles inland.

Devon has the most extensive road network of any place in the country and there are thousands of these lanes fracturing the county. Walking along, I feel I've been thrust down into the earth, the grass-topped fields far above me. The lanes offer a stratified, restricted view of the land, a close look at the Devon flora. At the bottom, I gently nudge loose scree and gravel with my boot, careful not to disturb the clinging soil. Then, tracing my eye up, the plants start to burst out, a massed wall of vegetation many feet high. Grass hanging slightly forlornly alongside ferns, catchweed and vetch. Foxgloves – varieties both towering tall and pink, and small, delicate and pale yellow. Hazel, ash and holly. Honeysuckle and dog roses knotting around and between all. It feels like at any second this whole lot of lush green could come tumbling down, burying me in north Devon. The rare breaks in hedge-line reveal views, bringing into focus that I'm walking in a wider world.

I come to the brow of a hill, where a cross stands on a pedestal of long wild grass, at a meeting of roads. This is known as the Eastacott Cross or the Stonen Hammer, a tall wayside marker of solid granite. Just one of hundreds of similar crosses by the roads of Britain, with the highest concentration in south-west England and North Yorkshire. Walking on another 500 feet, a whole valley opens ahead of me, a spot where the Eastacott Cross may have originally stood. This view out of the lanes is spectacular and comforting, a revelation of sorts, an unfolded familiar landscape of fields, woods and scattered houses. At the centre of it all, and framed by the lane, is the village of Chittlehampton, pinpointed by the tower of St Hieritha, known as the Cathedral of North Devon.[1]

I've come to this part of Devon after reading about the village in an article published in the *North Devon Journal* in June 1950. It was not a happy time for the parish council and the article declares that the village is in a state of 'open revolt'. Earlier in the year, a sixteen-page pamphlet had dropped through the doors of the parish councillors. The Reverend J. H. B. Andrews had read one of these 'three times, with increasing amazement'. The full title of this document was *Surveys and Maps of Public Rights of Way for the Purposes of Part IV of the National Parks and Access to the Countryside Act, 1949*. It was produced by the Commons, Open Spaces and Footpaths Preservation Society (now known as the Open Spaces Society) in collaboration with the Ramblers' Association. This document, endorsed by the County Councils Association and approved by the Ministry of Town

---

1 It's a sobriquet with impressive cousins across the country: the Cathedral of the Peak at Tideswell in Derbyshire, the Cathedral of the Forest in the Forest of Dean, the Cathedral of the East End on the Commercial Road in London and the Cathedral of the Industrial Revolution in Birmingham (alongside many more similarly nicknamed churches).

and Country Planning, advised local councils, voluntary groups and members of the public on how to map the public paths in their area. The guidance was clear and helpful, even if it wasn't always well received. The parish councillors of Chittlehampton were resistant, but they weren't the only ones. In the same year Home Secretary James Chuter Ede was reported to have told a meeting of the Ramblers' Association that some parish councils were 'too busy, too stout and too lazy to take the trouble to get the information required by the Act', and that 'ramblers should go and jog them up'.

The Reverend Andrews had strong feelings about the surveying of public rights of way. At the heart of his argument was that if paths hadn't been used for a number of years, then they simply should not be recorded as public rights of way and that recording them was just too much bother. As an example, he cited a path last used by the postman on his bicycle six years ago. He believed that 'no parishioners would benefit from the survey; children no longer walked to school, and the postmen of the future would have helicopters'. He suggested that this was simply a case of city dwellers bossing country people around, 'tantamount to the people in the rural areas telling MPs to survey the Palace of Westminster, and just about as much use'. When it was suggested that the paths be walked and mapped on Rogation Sunday (the sixth Sunday in Easter, a traditional time for fasting and prayer), this was rejected as inappropriate, 'an attempt to turn an act of supplication to God into a means to ascertain one's rights over footpaths'. Instead of the parish council undertaking this work, the Reverend Andrews proposed that Hugh Dalton, the former Chancellor of the Exchequer and at this point Minister of Town and Country Planning, should 'don a pair of running shorts and traverse the paths himself'. The Reverend Andrews felt that 'no ramblers come our way and, if they did, I do not see why we should maintain paths which are not used by parishioners'. But outsiders have been coming to Chittlehampton for hundreds of years and the Eastacott Cross gives a clue as to why.

Such medieval wayside crosses were placed along the old paths to show travellers the way, offering reassurance in unfamiliar or otherwise unmarked territory. Many of these had a religious function, guiding those on pilgrimage. The Eastacott Cross's position suggests it was exactly for this purpose, pointing a holy way to Chittlehampton, a place described by the antiquarian William Camden in the 1580s as 'a small Village where Hierytha, canonized a Shee-Saint, lay interred'. Hieritha was, in the words of one late-sixteenth-century historian, a saint 'whose miracles are able to fill a whole legend', but like so many other saintly figures, her renown has faded over the centuries. Even her name is contested; the usual spelling is 'St Urith' (which I will continue with). But the destination was not the grand St Hieritha's Church but a nearby holy well, which is known as St Teara's Well. At times the name was even masculinized to St Ercus or St Erth.

The cult of St Urith goes back to the seventh century and the very early days of Christianity in the west of England, where the traditions of this newly revived religion were still blurred with the 'pagan' beliefs of the land. This early date for the life of St Urith would place her among the beginnings of recorded saintly veneration and pilgrimage, although the records are all from much later centuries. The story goes that when she was young and a virgin (the sources all seem to make sure the reader knows this), she converted to Christianity. It was a conversion which was hated by her pagan stepmother who conspired to have her murdered by some local hay-mowers. One took his scythe to her. Miraculously, when her body fell to the ground, a spring burst from the spot and the spatter of blood around transformed into the scarlet pimpernel flower. Urith is most often depicted as a cephalophore, a saint who carries their own severed head, although curiously she is never shown decapitated but is instead two-headed, with one attached and one detached. St Urith's martyrdom lives on, and was re-enacted by the villagers of Chittlehampton in pageants in 1936, 1974 and 2000. The 70s pageant was captured by James Ravilious's camera: villagers in fancy dress, a band playing in the main square, a goat being led into St Hieritha's and a man with his head in makeshift stocks being pelted by tomatoes.

Despite its extraordinarily gruesome details, the death and martyrdom of St Urith is not unique and bears a remarkable similarity to two other West Country saints. Like St Urith, St Juthwara of Sherborne (in Dorset) and St Sidwell of Exeter were both targeted by jealous stepmothers who commissioned men with scythes to carry out their murders and springs emerged from the ground where their heads landed. St Sidwell's legend lived on the longest and the strongest, and she became the patron saint of Devon's second city. Today she looks down, in fibreglass form, on a street bearing her name in the centre of Exeter, scythe in hand but head in place, on a large relief mural commissioned by the Tesco supermarket in 1969.

The springs of water in all these saints' stories is important. The curative properties of sacred water in holy wells were the focus of many pilgrimages across England and Wales. The waters from the well in Chittlehampton, the destination for the pilgrimage of St Urith, were reportedly able to cure eye conditions.[2] The oldest continually visited pilgrimage site in Britain is St Winefride's Well, after which the town of Holywell in north Wales is named (St. Winifred was another beheaded

---

2 This sacred well, and its purported healing waters, is no longer accessible, having been deemed an unsafe, uncapped water source by the water board in the 1950s and concreted over.

virgin). Despite their enduring popularity, wells and springs were a contested destination for pilgrimage, due to their association with pre-Christian beliefs; for many in the church the power of their waters smacked of magic rather than orthodox religion. A thirteenth-century bishop objected to the pilgrimage to a spring in a Buckinghamshire field, warning that 'no profane place is to be frequented by the people by reason of veneration on account of audacious assertion of miracles which have not been approved by the church'. The bishop accused the local parish church of supporting the pilgrimage for reasons of 'cupidity' (i.e. greed). If indeed the local clergy encouraged pilgrims to their community for money, that wouldn't be surprising. Pilgrimage was big business. In Chittlehampton the peak of revenue from pilgrims was just before the Reformation, bringing in £76 16s 10d a year (in the region of £50,000 today).

There is not one accepted pilgrimage path to this holy well in Chittlehampton – no defined route taken by pilgrims marked out on old maps or waymarked on the ground. Those seeking solace and healing on their pilgrimage to the well of St Urith came from all directions. Tracing their journeys reveals how the network survives into the present day: extensive and complex. I walked nearly all of Chittlehampton's deep lanes, seven of which converge from the wider north Devon countryside into the heart of the village, alongside three footpaths which run right to its centre. There is also, to the south of Chittlehampton, a busy road which looks suspiciously like a bypass, and it was suggested to me that this was created specifically so that others going about their business could avoid the crowds of pilgrims (although I haven't been able to find any documentary evidence to back this up).

Undoubtedly thousands of people did come to Chittlehampton on pilgrimage. The bedroom window at the Bell Inn, my accommodation for the night, looks out on to the village square, once known as Town Place. The church of St Hieritha forms the northern boundary of the square, the threshold to the churchyard emblazoned with golden words shining on dark black wood: *Enter His Gates with Thanksgiving*. The square, sloping down to the main road, is an unusually large piece of land at the heart of the village whose shape has little changed since the eighth century. Now it is a place of low-level activity: the quiet greeting of two villagers by the ornamental planters; a woman sitting on one of the benches, resting her head on her left shoulder, her shopping by her side. The popular Bell Inn is the last pub standing, but there used to be eight inns on this square, places for the pilgrims to stay and an indication of the popularity of the cult of St Urith and the local economy it sustained.

We do not know from how far away these pilgrims came; perhaps the sliding of the veneration of St Urith into obscurity is because of its local nature. Thousands came here but maybe only from Devon and the surrounding counties. There is one possible record which casts some doubt on this picture, though, which is to be found across the continent in the Palazzo Vecchio in Florence. Within this Italian town hall is a trapezoid room called the Guardaroba, transformed by the Medici family who commissioned the painter, architect and historian of art Giorgio Vasari to refit it entirely in the late sixteenth century. The room was to be a place to display knowledge of the world and collect the finest objects of the Republic of Florence. A demonstration of wealth, power and learning. Cabinets line the walls, their doors featuring maps of the world, including a representation of Britain and Ireland. This map records Manchester, Caernarfon, Canterbury, Oxford and Gloucester, alongside dozens of other towns and cities. In Devon, Barnstaple and Bideford are shown on the north coast and Exeter, Exmouth and Honiton to the south. There is also the intriguing name of 'Chilmeal'. Perhaps this refers to the small market town of Chulmleigh further south or to the nearby village of Chittlehamholt, or maybe, just maybe, the pilgrimage to St Urith had put Chittlehampton on the Medicis' map, 900 miles away.

Whether they came from near or far, pilgrims journeyed on foot, wayside crosses guiding them to this holy site. Potentially, miles of the network around Chittlehampton remain unrecorded; over twenty paths are marked on the 1900 Ordnance Survey map which are not recorded as public today. Paths which seem to be missing cross fields, linking the deep lanes, winding through woodland and snaking alongside streams and brooks. It isn't just footpaths which appear to have dropped off the map. The 1840 tithe map shows a lane crossing a ford just south of the village, coloured in the same sienna wash as those on the current road network (therefore suggesting the same historical status) but that is not publicly accessible today.

If the pilgrims came to Chittlehampton to present an offering or to seek a cure in the waters, then the long-distance pilgrimage offered them the promise of a higher connection to God. But even at the height of pilgrimage in the medieval age these journeys were never taken by anywhere near the majority of the population; there was no mandatory requirement for pilgrimage such as the Islamic Hajj, which is usually expected to be performed at least once in a Muslim's lifetime. For the individuals who did walk the long paths to pilgrimage, the journey was as important as the destination; moving through different communities over multiple days was an experience of physical and spiritual distancing from everyday life (the Latin root of the word 'pilgrim' is 'foreigner' or 'stranger'). In this act of contemplation of and supplication to God, the hardship and difficulty of the journey was vital, an experience further enhanced for those who chose to walk barefoot. Others went even further by restricting themselves with heavy, cutting chains around the ankles or wrists.

Some of the most well-known pilgrimage destinations and routes were associated with Canterbury, especially after the murder of Thomas Becket in December 1170 and his canonization shortly thereafter. There are several signature routes to Canterbury (although it is likely that people came a multitude of ways). The route from London was made famous by Chaucer in his *Canterbury Tales*, which was inspired by watching pilgrims passing his home in Greenwich, and follows for a great part the Roman Watling Street. The path is still known as the Pilgrims' Way and trundles across south-east England from Winchester (itself a place of pilgrimage, primarily to the shrine of St Swithun) to Canterbury, and now forms part of the North Downs Way National Trail.

The use and history of the 130-mile Pilgrims' Way are contested. The path was the focus of Hilaire Belloc's *The Old Road*, which probably did the most to bring the route to the attention of a general audience and tie it to pilgrimage specifically. I share the same impulses as Belloc to trace the old paths through walking. Belloc desires to 'step directly in the footprints' of his ancestors, to follow 'their hesitations at the river-crossings', climb 'where they have climbed' and suffer 'the fatigue they have suffered'. What Belloc proposes is a path with two bright bursts of activity in its history: an ancient prehistoric trackway and a path used by pilgrims to travel to Canterbury. In *The Pilgrims' Way: Fact and Fiction of an Ancient Trackway*, Derek Bright picks through the evidence for the use of this path over millennia. The history is, in fact, more interesting than the simple story of an ancient track repurposed as this flagship pilgrimage route many centuries later.

This is not the clearly defined, singular pilgrim's path of Belloc's reckoning. The Pilgrim's Way is part of the whole, formed of many links in a wider network. The paths that make up the Pilgrim's Way have shifted purpose and meaning over time, their use by prehistoric Britons and later pilgrims just one part of the story. As the historian of medieval pilgrimage Diana Webb points out, it would be rare for new routes to be forged simply for the act of pilgrimage. The passage of pilgrims was one way in which the old ways were sustained and preserved. For instance, the Roman Fosse Way in Gloucestershire was used by those journeying to Hailes Abbey, which was placed firmly on the pilgrims' map after Edmund of Almain donated a crystal phial of Christ's blood in 1270. But those travelling to bask in the sight of the holy blood would have been mixed up with all the other traffic using this Roman road (the ruined abbey is a way-point on a modern path, the Cotswold Way National Trail).

While many of the paths used and created by pilgrims survive to this day, pilgrimage itself nosedived after Henry VIII's Reformation, despite Henry having travelled on pilgrimage himself, including to Walsingham, where he took his shoes off at the Slipper Chapel at Houghton St Giles in order to complete his journey barefoot. Shrines, saints and relics no longer had a place. Martin Luther, the spark of the European Reformation and himself previously a pilgrim to Rome, sharply criticized the practice:

> By these pilgrimages men are led away into a false conceit and a misunderstanding of the divine commandments; for they think that this going on pilgrimage is a precious, good work, and this is not true. It is a very small good work, oftentimes an evil, delusive work, for God has not commanded it.

The objects of pilgrimage were stripped away. Becket's shrine at Canterbury was dismantled, the holy blood of Hailes was declared to be honey coloured with saffron and removed (and the abbey in which it lay destroyed) and the statue of Our Lady of Walsingham was taken away, to be burned in London. In Chittlehampton, J. H. B. Andrews (the same reverend who complained of the path survey in 1950) unearthed records of a local inquiry of 1540 into why the vicarage income had suddenly dropped. The reason given was the 'Takyn away of Imagys of Sait Urithe and cessyng of offerynges used to be made here by pulgremes'.

But, like a pilgrim emerging healed from an ancient shrine, there has been a revival – of both the paths and the practice of pilgrimage. Waymarks and guidebooks are springing up all the time for new or revived pilgrimage routes across England and Wales. The Northern Saints Trails are seeking to position the north-east of England as the 'Christian Crossroads of the British Isles', harking back to the pilgrimage routes of the seventh century, the age of Bede, St Cuthbert, St Hilda and St Oswald. In Wales, the Way of St David retraces the path suggested in the twelfth century as a safe alternative to pilgrimage to Jerusalem – a path on which we can 'experience the inspiration of the land and experience a bigger reality'. Many of these routes and paths highlight the aesthetic and wider spiritual benefits of walking their ways rather than being strictly Christian pilgrimages. It's an inclusive and modern approach to pilgrimage; the *i* newspaper's travel section goes almost completely to the secular, urging us to 'think of a pilgrimage as a walking holiday with added benefits'.

At the forefront of this renewed popularity is the British Pilgrimage Trust, founded in 2014 'to advance British pilgrimage as a form of cultural heritage that promotes holistic wellbeing'. The trust lists a vast range of recommended pilgrimages on its website, some reworkings and rewalkings of old routes and others entirely new. One of the most prominent projects of the trust involves a possible lost path from one of the oldest surviving maps of Britain, which is being looked at anew. The Gough Map (named after a previous owner – its authorship is unknown) dates from the reign of Edward III and shows 3,000 miles of fourteenth-century road but only one leads to the most important British pilgrimage site of all: Canterbury. This thin red line on the Gough Map starts at Southampton (perhaps to receive pilgrims from the continent), passes through Chichester, Lewes and Rye and is now dubbed 'The Old Way' by the British Pilgrimage Trust. While it is unlikely to follow the exact paths of the fourteenth century, this pilgrims' way is going back on the map and being walked again after 700 years.

Water

10. Salt Ways

Salt: a necessity for human life which has become the stuff of nightmares. Public information campaigns proclaim it the 'hidden danger', the 'forgotten killer', the 'silent killer'. The amount we physically require – for firing nerve impulses, keeping our blood pumping and contracting our muscles – is minute, but we, as a society, eat much more than we need. Yet for millennia, salt has been a vital commodity. An importance that comes from its ability to preserve, to allow for food supplies to be built up and traded (crucial before modern processes of refrigeration and freezing). Salt became, in the words of the historian S. A. M. Adshead, 'a fact of culture rather than nature'. Pliny the Elder agreed, judging that 'civilized life is impossible without salt'. So for much of human history it has been a product to be gathered, processed and traded. On the back of salt, whole networks of trade were built, and paths created, across the world.

The geographical distribution of salt is uneven, whether it is extracted from seawater, dug out of the earth, or scraped off surface deposits. This meant that salt had to be carried overland and by sea across kingdoms, countries, and empires. A thousand years ago, Saharan Desert salt – extracted from dried-out lakes or shallowly mined in slabs – made its way to West Africa on camel trails via a series of trading cities. From the remote salt outpost of Taoudenni (in modern-day northern Mali), 23,000 camels plied the route to Timbuktu over 400 miles south, and 16,500 camels carried salt further on, east to the city of Gao. Salt routes in the landlocked Sichuan province of early modern China were driven by culinary tastes, an emphasis on vegetable dishes pickled and brined, or flavoured with ginger, mustard and newly introduced chillies as well as salt-rich soy sauce.[1] Salt was produced from the sea and traded along inland waterways in seventh-century Fiji, and in eighteenth-century Russia the quarry of Ilek, near the border of Kazakhstan, was transporting thousands of tonnes of salt overland by cart to regional population centres in Ufa, Kazan and Nizhny Novgorod.

Today many of these trading routes exist solely as subjects of historical research, traced back through the records, writings and accounts of previous generations. But some salt paths can still be walked, experienced somewhat as they were. The Col de Finestre (the Fenestre Pass), high up in the Alps and straddling the border of France and Italy, follows the old camin salie ('salty trail' in the Provençal dialect). This path took French salt from Nice to the Italian Piedmont region, where modern hikers now find themselves in the company of Alpine ibex picking their way over the rocky terrain.[2] Over another high mountain pass, in one of the remotest regions of the Himalayas, is a still-used path which for centuries carried salt by yak and sheep caravans from Tibet into Nepal. Perhaps the most famous surviving salt way in Europe is the Via Salaria, spanning much of the width of Italy from Rome to the Adriatic at Porto d'Ascoli. This route,

---

1 A British consular official, reporting to Parliament in the early nineteenth century, said of Sichuan, 'No province in China has a greater variety of vegetables . . . inhabitants indulge fearlessly in almost everything green.' He added, 'Several of the above vegetables are pickled by being steeped in brine from fifteen days to a month. Twenty pounds of salt are allowed for every 133.3 lbs of vegetables.'
2 The young of these ibexes seek shelter in the robust fortifications built here by Mussolini, thousands of feet above sea level, to guard against a French invasion of Italy.

established by the Sabines before the formation of Rome, is now mostly a busy highway, though sections remain accessible solely on foot.[3]

Britain has a history of thousands of years of salt production and its own distinct passages for its transport and trade. I'm tracing one of these salt ways, between the Worcestershire towns of Droitwich and Pershore. Its first section is an ordinary country road, light grey tarmac streaked with the dark shade of roadside trees. I walk in the hum of the M5, somewhere parallel to my left. In the verge, pink flashes of willowherb and the jewelled red-berried clusters of late summer lords-and-ladies thrive in the trees' thick shadow.

Following the ancient line of this southern salt path, I cut across a wide field of wheat – gilded ground with a picture-book blue sky. The path feels familiar, an almost forgotten memory, a fading dream. A breeze animates the whole field, a hazy, sluggish movement of crops softly swaying. Fifty feet to my west stands a single oak, a lonely vertical among the ears of wheat. The leaves still rustle at this distance but the tree seems to be suffering from dieback; the top branches reaching up to the sky are bare and dead, cracked into their final shape. A Saxon charter identified this salt way as being a 'made road', though the path doesn't feel substantial. The path I'm walking now isn't defined by having an obvious human-laid surface or from being hollowed out by hundreds of years of cartwheels. This section of the salt way is a footpath, its form coming from how it crosses this field, from where the wheat hasn't been planted across its course, a strip of dark brown earth in between flanks of yellow, and from the points it crosses boundaries, stiles buried deep in

3 The Sabines were a pre-Roman tribe from the Apennine Mountains.

pleasingly untidy hedges.[4] I stand for a minute or two in the middle of this field, the centre of the path. From the other side of the oak, dust rises. A combine harvester is making its steady way through the wheat. The field will soon change again but the path will remain.

In the next field, the harvest is more advanced, long wind-rows of piled wheat drying in the sun. A field clothed in corduroy, lines stretching up a slope, pointing to its rich green neighbour, a vivid contrast to the gold around me, and the small village of Bredicot at the brow of the hill. The path runs dir-ectly to the church of St James the Less. A small, solid medieval building, without electricity, open only for a handful of ser-vices in the summer. It now sits in the rectory garden, cut off from the rest of the village by a railway line which splits the countryside. Although the trees bordering this small space are not deep, it feels like an intimate glade, a private place. It is just south of St James's that the path meets the western branch of the same salt way from Droitwich, a meeting point now defined by where it crosses the railway line.

The story of why this salt way exists in the first place begins with the River Salwarpe. Bounding the east and north of Droitwich, the 'warpe' in Salwarpe perhaps comes from the Old English 'to throw up' and the 'Sal' from, well, 'salt'. The river is vomiting salt. The town sits on a Triassic mixture of lime-rich mud and sandstone, streaked with beds of rock salts. These deposits are the trace of a shallow sea which periodi-cally covered the area 200 million years ago. Water percolates through the beds, taking up salt and turning into streams of brine. Pressure forces the brine up through fissures in the earth to the surface and forms springs that are unusually pure

4 Crops (other than grass) have to, by law, be clear of a public path to the width of at least one metre on a footpath or two metres on a bridleway.

and rich in the salt we eat (sodium chloride) and lacking in less desirable salts and other impurities. It is ten times saltier than seawater, a concentration rivalled only by the Dead Sea. People have been exploiting this extraordinary geology since at least the Iron Age, although it is likely that the tradition of salt production goes back even further. A dense layer of 'briquetage' vessels, for storing and processing salt, were excavated in the town centre and dated from the third and second centuries BC. Similar fragments have also been discovered in other sites in Worcestershire and neighbouring Herefordshire, evidence of the robust trade – and carved-out paths – for salt.

My bed and breakfast in Droitwich is in a cul-de-sac, near the town's centre, across from the Working Men's Club and Waitrose's massive car park. This is also the area where the Romans produced their salt, in Vines Park, sandwiched between the River Salwarpe and the recently restored Droitwich Canal. In the early morning, it is peaceful: a slight mist and the greetings of lone dog walkers. For centuries this park was a place of hot and hard industry – the nearby church of St Augustine is still stained from the burning fires of salt production. The darkened church rests on Dodderhill, the site of a Roman fort. The road running beside it was Roman too, one of six of their salt ways which radiated out from the town. Under the earth of Vines Park, in a settlement they called Salinae (literally 'the salt works'), the Romans dug timber-lined pits to tap into the springs. Wooden buckets were craned in to extract the brine for intense boiling.[5]

The surviving Saxon records detail the movement of salt

---

5 An alternative etymology of the River Salwarpe associates its name directly with the Roman name for the town. Either way, the river's name has a salty source.

south of the town but also provide a glimpse of the places clustered around where the salt came from – places of royalty and
power. The kings of Mercia established a palace at Wychbold,
just north of Droitwich, holding their royal councils there in
the eighth and ninth centuries. By this time Droitwich was
known as Saltwic, with the Mercian royal household control-
ling the production and trade of salt but granting rights to
other powerful Worcestershire landowners. Naturally the
church was to be counted among those with royal permission –
abbeys at Pershore, Worcester and Evesham profited from this
valuable commodity.

The fame of the salt springs was widespread in learned Saxon
circles. In the ninth century a monk called Nennius documented what he regarded as the 'Wonders of Britain', aping the
Seven Wonders of the Ancient World (the Great Pyramid of
Giza, the Colossus of Rhodes, the Hanging Gardens of Baby-
lon, etc.). Nennius' list of British wonders is a tantalizing
mixture of the fantastic and the real: an altar which levitates
simply 'by the will of god', the grave of King Arthur's son,
which magically changes dimension every time it is measured,
and a stone which mysteriously and independently rotates
three times a year. However, many of Nennius' wonders have
been, with varying degrees of certainty, grounded in the real
world, identified as natural features. Wonders from the land
itself, many watery, unsurprising in a place crossed by rivers and
bounded by the sea. Nennius' 'Lake Lumonoy' is now taken to
be Loch Lomond in Scotland, the thermal springs at Bath are
tentatively documented, as is the extraordinary tidal bore of
the River Severn, which still produces a continuous wave running far up the river (the thrill of riding this wave now chased
by Severn surfers and canoeists). For his fourth wonder, Nennius talks of the 'fountains discovered in the same [place] of
salt, from which fountains salt is cooked: from that place

diverse plain-foods are salted and they are not near the sea, but from the earth they emerge'.

I've left the quiet and contemplative field paths behind, joining busy roads which have been imposed over the old salt way. But even here, attempts have been made to make it a pleasant walk; the footway is separated by a grass verge and a sparse avenue of fruit-bulging plum trees, standing between me and the cars. The charters declare this section as Salt Straet, as it goes south-west to the hamlet of Edgon, where the Saxons recorded a Salt Broc ('salt brook') alongisde a place called Seltera Wul ('salt carriers spring'). I imagine these salt carriers stopping here on their journeys by the cooling stream for a refreshing drink.

While fresh water may have been welcome for the transporters of salt, it would have been even more so for its producers. The creation of salt from brine is a hot, fuel-intensive industry, workers labouring over continually burning flames and through steam. The salt paths from Droitwich would have seen two-way traffic – salt out and timber in. To produce 112 pounds of salt in the fourteenth century would have required twice the weight of wood. Further back in time, with less efficient production, the amount of wood required would have been greater still. Vast tracts of woodland, for miles around, would have been managed and felled to keep the salt fires burning. There is no trace of this woodland now on my walk along the Droitwich to Pershore path – only lone trees, like the wheat-field oak, or a few trees in the hedgerows alongside a smattering of small copses and plantations. The heavily wooded landscape has slipped out of memory, and alongside it this path. I've chosen to come to this particular path *because* it has largely been forgotten. A personal retracing and reconnection to one of the premier Saxon salt ways.

Transporting the Droitwich salt just eleven miles to an

outlying town might not seem worth it. But this salt way's destination, Pershore, is on the River Avon, a connection to the wider world, a node on the salt-trading network which didn't start and end in the West Midlands. The production and trade of salt took place across the land, bringing its riches to a multitude of communities. Identifying these sites, and the connections between them, we can create a salty map of England.

On our fresh blank map, we can first add the major sites of salt extraction and production. Alongside Droitwich go other key salt areas just a little further north, all of which spring from another Triassic salt pan, under modern-day Cheshire – Northwich, Nantwich and Middlewich (the latter is now the largest producer of salt for the table). Also in Cheshire is Winsford, a town created by salt, following its discovery here in the 1830s. At Winsford rock salt is extracted to be laid on the nation's icy roads and it is one of only two places in England where salt is still mined for this function (the other being Boulby in North Yorkshire – another place to add to our salt map).[6]

When mapping our salt history, we cannot forget to add the thousands of miles of continually seawater-washed coastline. Places like the village of Ingoldmells, the site of the first-ever

---

6 As the salt was extracted under Winsford, a great void was created under the earth, the size of 700 football pitches. This has now been repurposed as DeepStore, a place to keep valuable documents free from vermin and ultraviolet light in a vast temperature- and moisture-controlled archive. Historical records from the National Archives, pottery and human bones from Cambridgeshire County Council's archaeological service, valuable paintings from an anonymous art collector and financial documents from a Japanese bank are among the many objects that reside underground where there was once only salt. At Boulby, a mineral salt is now being mined which may be just as precious – a mineral salt called polyhalite. A fertilizer which is only mined here and is the apparent secret ingredient in how Wimbledon keep their tennis courts so green.

Butlins camp just north of Skegness in Lincolnshire, exploited for salt in the Iron Age and, a millennium later, recorded in the 1086 Domesday Book. Joining these on the coast are the salt pans in the marshes of Lymington in Hampshire, which produced up to three tons of salt a week from the eleventh century until the nineteenth, and the River Blackwater in Essex, home of the famous Malvern Sea Salt, celebrated and popularized by the celebrity chefs of the early 2000s.

We can now fill in the connections on our salt map. Alongside the Droitwich to Pershore salt way and the River Avon we can trace other routes out of town. A road which begins in Vines Park (where the Romans boiled brine) and goes east is even today called 'Saltway'. It is possible that this path would have stretched across the entire country, terminating at East Anglian ports for onward international trade. Fragments of it have been identified in communities across a broad sweep of the Midlands and the south. From Droitwich it passed through Stratford-upon-Avon, and it has been found in the village of Wormleighton in Northamptonshire (abandoned after the English Civil War), whose northern parish boundary was recorded as 'baore saelt street' in AD 956. This clue, along with many others, was found by local historian Tony Marsh, who tracks the path either side of the parish of Blisworth. Further east, he has found records of a 1715 curate noting 'a place called Salt-Way', a field in 1727 named 'Saltway Furlong' and a 1775 estate map showing 'Salt Lane'.

A similar path, again known only as 'Salt Way', can be found in the Cotswolds. The Ordnance Survey map from around 1900 records this name in five separate parishes, a seemingly continuous road over gentle hills. Still there as a trail of small country roads, straddling the Area of Outstanding Natural Beauty, with sparse, gappy hedgerows framing the valleys. The path is shown on the modern Ordnance Survey map, marked out in that particular Gothic font used to denote something of the past. But it's not really clear where the idea of this path came from. Some talk of it as if it has existed for ever, a truly ancient road surviving into the present. Or perhaps it was a medieval drovers' road: still interesting but less romantic to some. I'm sure that salt was carried over these hills, though it is impossible to prove.

In creating our salt map there is a danger that we systematize the landscape. Taking our idea of a network of roads and paths as fixed on modern maps and reflecting this back into the past (when looking into the Cotswold Salt Way, one website even includes the path in a list of 'ancient motorways'). Perhaps this is an attempt to impose some semblance of order on what is, in fact, a wonderfully disordered history. In his influential book *The Old Straight Track*, the amateur archaeologist and writer Alfred Watkins saw lines in the landscape, 'a fairy chain' of 'leys', which connected places of spiritual and historical importance. He applied these to ancient monuments, mounds and stones, and to place names. He saw connections in salt, what he calls 'the white group', place names which stand in a line from the Black Mountains in Wales to Suckley in Worcestershire: White House, Whitwick Manor, White Stone, White Cross. Watkins boldly links these with salt production and trade, asserting that 'these places are quite plainly not so called because they have ever been white', and draws one of his leys, confidently asserting real-world material ways between them.[7]

---

7 The fundamental problem is which point to select when drawing your lines. There are a multitude of potential data points Watkins could have picked, a seemingly endless array of mounds, cairns, wells, fords, strange lumps, rocks and place names on which to superimpose some sort of system. You can only really get the nice straight lines identified by Watkins if you pick and choose the most convenient markers (and ignore the very differing periods in which some of these monuments stood). The archaeologist Richard Atkinson, who excavated Stonehenge, once used a Watkins-like system

For me, the truth is much more interesting. We have a modern-day network where some paths have survived for thousands of years to be walked today. But over the centuries paths have existed that were used, created, abandoned, reborn, transformed, lost and found. Paths which float under the map and then suddenly rise for air before dropping back down into the noise. Paths which are disjointed, sections used for local journeys for local people and sections for long-distance travellers. A collection of paths which looks different from one year to the next, let alone from one millennium to another. Paths which take into account topography and geology, and a human, almost unconscious instinct to adapt their direction accordingly. In imagining a continuous, overarching system on to our paths, we are in danger of losing the joy in the mess of how our paths evolved.

There is nothing mystical about today's A38 (even if you try and picture the Romans coming this way from their salt works at Droitwich or their fort on Dodderhill). If you stand on the earth-sprayed pavement of this busy road, looking past a stand of towering pine trees and soft, landscaped mounds, you can see the top of a country house. A bombastic confection of many bays, windows, pinnacles and balconies – grey slate, red brick, stone and ironwork. A wonderful chaos of ornament, described by Nicolas Pevsner as 'the showiest in the county', this Louis XIII-style pile, Chateau Impney, was commissioned by the man who saw the beginnings of

---

to demonstrate the existence of 'telephone leys', drawing lines where telephone boxes are located to make a perfect pattern, even though we know for sure that they weren't laid out like this. The same techniques have been used by the mathematician Matt Parker to pleasingly show that the placement of Woolworths stores also seems to conform to some ancient and mystical grid.

the decline of salt production in Droitwich and aimed to revive the local brine springs for a new Victorian use. This was John Corbett, the man who became known as 'The Salt King'.

Corbett was born in 1817 in Staffordshire. As he was growing, so was his father's business and wealth, which was focused on the canal trade in the West Midlands. In his late twenties, John became a partner in the business, selling his share in the 1850s. With these funds Corbett began buying up salt works in the Droitwich area, ultimately moving most of the production to Stoke Prior, three miles outside the town. The Stoke Prior Works became the largest salt works in Europe, with Corbett introducing new methods of industrial production to increase the efficiency at which the brine was boiled. He made major changes to the workforce, firing all female employees. This was seen then as a moral decision, removing them from working conditions evocatively described in one newspaper report: 'The boiling brine was manipulated in vats by half-naked women, whose nudity was only partially concealed by the atmosphere of steam and mist'. This 'enlightened' act was made alongside the increase of his male employees' wages, so that, in the words of an effusive *Country Life* article published after his death, 'they should not feel the loss of the women's wages. In turn he expected the women to make the men comfortable at home, so that they could do a good day's work.'

Beyond his salt works, Corbett sought to make an impact on the town itself. He was elected as a Liberal MP for Droitwich in 1874, taking over from his great rival the Conservative John Pakington (he had previously unsuccessfully challenged Pakington in the election of 1868, a bitter and personal campaign in which the pro-Pakington newspaper the *Worcester Journal* had compared electing Corbett to replace Pakington as like replacing an oak tree with a mushroom).[8] It was this rivalry which led Corbett to build Chateau Impney in a bid to have a grander country house. But his building extended beyond the domestic and included the 'establishment of a hospital for the treatment and relief in sickness and accident of poor persons'; a 'Salter's Hall' (a place of dances, lectures and concerts for the workers) and the infrastructure needed to turn Droitwich into a fashionable spa town.

There had been a salt bathing pool in Droitwich before Corbett came to town, with the allegedly curative properties of brine identified during the cholera epidemic of 1832. However, these baths had failed to attract sufficient custom, mainly due to their proximity to the heavy, smoky industry of salt production. Having moved the salt works out of town, Corbett revitalized the idea of Droitwich as a spa town, with a local newspaper trumpeting the visit of an 'Indian prince and his retinue'.[9] A resort town needed fancy buildings and infrastructure, and Corbett set about creating the new St Andrew's Brine Baths; the aforementioned Salter's Hall and hotels with croquet lawns and tennis courts; parks with an orchestra playing during the summer season; and boulevards and roads – new urban ways for salt. It was an attempt to put Droitwich Spa alongside the likes of Harrogate, Buxton, Leamington, Cheltenham, Bath

---

8 The vicious campaign also focused on Corbett's wife's religion, with posters around town reading 'The wife of the Liberal Candidate is a Roman Catholic, and brings up her children in the same faith. Electors, what must Mr Corbett's real opinions on RELIGIOUS MATTERS be under such influence?'

9 It was around this time the name of the town changed to Droitwich Spa, a symbol of the transformation, which was described by a local newspaper in 1894: 'By and bye there will be a new Droitwich and an old Droitwich. The old Droitwich will be the lingering remnant of the manufacturing town; and the new Droitwich a fashionable healthy resort.'

and Tunbridge Wells. By the time of his death in 1902, Corbett owned nearly half of Droitwich. He was praised in the press as a man who set about on business with the 'methods of Julius Caesar', who became rich through hard work, whose 'every portion of his public life has shown the greatness of his fortune as well as the greatness of his soul'.

Droitwich as a spa town was only ever moderately successful, despite the claims in one newspaper that 'a stream of the halt and lame flows without ceasing . . . where crutches are left behind in a memento of relief that is sometimes so rapid and complete as to seem like the work of a magician'. A sluggish population rise meant it never reached the heights of Leamington or Bath, and the original brine baths were closed in the 1970s.[10] Whereas Buxton and Harrogate grew by over six times between 1841 and 1901, Droitwich Spa didn't even double.[11]

Salt works more generally didn't fare well as the world entered the twentieth century. The Stoke Prior works were practically finished by 1912 (though they just about limped on until 1972). And yet the legacy of salt in Droitwich still lingers in its paths. It can be seen in its urban Victorian spa streets (Corbett Avenue and Corbett Street are named proudly in the town centre) and through the paths which left town, the traditional salt ways, conveying this 'white gold' to the wider world. Suburban streets and pastoral ways which perhaps deserve to be as treasured and celebrated as the ancient Saharan camel trail from

10 However, the outdoor lido has been brought back to life – one of the very few open-air saltwater swimming pools in the country.
11 Buxton grew from 1,569 inhabitants in 1841 to 10,181 in 1901; Harrogate from 4,785 to 29,885; and Droitwich from 2,832 to 4,154.

Taoudenni to Timbuktu, the Himalayan salt ways and the Sabinian Via Salaria.

Before tracing the salt way through the wheat fields south of Droitwich, I took a path between the River Salwarpe and the canal to Churchfields Farm, just outside the town. Like many similar businesses, the farm has become adept at diversification. It's the middle of the summer holidays and alongside fields of cows, kids are everywhere, enjoying the 'Fairy Trail', 'Adventure Farm Barn', and the 'Everyday Superhero Maize Maze'. But for me what is the most interesting attraction of all is away from the running toddlers. The farm has opened the first salt works in decades and exports it around the world, putting Droitwich salt back on the kitchen table. I leave with two bags tucked into my rucksack, as I walk the old salt way south.

11.   The Climate Coast

The path snakes pleasingly, its borders blurred by vibrant ferns and ivy and a gentle accumulation of leaf litter. Small indistinct noises penetrate from the outside world. There are thousands of people a short distance from here, shielded by the trees, but in these north Wales woods I am seemingly alone. Standing at the top of a hill, you gain an idea of how the earth fits together. But it is in the woodland that you see how this tree – that one, right in front of you – connects to the next. How this long branch pierces the dense umbrella of a neighbour. How the suckers have marched across the woodland floor. The geometry of tree trunks, which never seem to run truly straight. Looking up, you might see overlapping tree canopies obscuring the breadth of the sky, or how the trees don't touch, keeping a respectful distance from one another. So-called 'crown shyness' creating its own paths in the sky, like viewing a map from underneath.

A dense enough woodland can feel small and closed, even constricting, and yet at the same time never-ending – like standing in a forest which stretches around the globe. My greatest joy comes from woodland walks where you get the mystery, the pleasingly tight sense of being bound in but are allowed glimpses into the wide world. In these woods, I get fragmentary views of water and the shores of an island. I'm looking out on to the Menai Strait, a strip of sea separating mainland north Wales from the Isle of Anglesey (the Welsh for 'narrow water', *main-aw*, gives its name to this stretch of sea). The Strait is notoriously dangerous, particularly a section known as the Swellies, between the Menai Suspension Bridge (the first of its kind, Pont Grog y

Borth in Welsh) and the Britannia Bridge (Pont Britannia). Here water swirls and surges among rocks, shallow shores and a smattering of islands.

In their sumptuously detailed book, *The Fabled Coast*, Sophia Kingshill and Jennifer Westwood recount the thousands of stories and legends which have been told and retold about the coast of Britain and Ireland. Bells which ring in drowned villages, ghost ships on the horizon; spectral figures which haunt the shore; serpents and monsters rising from an unknowable deep. Birds, rats, dogs and even eggs as omens of bad luck. Kingshill and Westwood tell the story of a boat laden with seventy people which tried to cross the Menai Strait in 1665 (the only way before the bridges were built). The boat was overturned, leaving just one survivor, a man named Hugh Williams. It was said that this vessel was made from timbers stolen from the church of Llanidan on Anglesey, a sacrilegious act which destined it for the bottom of the sea. But the legend continues, documenting that in 1783 and 1820 further boats sank here, again each with only one survivor, and in both cases this was a man named Hugh Williams. An extraordinary coincidence which in legend reveals the power of the sea to baffle and terrorize.

These coastal woods are part of the Treborth Botanic Garden, owned by the University of Bangor. It is a small section of ancient forest, with sessile oak and ash surrounded by many more trees planted over the last couple of hundred years. The core of this designed and planted woodland was created by Joseph Paxton – Member of Parliament, landscape gardener, designer of the Crystal Palace and cultivator of the modern banana – who in 1855 successfully presented a proposal to Parliament for the Great Victorian Way, a ten-mile-long arcade covered in glass, 'in the same style as the Crystal Palace', which would encircle central London and under which would be shops, houses, a road and a railway powered by air pressure.[1] In the Treborth woodlands there are an array of trees planted by Paxton and his successors – lime, beech, birch, turkey oak, yew, Scots pine, whitebeam, cedar, spruce and larch all jostle within 16 hectares. Where the trees meet the shore, they occasionally slump into the water, and through this gentle erosion fossilized plants appear, uncovered from a muddy tomb after 300 million years. From one gap in the trees, I see a statue rising from the water, where it almost touches the opposite shore. Created by Lord Clarence Paget of the nearby Plas Newydd country house, this figure of Nelson was an early experiment in sculptural concrete and a navigational aid to help ships negotiate the treacherous waters.[2] The statue lies just outside the village of Llanfairpwllgwyngyll, famous for the longer form of its name Llanfairpwllgwyngyllgogerychwyrndrobwllllantysiliogog-ogoch. Buried in the name is a reference to the Swellies, the full translation being: 'St Mary's Church in the hollow of the white hazel near to the rapid whirlpool of Llantysilio of the red cave' (its great length was probably a Victorian marketing ploy).

As I follow the coast to the west, the woods seem to become lusher and the path rides undulating ground. Trees are painted with the luminous green sheen of damp lichen. Salt and the taste of decomposing leaves are caught in the back of my throat and up the sides of my nostrils. Despite the clear path, this feels like a wilder, more elemental place. Suddenly a high stone wall topped with spiky slabs of grey slate cuts through the trees. I wasn't expecting this solid man-made line to cross my path, an

1 The proposal was authorized by Parliament, but the cost turned out to be too great. Another Victorian way, of a kind, was built instead: Joseph Bazalgette's great sewers under London.
2 Originally a statue of Neptune, the Roman god of the sea, was to stand here, but the sculptor Lord Paget objected to the mayor of Caernarfon, 'What has Neptune done for us? Nelson is the proper subject.'

interruption to my gentle walk. Set in the stone wall is an ornate gate, and from this side it feels like a portal to a secret garden. Beyond is the National Trust owned land of Glan Faenol. Upon passing through the gate, the trees change. Towering pines emerge from a dense green undergrowth, ivy climbing their trunks. The green lichen from before has gone, and these trunks are splodged bright orange. Walking further, the trees change again: the blotched, cracked and streaked bark of a stand of shorter silver birch, more numerously planted. The way between these trees is new. The National Trust, working with Gwynedd Council, have created this new path which hugs over a mile and a half of coast to the village of Y Felinheli (the port where slate from the Dinorwic Quarry was shipped from). Walking the Wales Coast Path six years ago, I would have been guided inland here. My walk would have taken me along the busy A487, alongside a different section of the same solid wall topped with slate, shutting me out from the coast.

From points on this new coastal path, you can glimpse Plas Newydd on the opposite shore, the country house of Lord Paget and generations of marquesses of Anglesey. In this house is an extraordinary mural by Rex Whistler, the largest painting on canvas in Britain. The fifty-foot-long mural spanning the dining room faces a spectacular vista – the mountains of Eryri, in grey, white and blue, suspended above the waters of the Menai Strait. Whistler's mural reflects the view, with mountains and sea, but he places them in a fantastical landscape. A confection of Italian and British buildings, some real (Trajan's Column and the steeple of St Martin-in-the-Fields feature) and some imagined. While at Plas Newydd, Whistler pursued an unrequited love for Lady Caroline Paget, played out in their letters and in his many portraits of her (including a startling nude, which may have been the result of Whistler's fantasy). Allusions to this may be glimpsed in the mural. Whistler stands, solitary and

Romeo-like, under a balcony. Caroline is in a rowing boat at the heart of the scene. The mural, called *Capriccio of a Mediterranean Seaport with British and Italian Buildings, the Mountains of Snowdonia, and a Self-portrait Wielding a Broom*, is a depiction of a mythical British coast.[3] The mural and the house, along with 169 acres of land and a mile and a half of coastline, are no longer hidden away for aristocratic eyes only but open to the public, having been gifted to the National Trust in 1975.[4]

The National Trust was founded on 2 January 1895 by Octavia Hill, Canon Hardwicke Rawnsley and Sir Robert Hunter, in a key part of an early movement to protect and ensure that land could be open for all. The trust, alongside the Open Spaces Society (also co-founded by Sir Robert Hunter), sought to counter the threats of scattered development, enclosure and game hunting which restricted public access. Twelve weeks after the founding of the trust, they acquired their first piece of land, a place round the Gwynedd coast from where I have been walking, five acres of cliff top called Dinas Oleu, Citadel of Light.

3 Caroline went on to marry Sir Michael Duff, who owned the Vaynol Estate, despite what her cousin and historian John Julius Norwich called 'lesbian tendencies'. The National Trust property at Glan Faenol once formed part of this larger estate. It was Sir Michael's family who built the seven-mile wall through which my path along the coast passed. Whistler went off to fight in the Second World War and was killed near Caen on 18 July 1944.

4 While Plas Newydd was a very comfortable family home for a grand family, the Pagets used to be much richer. Their fortune was frittered away by the fifth Marquess of Anglesey, Henry Cyril Paget, whose exploits and spending were legendary. This was a man who walked around London clutching a pink-ribbon-bedecked poodle, retrofitted his car so that the exhaust would belch out perfume, staged lavish plays in which he often starred (one Aladdin costume cost £100,000) and was said to buy 'diamonds as an ordinary man buys cigarettes'. While Henry did marry, many think he was gay (instead of sleeping with his wife, who he later divorced, he would lay her in bed and decorate her body with jewels from head to toe).

The land was donated by Miss Fanny Talbot, a friend of Octavia Hill and Canon Rawnsley, who had 'long wanted to secure for the public for ever the enjoyment of Dinas Oleu' and wished to place it into 'the custody of some society that will never vulgarise it, or prevent wild Nature from having its own way'.

In its early days, a few further tracts of coastal land were purchased by the National Trust, including Blakeney Point in Norfolk and the Farne Islands in Northumbria, but much of the focus was inland. The trust secured entire mountains in the Lake District and Peak District, bought pretty much a whole village in Buckinghamshire, and purchased farmland around Stonehenge alongside numerous stately homes. In the mid-1960s, the National Trust turned once again to the sea, launching Enterprise Neptune, which aimed to raise £2 million (equivalent to £35 million today) so they could buy up stretches of the English, Welsh and Northern Irish coastline. Initially planned as a temporary effort, the campaign continues today (under the name of the Neptune Coastline Campaign), and the National Trust now own 780 miles of coastline, almost seventy-five per cent of that having been purchased since 1965.

Enterprise Neptune was inspired by the work of geography lecturer John Whittow who, alongside thirty-four students, walked and mapped the coastline in 1965. On their journeys along the coast, they noted areas which were publicly inaccessible or under threat from piecemeal development. Their maps for the section of Welsh coast I've been walking show the built-up areas as a creeping tide, spreading mainly from Bangor in the east. A stretch along from me is noted as 'a coastline of superb views in all directions', but at the same time 'Not very accessible coast, poor bathing beaches'. A map is dotted with annotations which give some flavour to what the National Trust, then and now, are trying to guard against: 'new industrial site', 'saltmarsh used as refuse tip' and 'stone quarries, excessive disfigurement'.

The National Trust's focus on the coast from the 1960s has not only helped prevent its disfigurement but has undoubtedly secured hundreds of miles of public paths alongside the sea, protection of which was bolstered by the rapid expansion of the Wildlife Trusts in the second half of the twentieth century (at the beginning of the 1960s the Wildlife Trusts owned forty-six nature reserves; by 1970 this had increased to 547).[5] These efforts to secure coastal landscapes came after nearly two centuries in which seaside resorts had blossomed along the coast, a time which, in the words of Historic England, saw transformation 'from a natural environment to a highly regulated man-made space'. The mid-eighteenth century onwards saw places like Brighton and Margate developed into destinations for the wealthy (and in the case of Brighton, the royal) to escape, play and 'take the waters'. The seaside became a place of leisure in which walking played a central role. Sea air was regarded as best taken on foot, and walking alongside the coast was recommended following bathing in the curative seawater (as well as being a fashionable way to be seen). Small fishing villages were transformed in a matter of years. The London MP and businessman Sir Richard Hotham turned the tiny community of Great Bognor into a resort named after himself – Hothamton, which later became Bognor Regis (the 'Regis' was added because of George V's convalescence in the town following surgery).[6] Blackpool, named after a dark peaty stream disgorging into the Irish Sea, grew from a population of 1,658 in 1801 to 62,302 by 1911. The Victorians, and their railways, brought people to the sea

5 The Wildlife Trusts, like the National Trust, also started at the shore with the establishment of the Norfolk and Norwich Naturalists' Society, which secured the Cley Marshes in 1926.

6 Although the king was not the greatest fan of the town either, supposedly uttering the famous quote 'Bugger Bognor', either when it was first proposed to affix 'Regis' to the town's name or when he was on his deathbed.

and solidity to their coastal paths – promenades, piers and pleasure gardens.

Recent figures show that, in just a six-month period, almost 30 million people made walking trips to the sea, boosting coastal economies by £350 million. Walking the coast now, we are less likely to stay stuck within the bounds of a resort town on manmade ground. Our walking horizons stretch into more natural land, along an evolving network of designated coastal paths. Since the 1970s recreational walks have been created which stride out along the coast. The Pembrokeshire Coast Path (opened in 1970) became the first National Trail in Wales, and the South West Coast Path (opened fully in 1978) was established as Britain's longest National Trail, formed in part from paths used by the coastguard to patrol the cliffs and beaches, on the lookout for smugglers bringing illicit tobacco and spirits ashore. Alongside these came a whole host of regional coastal trails, many established by the Ramblers, including paths round the Isle of Wight and Anglesey and along the coastline of counties such as Kent, Northumberland and Lancashire. Then, in the 2000s, the Welsh government announced a plan to create the first trail in the world to follow an entire nation's coastline.

The Wales Coast Path was officially opened in 2012 with ceremonies at Aberystwyth promenade, Roald Dahl Plass in Cardiff Bay and Flint Castle, and a Big Welsh Coastal Walk organized by Ramblers Cymru. The footpath starts on the outskirts of Chester (it appears at the precise point where Wales becomes England on the River Dee) and runs all the way around to Chepstow on the Wye in the far south-west of the country. In creating this ground-breaking coastal path, new rights of way were established, already recorded rights linked up, and new paths physically laid down and signposted (continual improvement has taken place – as we have seen, the new path through the pines and birch at Glan Faenol was created in 2018, six years after the Wales Coast Path was launched). It follows the coast as closely as possible, but there are points where it darts inland. Our coasts are not just places of leisure and nature but of industry, trade and militarism. A Ministry of Defence missile launch site, a seaside railway line and a natural-gas-fired power station all divert the Wales Coast Path away from the shore. Even if it were to follow the exact course of the Wales coast, how long would the path be?

In the 1950s the mathematician and meteorologist Lewis Fry Richardson stumbled across a problem: how long exactly is the British coastline? Perhaps that seems easy to answer. The Ordnance Survey says 11,072 miles. The CIA World Factbook looks at mainland Britain plus Northern Ireland but comes up with a significantly smaller figure: 7,723 miles. Richardson had originally set out exploring the mathematics within a completely different problem, the probability of two countries going to war. Did the length of the border between two countries increase or decrease the chance of conflict? He combed through encyclopedias to gather his data, simply looking for the length of the Spanish/Portuguese and Dutch/Belgium borders. But none showed the same length, and they weren't just a bit out; there were discrepancies of up to twenty-five per cent, with the length of the Spanish/Portuguese border variously quoted at somewhere between 600 and 750 miles long. What Richardson soon realized was that, when looking at features like a coastline or a national border, the length depends on the size of your ruler. Richardson's ideas were taken up by mathematician Benoit Mandelbrot, who established the Coastline Paradox as part of the emerging field of fractals. There isn't a perfect ruler to measure the coastline; the closer you look, the longer it gets, and ultimately the coast is infinite.

Unlike the shore that it follows, there is a defined and

advertised length (870 miles) to the Wales Coast Path, but even this is subject to change. As I write, there are seven diversions posted on the Wales Coast Path website. A storm in 2014 breached a medieval seawall at Llanmadoc on the Gower, necessitating a diversion, which may become permanent. On the Llŷn Peninsula, a landslip has meant an almost two-mile diversion inland (or a walk on the beach when the tide is out). There are paths currently rerouted in Conwy and Denbighshire to enable coastal defences to be beefed up. These changes are all due, in one way or another, to erosion. Where the sea touches land, in gentle strokes and mighty punches, it gradually wears away and shifts the coast, a landscape that Paul Carter described as 'obstinately discontinuous . . . anti-rational, impossible to fix' – the coastline as a rebuff to those who need to define everything.

A recent study published in the journal *Ocean and Coastal Management* details that, in England alone, 200,000 properties may have to be abandoned or relocated by 2050 due to rising sea levels (just one of the many costs of national and global lack of action to tackle climate change). This is a process that has already started – whole communities have either already been lost to the changing shape of the coastline or live with the threat of loss. In Wales, under the dunes of Kenfig, crisscrossed by public paths and looking out to the Bristol Channel, once stood a town and a castle founded to impose Norman rule on the Welsh. By 1510 both castle and settlement had largely disappeared or were in ruins, the antiquary John Leland reporting that it had 'devoured with the sands'. Another community, the town of Amroth, situated on long sandy beaches in south-west Pembrokeshire, has long been predicted as one that will be lost to the sea. A news film from 1939 shows residents rescuing their possessions from half broken-down houses which teeter atop land battered by waves. Men in caps attempt to fill the breach in a struggle that the film describes as 'a losing battle against the Atlantic'. In north Wales, a more orderly but no less devastating evacuation is planned. Fairbourne lies on a wedge of flat ground between the sea and the mountains with no easy land to roll back to. By 2054 the village will, in the clinical words of the *Fairbourne Preliminary Coastal Adaptation Masterplan*, be 'decommissioned'. The villagers, described by the *Guardian* as potentially 'Britain's first climate refugees', are to be relocated and the village infrastructure – houses, roads, pipes, cables and all – will be dismantled and the area returned to salt marsh (and the Wales Coast Path will presumably move inland too). The plan is being resisted by many of the residents, with one telling the BBC: 'Everyone knows each other and talks to each other. If we have to move, we've got to abandon this way of life and learn to live in a new way. It's more than just losing your home; it's losing your whole identity.'

The greatest impact of erosion on Britain's coast is seen on the eastern seaboard of England, where a soft shore of sand and clay is being lost to the inescapable power of the North Sea. On a spit of land that juts out and protects the Humber Estuary once stood the town of Ravenser Odd, which rivalled its near neighbour Hull in terms of economic power. Granted a royal charter in 1299, the town was a centre for fishing (primarily for the herrings known as 'silver darlings') and a trading port. French wines, timber, skins, oil, salt and pitch were just some of the goods unloaded here. The town, always vulnerable at the very end of a spit on the Holderness peninsula, was wiped out in the storm known as St Marcellus' flood in 1362. All the streets of the town, some of which we know the names of (Newgate, Kirk Lane, Hull Street and Locksmith Lane), washed into the sea – urban paths which disappeared for ever. Ravenser Odd was just one of many communities lost on the same stretch of Holderness coast; over thirty have been identified, places like

Monkwike, Colden Parva, Dimlington, Southorpe and Out Newton. The settlements didn't exist in isolation but were connected by paths and lanes, now never to be seen again.

A hundred miles to the south-west of Holderness, on the Suffolk Coast, is perhaps the most famous lost community of Britain. The story of Dunwich is that of a town of great importance which suffered a slow death. In the eleventh century, Dunwich was the tenth-largest settlement in England and at its height it sustained a dozen churches and ecclesiastical buildings, a guildhall, market and mint. From the 1230s, the town started to fall into the sea. It was a transformation, as described in 1831, from an 'opulent and commercial city' to a 'mean village'. Today the village of Dunwich has under 200 residents and the pottery and bones of its lost inhabitants wash up on the shingle shore. In the 1830s, Dunwich would secure its place in one of the most contested political debates of the era. Since the thirteenth century, Dunwich had returned two Members of Parliament, an indication of its historical status. However, with its gradual disappearance into the sea, the number of voters for the seat dwindled dramatically and by the 1830s there were less than 250 people living there, under a fifth of whom could actually vote.[7] This tiny base meant that two local landowning families were able to control the voters and install who they wanted in the two parliamentary seats (the Barne family occupied one of the seats themselves continually from 1764–1832).[8] Dunwich had

7 It was rumoured that some would ride horses out into the sea or go by boat to where the town hall once stood to cast their vote.

8 Miles Barne became MP in 1764 and was succeeded by Barne Barne (yes, really), and then it was Miles Barne again, who was followed by Snowdon Barne, Michael Barne and Frederick Barne. The absurdity of elections in the rotten boroughs is satirized in *Blackadder the Third*, where the fictional constituency of Dunny-on-the-Wold takes the place of Dunwich. Dunny-on-the-Wold is described as 'half an acre of sodden marshland in the Suffolk

become, in the parlance of the time, a 'rotten borough'. The Great Reform Act of 1832 extended the number of those who were able to vote, 'the franchise' (although for the first time it was specifically stated that the vote was reserved for men and after the Act only eighteen per cent of the adult male population had the vote), and it did away with the rotten boroughs. For the first time in over five hundred years, and many years after most of it had fallen into the sea, Dunwich had lost its oversized place in Parliament.

What the stories of Kenfig, Amroth, Fairbourne, Ravenser Odd and Dunwich tell us is that the coast of Britain is as unfixed as the swirling sea. Like the deep holloways which are gradually worn out by the passage of feet and hooves, the coastline is endlessly diminishing, and the island of Britain is shrinking. We simply don't know how many miles of path have been scattered to the bottom of the sea, how many walks have been washed away. Britain's cliffs and shores are already among some of the fastest eroding in Europe and the shifting form of our coast is only set to accelerate. The national and global failure to tackle the climate emergency will lead to a rise in sea levels and an increase in the frequency of extreme weather which will batter our coastline and our coastal paths (one map from the organization Climate Central shows the potential impact of a one-metre rise in sea levels: flooding inland as far as Peterborough, Doncaster and Lincoln). A report from the Committee on Climate Change published in 2018 sees trouble ahead for our paths, with local authorities 'often unable to respond quickly to coastal erosion or landsliding because diverting the PRoW [Public Rights of Way] involves complex and often protracted legal processes'.

Fens . . . population: three rather mangy cows, a dachshund named Colin and a small hen in its late forties . . . only one actual person lives there, and he is the voter.'

In Cornwall, which has seen dramatic storms over the past decade, more and more signs are popping up which read 'This public footpath has foundered / No public access'.[9] Creating a path around an infinite and ever-shifting coastline is a perennial problem, which the England Coast Path is attempting to solve.[10]

The plan for a continuous coastal path around England was launched by the then Labour government in 2007. In a press conference at the White Cliffs of Dover, David Miliband proclaimed that 'We are an island nation. The coast is our birthright and everyone should be able to enjoy it. I want families to have safe and secure access to walk, climb, rock-scramble, paddle and play all along our coastline.' In the subsequent years, the England Coast Path has slowly been formed, section by section, with hundreds of Ramblers volunteers carefully studying, surveying and commenting on the proposals. The 2,700-mile England Coast Path is now nearing completion and is soon to be one of the world's longest coastal paths. This trail uses many stretches of existing rights of way and also creates new paths in areas the public have previously been excluded. Instead of just being a narrowly defined liner path, the Marine and Coastal Access Act (2009) creates a corridor of access land with most land falling seaward of the trail becoming publicly accessible. This gives people the right for the first time to fully enjoy the beaches and cliffs of the English coast, allowing picnicking, climbing and exploring right up to the water's edge.

9 As Caitlin DeSilvey points out in an essay in *After Discourse: Things, Affects, Ethics*, 'foundered' is an odd word which has an etymological link with the Latin word *fundus*, meaning bottom. Alongside paths, it seems that only a few very specific things can be said to 'founder' or are 'foundered': companies in dire straits, difficult diplomatic talks, troubled ships and unwell horses.
10 A similar problem besets riverbanks because a quirk of rights of way law means that a path can be diverted along a gently eroding river, but if there is a sudden landslip, then the path and its public rights of way are lost.

This right of access reflects the fact that, in the words of Jules Pretty, 'the coast and shore is not really a line. It's more of a zone'. The zone of access on the England Coast Path guards against the issue of coastal erosion. If a cliff top or foreshore carrying the path falls into the sea, the path will roll back, allowing the continuous walking line round the coast to continue. The England Coast Path, like its Welsh equivalent, will achieve public access to what was described in the Hobhouse report (which led to the creation of the National Parks and Access to the Countryside Act) as the:

> Infinite attraction in the varied beauty and changing moods of coastal scenery, the rugged grandeur of the Cornish cliffs, the luminous beauty of the white chalk headlands of Sussex, the soft colouring and fine contours of sand dunes, the secluded coves and beaches of Pembrokeshire, the wide prospect of sand, sea and sky along the Norfolk Coast.

The England Coast Path will trace the border, the edge and the end of the land, but through flood, storms and slips the path will endure; it will not founder and instead be a permanent continuous line around an erratic, infinite coast.

12.   Drainage

On a winter's day in 1970, peat cutter Ray Sweet was out on one of his regular jobs on the Somerset Levels, clearing a ditch filled with the detritus of the season before. Probing down with his spade, he hit a chunk of submerged wood. Scraping away the thick mud a plank of ash was revealed, sitting atop a mess of smaller pieces of wood, later identified as sharpened sticks and staves of hazel, alder, elm and holly. These trees had been felled over 5,000 years before; subsequent tree-ring analysis dated the wood precisely to the spring of 3806 BC. Ray had uncovered a buried Neolithic world, a preserved path. At the time it was the oldest known track on the planet.[1]

In the Shapwick Heath National Nature Reserve there is a reconstruction of what became known as the Sweet Track (named in Ray's honour). Walking along the slightly wobbly boards, clutching drawings from the original excavation, I can see clearly that this wasn't simply wood haphazardly piled up in the boggy earth but a sophisticated construction. A series of long poles were driven deep into the ground crossways, with oak planks laid on top to walk on, secured with more poles threaded through holes drilled in the timber and short, sharpened staves. Photographs of the excavated wood show fresh cuts

---

1 This title has been superseded by the discovery of a nearly 6,000-year-old trackway in the grounds of Belmarsh Prison in 2009, built 500 years before Stonehenge. Similar trackways have been found across Europe, with a particular concentration around the southern Baltic, on the Jutland peninsula and the Elbe estuary.

in their surface and clear indications of timber specially selected, shaped and curved to fit. Millennia-old marks made with the blades of stone knives and axes.

As remarkable as the track itself is the ancient snapshot of the environment preserved alongside it: tiny pollen particles of birch, alder, oak, elm and heather; the exoskeletons of beetles and other insects; whole preserved pieces of reed stems, leaves and chunks of sphagnum moss; and in places the timber shows the delicate tracery of thousands of years of fungal threads which have spread through the wood – all caught and kept by the peat. The builders of this path and their descendants left a personal trace in the objects placed and lost here. Ray Sweet found an arrowhead on his initial discovery of the track and subsequent excavations have uncovered a rare surviving wooden platter, axe heads and a longbow used for the hunting of wildfowl – preceding, by almost 5,000 years, the famous deployment of these weapons in the battles of the Hundred Years' War. For me the most moving objects are the pottery that was moulded directly in human hands. These finds tell of simple and singular uses. A pot still with its accompanying wooden stirring spoon. A smashed jar preserved alongside its contents of hazelnuts, perhaps the result of a momentary slip or trip on the slick path, a moment caught in time.

Later investigations showed that the Sweet Track was partially plotted over an even older example, the Post Track. A complex of further wooden walkways was uncovered, tracks such as the Meare Heath and the Abbott's Way. Tracks which were named after their discoverers or the peat companies and farmers who owned the land where they were found: Baker, Eclipse, Garvin's, Tinney's, and Rowland's. These paths were laid down to navigate land that was managed and farmed but fundamentally waterlogged. It wasn't just raised paths used to travel here; four ancient canoes were also found preserved in the peat.[2] While the Sweet Track and its neighbours are relatively short, providing dry routes to local high ground, they also formed part of a larger network navigated by feet and boats, which ran far beyond the Levels and even beyond Britain. Found next to the Sweet Track was a polished jadeite axe which came from high up in the Alps. It's an object that travelled thousands of miles to be placed here, unused, as an offering in a watery world.

The Somerset Levels are on low ground, framed by the Bristol Channel and a tryptic of high land. To the north are the Mendips, hiding in their craggy folds Cheddar Gorge, Wookey Hole and numerous other nooks and caves for underground exploration. To the south are the Quantocks, which are streaked with ancient ridgeways, and the heathland and grassland of the Blackdown Hills. Reaching between are the Polden Hills, gently dissecting the lower ground but not quite reaching the sea. From the Levels themselves rise a few islands, ridges and hills of sand and rock.

Some 10,000 years ago, with ice sheets melting in the northern hemisphere, seawater flooded this flat plane, and for three thousand years the Levels were completely under water. Only small islands of land peaked above the salty water, which deposited clay and silt on the drowned earth. Around 4500 BC, almost a thousand years before the Sweet Track was built, the water started to retreat. The receding sea created a low ridge of clay and sand where the Levels now meet the Bristol Channel, trapping some of its water behind. Reed beds flourished and died and flourished again. As they died, they sank into the water, forming the first layers of peat, and, as the peat built up, the

---

2 Coracles, small circular boats made from woven reeds and wood, seem not to have survived but were probably used and are still produced on the Levels to this day.

ground surface of the Levels was raised, encouraging the growth
of new plants alongside the reeds – willow, alder, birch, moss
and sedge. This was the environment in which the people of the
Levels built the Sweet Track.

Snaking across the Levels are rivers, tributaries of the Severn.
The Axe, Banwell, Brue, Cary, Isle, Kenn, Parrett, Tone and
Yeo all feed the damp earth. They are listless, slow-moving
rivers which very gradually move towards the sea, with hardly
any drop in height between their upper and lower stretches.
Rivers liable to gum up with silt and debris. They run into the
Bristol Channel, whose high tide is many feet higher than the
lowest moors on the Levels. When the sun and the moon are
aligned once a month and exerting their greatest gravitational
pull, the tides of the River Parrett and its tributaries can be seen
nearly twenty miles inland. Into this environment comes rain,
brought by the south-westerly winds, which falls on the Mendips, Exmoor and Blackdown Hills, washing down to the flat
ground below. Water seeps, sits, pools and flows on the Somerset Levels, defining the past, present and future of this land.

In the Iron Age, more than three thousand years after the
Sweet Track, the extraordinary lake villages of Glastonbury and
Meare were built. The settlements were formed by laying down
wood, bracken and clay directly on to swampy ground. Artificial
islands were created among the reeds, marsh and damp, an
attempt to adapt to conditions rather than change them. Communities were established on similar ground in the Swiss Alps,
people carving out a life in the liminal space between water and
earth.[3] At the Glastonbury Lake Village, less than two miles from
Glastonbury Tor, up to forty roundhouses were built on this

---

3 A few hundred years after the Sweet Track was being laid down, whole
artificial islands – defensive houses called crannogs – were being built directly in the water of Scottish lochs.

new land, along with sheds, barns and animal pens. Paths spread through the site and there was a sturdy internal roadway and a jetty of sorts, places of connection and places of supply, including for the masses of clay needed to keep the village high and dry – local infrastructure now buried. Whole lives were focused on these new patches of ground, people working as well as living here. Discarded fragments from spinning and weaving, antler, bone and shale working, and glass bead-making have been found preserved in the peat or trapped between layers of clay.

The Romans largely avoided settling on the bulk of the Levels and moors, instead utilizing upland Iron Age sites. They built roads along higher ground, away from lower areas that were liable to flood. The Romans came to the low moors of the Levels for salt, as these areas at the time were still touched by tidal seawater, not the freshwater of today. They established salt production sites; at Droitwich brine was boiled in vats but here it was left to dry naturally, laid out in lead pans under the Somerset sun. On a burning-hot day in June, walking past one of the sites of the Roman salt works, I can imagine the water evaporating quickly. It's a still day, and, as I walk, I'm yearning for some shade or a breeze. The long track, a local drove road, points to the distance, a seemingly never-ending flatness of hard, crushed gravel. This path is called Shaking Drove. In 1845, the self-styled 'practical farmer' Erasmus Galton describes the experience of travelling in the area before the land was fully drained and reclaimed, a place known as the Shaking Bog. In the *Journal of the Royal Agricultural Society of England*, he writes that 'the bog is so soft . . . that a person trotting his horse on the turnpike road abreast of the land . . . will see the water quite ruffled by the concussion of the horse's feet on the road'. There is a natural softness and wetness to the ground of the Levels. Nothing is solid; the earth isn't fixed.

It's a feeling I experience as I turn the corner from Shaking

Drove on to West Drove. Here I'm walking on the soil and grass. It doesn't feel like people come this way often. I'm shepherded through the long grass by needles of electric blue damselflies, some of the most ancient creatures flying around the planet. At points where the wall of vegetation is high, coming from the sides and below, the earth has stayed moist. I feel myself slightly sinking. The track widens out a little and cows which jostle in the same space have dug into the ground, exposing the underlying peat. When commercial peat cutting took place on the Levels, when people like Ray Sweet were working, hot days like these would have seen steam rising as the fresh peat was exposed to the sun. Blocks of the soft, dark peat were formed into beehive stacks, the water they held instantly starting to evaporate. The churned-up peat under my boots has formed into brown crests and waves, and parts of it crunch under foot, like walking through snow. I reach down to scoop up some of the earth. This peat has dried out and leaves a rich dark biscuit crumb between my fingers.

The Saxons, like the Romans, generally avoided living on this unstable ground. They largely settled on the dry uplands fringing the Levels and on the belt of higher ground which sealed the area from the Bristol Channel. Tracks and paths presumably connected these communities, taking the high routes away from flooding and also serving parts of the lower ground, where peripheral moors were used for pasture during the hottest and driest of the summer months. The Levels became a place of refuge, their very inaccessibility a positive. The islands which rise out of the impenetrable and complex moors and marsh provide a perfect location for contemplation and separation from the world. Now hills, these areas are identified as Saxon by their names, taking versions of the Old English suffix for 'island' – *iey* or *ey*. These names can be found scattered across a map of the Levels, places like Athelney, Muchelney, Chedzoy,

Middlezoy and Thorney.[4] Towards the north of the Levels, one of these former islands rises abruptly from the low-lying ground. On this famous island, at Glastonbury, a monastery and abbey were founded.

I've walked the many steps up Glastonbury Tor early in the morning, and while I feel no sudden metaphysical realization, looking out at the mist and sun rising from the watery plain below, I can understand why this place became shrouded in a veil of myth and legend. Wishful thinking and conjecture obscure the history of this religious community. Saxon charters seem to point to the formation of the abbey back in at least the eighth century. A parade of legendary people are said to have walked through the settlement and abbey, a place that one archaeologist called 'the Mecca of all irrationality'. Glastonbury's tor, the dramatic hill, was said to be the Isle of Avalon, the burial place for King Arthur. The monks at Glastonbury cultivated the Arthur connection, claiming to have discovered a grave bearing the words 'Here lies Arthur, king'. It was a handy discovery for a community who wanted to attract the wealth of pilgrims.[5] The supposed grave of Arthur was 'found' at Glastonbury following a fire which destroyed much of the monastery. Like the nineteenth-century gentry who built their country houses as medieval 'castles', the monks deliberately rebuilt in an old style, a ploy to give their monastery an ancient lineage. By the thirteenth century, this sham history had been

4 Thorney appears as an island name elsewhere in England. The West Sussex Thorney Island was for many years an RAF base, which in the 1970s hosted refugees from Vietnam. The London Thorney Island, now buried beneath city streets, is the site on which the Houses of Parliament and Westminster Abbey were built.
5 The mystical connection continues, as a collection of nature reserves on the Levels are today branded as the 'Avalon marshes . . . a magical wetland landscape'.

extended back to the age of Christ. A story was created that Joseph of Arimathea, the man who buried Jesus after the crucifixion, had come to Glastonbury and died there (in another version of the tale, Jesus himself is said to have visited Glastonbury to 'learn about spirituality').[6] In 1342, John of Glastonbury retold a prophecy from a bard called Melkin (a predecessor to Merlin) that upon rediscovery of Joseph's tomb, 'neither water nor heavenly dew will be able to be lacking for those who inhabit the most noble island'. It seems a strange prophecy in an area so defined by water already.

As the Middle Ages progressed, generations of landowners, residents and communities didn't simply live with the landscape they had inherited on the lower moors but sought to tame, channel and manage the water of the Levels. There is a clear dividing line – 'pre-drainage' and 'post-drainage' – as hundreds of years of interventions and improvement, the man-made creation of land through drainage, with varying success, took place across England and Wales. In East Anglia, the Fens and the Broads, and, just to the south, the Essex Marshes. In Kent, the Pevensey Levels and Romney Marsh, the place that the cleric and writer of ghost stories and myths Richard Harris Barham called the fifth continent ('The world, according to the best geographers, is divided into Europe, Asia, Africa, America and Romney Marsh'). The meres and mosses of Shropshire, Wrexham and Cheshire. In Humberside, the Hull Valley and the Humberhead Levels and the Isle of Axholme, an island which has lost its sea.

The monasteries spearheaded the first systematic drainage work on the Somerset Levels, as they grew in wealth and power in the

6 This claim was made, among others, by Gordon Strachan in his 2009 film *And Did Those Feet*, leading to headlines such as the following from the otherwise respectable Reuters news agency: 'Did Jesus headline Glastonbury before Springsteen?'

Middle Ages. Some areas of low-lying moor, once held in common for the seasonal grazing of cattle, were drained. These efforts were localized and piecemeal, some parcels of better-grazing land created by the cutting of deep ditches called rhynes, which left the ground around relatively dry (the word 'rhyne' exists in various forms, such as 'reen' and 'rhines', in only a few places in Britain including Somerset, Gloucestershire and south Wales). It is in the Middle Ages that we see an emergence of a larger network of identifiable, and sometimes named, paths on the Levels. From the mother church at Moorlinch at the edge of the Polden Hills, radiating paths went to outlying chapels, such as the old route known as the Padenayshe Wey or Lychewey to nearby Sutton Mallet, or the road to Stawell, along which is a crossroads called Righton's Grave (likely to be the final resting place of someone who died by suicide, as they were often buried at crossroads, away from the churchyard).[7] A track simply called the Herpath (usually associated with the movement of armies) near where the Levels meet the Bristol Channel is now known as Sloway Lane, perhaps to differentiate itself from the later, straighter, drier and faster route called Main Road which runs a quarter of a mile parallel. Leading off Sloway Lane is a track called Slow Way Drove which leads to the new England Coast Path. It has been shown on maps for hundreds of years but remains unrecorded and unprotected.

On 20 January 1607 a storm surged up the Bristol Channel, causing disastrous flooding in south-west England and south Wales. In Somerset it left 'whole villages [to] stand like Islands . . . and in no short tyme were those Islands undiscoverable, and no

---

7 I find these solitary grave sites desperately sad. People shunned from their communities even in death. Perhaps the most moving is Kitty Jay's grave on Dartmoor, the burial place of a late-eighteenth-century woman who died by suicide. All year round, you can still find fresh flowers laid on her grave. No one knows who leaves these touching tributes.

where to be found. The tops of trees and houses onely appeared . . . as if at the beginning of the world townes had been builte at the bottome of the Sea'. Events such as these could only help galvanize a renewed interest in flood alleviation and drainage, something to try and turn back the devastating sea. The Crown had a vested interest in getting drainage right, having acquired large amounts of the land on the Levels (and elsewhere) following the dissolution of the monasteries. Activity, at the prompting of the king, was intense from the early 1600s. A survey from 1638 of the 'Moores and Lowe Grounds' of the Levels showed that of the land liable to flood, over one third was reclaimed ground – meadows which could, in a good year, be used through all four seasons. This survey was produced just four years before the English Civil War broke out, a conflict which saw the Levels become a battleground, with skirmishes, full-on confrontations and sieges at Langport, Bridgwater and on the Isle Moors.[8] The war also set back the course of land reclamation on the Levels for almost 130 years, with renewed attention only starting again in the late eighteenth century.

Parliamentary enclosure in the eighteenth and nineteenth centuries created much of the Levels we walk today. From 1770 to 1790 there was a rate of two enclosure Acts a year for the area. The enclosures here focused on the 'wastes' rather than the removal of the old open-field system as seen in other parts of the country. Open moors on which commoners had the right to graze their cattle were split by a network of rhynes and drains, backed up by the installation of sluices and pumps. The rate of enclosure quickened as the eighteenth century drew to a close, partly as a response to the scarcity of wheat caused by almost

8 A key battle in a later civil war also took place on the Levels. The Battle of Sedgemoor was the last in the Monmouth rebellion which had attempted to overthrow James II in 1685.

twenty years of war with France from the mid-1790s. Ultim-ately sixty-two enclosure Acts were passed by 1859, affecting nearly 100 square miles of land. Former communal rights to dig peat, fish, catch wildfowl and cut reeds were lost, and it is not surprising that this ripping away of collective rights led to bit-terness and anger. The commoners of Sedgemoor burned the backers of one enclosure Bill in effigy.

New paths were formed as drove roads were driven across previously dank ground. Hundreds of named drove roads cre-ated an angular network, paths that show on the map as a web of straight lines, fracturing the earth. Drove roads were not just used for moving animals but as paths for the whole community. Some of these tracks are now recorded as public paths (Lyng Drove, Gold Corner Drove and Burrow Drove), but maybe hundreds more are not (Yellow Batches Drove, White Horse Drove, Skimmers Drove and Shepherd's Drove).

People are missing out by not going walking on the Somerset Levels. We have an outdoors culture that lionizes getting to the top of a mountain, while flatlands are often seen as lesser, maybe even as boring. It is perhaps telling that many of the first National Parks were created in our hilly lands – the Peak Dis-trict, the Lake District and Eryri (Snowdonia) – to be joined only later by the woody lowlands of the New Forest and the drained land of the Norfolk and Suffolk Broads. But what you get on the Levels is the anticipation of surprise or discovery, akin to wandering around a city. When you are down on the lower moors, the landscape doesn't reveal itself fully; it isn't laid bare. The drove roads, largely devoid of fellow walkers, create quiet corners in their turns. At the meeting of two rhynes on the bend of a long track a solid, crooked willow emerges from the ditch, its bark spiralling as if frozen mid-twist. Sprinkled lights on a reed bed, the slips of yellow irises, and beyond, a deep, extended plane of meadow and sky.

However, if you walk on the Somerset Levels and only follow the recorded rights of way, you might be in for a frustrating experience. Footpaths that seem to cross drains and rhynes but there is no bridge in sight. You stand stranded on one side of the ditch, looking down into the treacle-black water, considering whether leaping across would be a good idea.[9] There are fields bounded with water where the only way out is blocked by a mass of inquisitive cows, and the alternative option is to walk alongside a busy road. In places, the line of a path on the map seems to go straight down the middle of a drain – you pick a side, invariably the wrong one, and need to retrace your steps. Many of these footpaths are the really old ways, routes across the common land before enclosure. They wiggle and snake, whereas the post-enclosure drove roads run straight. Once you see the drove roads as the public rights of way that they were and are, the whole history of life and travel on the Levels starts to make sense. A myriad of possibilities is revealed for walking, riding and cycling along these long, angular ways.

Coming over the Polden Hills and looking down into the southern Levels it's easy to imagine water stretching out to the horizon. A dry sea. On the map, I linger on the settlements which seem to have been named with a baroque, free-wheeling attitude. Westonzoyland, Hatch Beauchamp, Thornfalcon, Curry Rivel and Kingsbury Episcopi. I'm heading for Curry Moor, which lies in the direction of Taunton. The moor is

9 It's probably not. While the wetlands of the Levels are noted for the wide ecology they support, the rivers harbour a dark secret. All Somerset rivers are polluted 'beyond legal limits'. The Brue contains polybrominated diphenyl ethers, chemicals used to make electronics flame-retardant. A stretch of the Parrett is polluted with the insecticide and neurotoxin cypermethrin, and the Tone records mercury compounds and perfluorooctane sulphonate, used in metal plating and foam fire extinguishers.

beyond two of the most prominent islands on the Levels. Burrow Mump (meaning 'hill hill') has the same distinctive steepness as Glastonbury Tor. Rising at the confluence of the Tone, Cary and Parrett rivers, this cone of earth can be seen for miles around. It's unsurprising that the Normans found it to be the perfect location for a defensive outpost. A mile away is another former island, a gentler, less obtrusive hill. On top sits King Alfred's Monument, surrounded by a stout set of iron railings and a small square of paving, looking out over cultivated fields. Underneath lies the buried remains of the Athelney Abbey, founded by Alfred the Great to give thanks to the safety that this small promontory offered him when he was fleeing the Danes in 878.

I'm meeting Sarah Bucks in the middle of Curry Moor. Sarah is the author, along with Dr Phil Wadey, of a textbook which details the process to save unrecorded rights of way. We walk alongside her dog Frankie, who delights in a shaggy wallow in the few muddy puddles that have collected and remain on the drove under the hot sun. We walk along Currymoor Drove and Westmoor Drove, both fully accessible and well used but not legally recorded. These are just two of the dozens of paths which Sarah has spent hours researching so that they can be reclaimed for the public. Currymoor Drove was created through an Enclosure Act of 1797, which made clear that we have the right to be here. The enclosure commissioners intended that this drove was for the public who 'shall or may have occasion to go travel pass and repass . . . at their . . . free wills and pleasure'.[10] These drove roads were,

---

10 Sarah Bucks's application for the recording of Currymoor Drove as a public path includes, alongside the Enclosure Act, evidence from early Ordnance Survey maps, turnpike and tithe maps and documents from the sale of land on the Levels.

and are, maintained by drainage boards, the records of which can be used to help save these old paths. The preamble to the Somersetshire Drainage Act of 1877 makes clear the need for cooperation and enforcement, and describes the previous situation where 'every man would then be dependent upon the forbearance of his neighbours . . . it would be in the power of the neighbours on the higher level to pour down any amount of water' on his fellow landowners below. This wasn't just a theoretical threat. In *The Farming of Somersetshire*, published in 1851, the authors write of 'a feudal war' between occupiers of adjacent lands, which necessitated an all-night patrol of thirty men to ensure that a crucial dyke wasn't deliberately cut in a time of flood.

Walking through a heatwave on Curry Moor, it is difficult to comprehend how different this area looked in the early months of 2014. In January of that year, devastation came to the Levels. An estimated 65 million cubic metres of floodwater covered an area of sixty-five square miles, one of the largest floods ever known here. Along with the water came perennially vexed questions of drainage, dredging and flood defences. Climate change will bring more extreme weather, and we have to face up to the reality that, in the words of Professor Keith Beven, 'total flood defence is a myth'. Eighteen per cent of Somerset is below high tide, and the county has hundreds of miles of raised defences, most of which are focused on protecting the Levels. The moors of Somerset hold millions of tons of water, 17 million in the case of Curry Moor alone. After every major flood event, action plans are created and investment is made, but then the spotlight fades and works go quiet until the next one. As John Rowlands from the Adapting the Levels project tells me, perhaps we need to accept that we can't tame the water and instead focus on adapting to it (a process which has already started for some local farmers – water buffalo, producing

Somerset mozzarella, can now be seen grazing at the edge of the Levels).

Over ninety per cent of the UK's wetlands have been lost – drained and dried for agriculture and housing. But in places change is afoot, with new wetlands being created. These are attempts to restore our lost biodiversity, with beavers, frogs, birds and plants returning to alleviate the threats of flooding and wildfires. In newly wetted lands, where we perhaps don't seek greater and greater protection but let water naturally return, this raises fundamental questions – how and where do we live and how do we move across the landscape? The drove roads of the Somerset Levels are the inverse of the archetypal old path; unlike a holloway ground down by centuries of feet and hooves, they rise from and above the earth – perhaps they will survive as the water truly returns, safe and critical infra-structure through reflooded ground. But what of the older paths, the sinuous footpaths of the Levels which run through fields already boggy and waterlogged? Perhaps these are paths that we must accept losing, to be forever washed away.

Conflict

13.   The War at Home

Pevensey Castle has been protecting the south coast of England for 1,700 years. A Roman fort, a temporary encampment for the invading armies of William the Conqueror, a Norman castle, a fifteenth-century prison and a defence against the Spanish Armada. Ruined for hundreds of years, it is now an ancient monument, preserved in a state of frozen decay. Corner towers with tattered holes and narrow vertical slits and a thick degrading wall, let its insides show, a mass of grey stone. Across the top of these stones a black horizontal line catches the eye, something that looks slightly out of place. Almost hidden in the ruins of Pevensey Castle is part of much more recent defences. A machine-gun placement has been built directly on top of the walls, designed to blend in. A small, incongruous glimpse of a war from eighty years ago.

The remnants of the physical infrastructure of the Second World War can be found scattered across the country. Pillboxes, flecked with yellow lichen and topped with grass, flank the roads to a village in Northumberland or sit on manicured Oxfordshire lawns as seen from the Thames Path. Concrete cubes, slowly crumbling, lie across a field in Carmarthenshire or can be found buried in leaf mould beside a busy road in the Surrey commuter belt. These are just the ones we can see; it has been estimated that up to seventy-five per cent of surviving defence infrastructure is now hidden from view, inaccessible and completely buried, swallowed by nature in pockets of ivy, brambles and scrub.

The plan for defending Britain from invasion started in

earnest after the retreat from France at Dunkirk in May 1940 (an urgency compounded by the relative ease that the Channel Islands were captured in June that same year). Britain had to work out how to protect itself despite having lost so much equipment and guns on the beaches of northern France. Pevensey Castle was one part of a long shoreline defence, focused on the south and east, and parts of the west (from where invasion through neutral Ireland was feared). Thousands of miles of barbed wire, earthworks and field defences were thrown up around major ports. Thousands of civilians were moved away from their seaside communities, and coastal paths were closed, to be replaced by minefields, anti-tank scaffolding and coastal guns.[1]

France had built the Maginot Line, an extraordinary belt of fortifications along its border with Germany, which was designed to deter, stop and slow invasion. But this was not the model for Britain. The idea of stopping invading forces at the border, of a solid impenetrable line, was seen, mainly in hindsight, to engender a false sense of security. In the end the German army invaded France through Belgium and Holland, bypassing the Maginot Line almost entirely. Britain had learned a salutary lesson. Strategies were put in place to prevent enemy planes and gliders landing, to stop tank columns from breaking out along roads and to protect vulnerable infrastructure including factories, reservoirs and radar stations. The country was carved up into stop lines hundreds of miles long that were designed to contain any potentially rapid advance. The main stop line, the GHQ (General Headquarters), stretched from the Bristol

1 For instance, early in the war the cliff path near Dover was, unsurprisingly, closed to the public as it ran through a prohibited area. Perhaps more surprisingly, as the local paper reported at the time, the 'Dover Golf Links lie in this area, but they will remain open for play'.

Channel across the south and under London to the north Kent coast, with an additional long stretch running a few miles inland up the eastern coast. A web of shorter lines was formed around key cities: London, Hull, York, Bristol and Newcastle, and a few concentric radiating lines from key points on the coast.

The traditional British idea that defence was something that happened at the coast had been thrown away. The physical imprint of a potential war on home soil was to be seen in every county.[2] An engineer on the GHQ line describes the impression of these defences on the locals, who watched 'open-mouthed at the way earthworks were being thrown up'. The military juggernaut crashed down hard on the old paths: anti-tank ditches severed ancient footpaths, roadblocks cut public access, old ways were ploughed away in the dig for victory, and whole areas of the country – along with their path networks – were now out of bounds.

Even during this time of national crisis, the protectors of paths were looking towards the future and urging that the ancient ways were not to be lost for ever. A little over a week after the evacuation of Dunkirk, the Pennine Footpath Preservation Society held its annual 'Footpaths rally and demonstration' at Downham in the Forest of Bowland. Speakers urged walkers to be vigilant, to record in their memories every path which had been temporarily closed so that 'when the liberty of the world had been restored, the same should apply to our rights of way'. Philip Milner Oliver, the former Liberal Member of Parliament for Blackley in Manchester, in

2 One aspect that perhaps points to the ubiquity of these defences is that they were given nicknames. 'Pillbox' is probably the most famous, such that it is now the common name for these concrete fortifications, but there were also 'dragon's teeth', which were pyramidal lumps of concrete laid in a field and designed to stop tanks and other vehicles. A short section of Switzerland's defences, using dragon's teeth, has been nicknamed the 'Toblerone Line'.

his speech to the assembled walkers and cyclists, urged that 'if the German parachutist was to be hampered, the native ramblers, after the war, should be welcomed and not subjected to the threat of persecution'. For Oliver it was the land itself, a place of 'memories, traditions and long history' with its ancient paths, that was the cause worth fighting for. He fervently hoped that 'the greatest memorial of this war will be the completion and establishment of the Pennine Way'. This was public access as patriotism, the audience told that there would be 'nothing in notices against trespassing that could ever uproot from the heart of an Englishman the love of his land'.

The detailed plans to prepare for invasion, the stop lines on the map, give a terrifying picture of what war in Britain might have been like, but British land never saw the ground battles which ravaged continental Europe, and the tens of thousands of pillboxes and fortifications were never used. It was to be the war in the air which made the greatest impact. An impact felt in the physical destruction of cities and in the lives changed and ended by aerial bombing.

Walking from my home in south-east London, I can see the scars of this bombing on the urban streets. Rows of red-brick bay-windowed Victorian and Edwardian terraces, interrupted by 1950s or 60s infill. A small green and a few benches where a house once stood. The public footpath through the green following the lines of garden paths which ran to the front and back doors of a home that disappeared eighty years ago.[3] The words 'SHELTER FOR 700' in faded white paint pointing down a

3 This is an unrecorded footpath, as inner London boroughs are not required to keep a definitive map of public rights of way, but it's a footpath nonetheless.

set of steps on a railway bridge. The estate of prefab houses (alongside a prefab church) in Catford, designed to temporarily house those bombed out but which lasted well into the twenty-first century.[4]

It wasn't just London that was subject to bombing from the air. Cities with docks and industries were heavily targeted, but the bombs landed indiscriminately across these urban areas – whole streets destroyed and communities devastated in an instant. Raids on Manchester just before Christmas 1940 killed nearly 700 people when over 2,000 incendiary bombs were dropped. In Hull almost ten per cent of the population were made homeless through bombing. Liverpool was the most heavily bombed city after London. Merseyside was the main entry point for the country's supply chains from North America, and air raids, which peaked during the May 1941 blitz, killed 4,000 people and destroyed 10,000 homes. Coventry sustained such devastation that a new German word was coined – *coventrieren*, meaning to raze a city.[5] To guard against this aerial threat, a chequerboard of searchlights was established across Britain. By 1941, 4,000 of these searchlights – with accompanying huts for their operators, generators and a single pillbox – were built, spreading the defence of Britain even further across the country.

Most structures didn't last long after the war ended. Between 1946 and 1953, the Ministry of Works spent £3.5 million

4 The Excalibur Estate was built just after the war and consisted of 189 prefab houses and the church. I used to look in wonder at this strange collection of houses from the bus window on the way to my nan and grandad's house. The site is currently undergoing redevelopment with the building of over 300 new homes, with only six of the prefab homes and the church preserved.

5 Of course, it shouldn't be forgotten that the British (and Americans) also undertook devastating aerial bombardment of German cities, including the razing of Dresden in 1945, which killed 25,000.

(equivalent to over £100 million today) dismantling physical defences. Of the 28,000 hard fortifications built, about 6,500 survive today (the vast majority, 5,500, types of pillbox). Removal focused on public land or where there were potential risks to public safety. Roadblocks were taken down, seafronts cleared of barbed wire, scaffolding and concrete removed, anti-tank ditches infilled and the old paths re-established. However, there was one part of our defence (and indeed offence) that would continue to leave a mark to this day: the airfields.

When Britain started to prepare for war in response to German rearmament in 1935, there were around 100 permanent airfields across the country. The majority of these were for civilian use and only nine had hard runways. In the second half of the 1930s when war seemed inevitable, the government undertook a large-scale programme of building and rebuilding airfields. When war was declared in September 1939, work ramped up significantly, and during the peak of construction in 1942, new airfields were being finished at a rate of one every three days. The concrete used to build the airfields (excluding cement and other building materials) could fill a convoy of lorries stretching one and a half times round the Earth – 30 million tons. Sir Archibald Sinclair, speaking in Parliament, compared the lengths of wartime airfield runways to a continuous concrete road '9,000 mile long, 30 foot wide' running 'from London to Peking'. In total, during the war years, 444 RAF stations were built across Britain and Northern Ireland. By 1945 they occupied 360,000 acres of land, equivalent to almost a quarter of a million football pitches (and, put together, would be bigger than modern-day Bedfordshire). The *Aeroplane* magazine, in an article published just months after the war ended, described Britain as 'one vast aircraft carrier anchored off the north-west coast of Europe'.

For reasons of practicality (flat land and easy draining surfaces) and strategy (proximity to Europe and potential invasion sites), airfields were concentrated in the east and south of England. Yorkshire had forty-three airfields, Norfolk thirty-seven, Suffolk and Hampshire both had thirty-four. Essex, Wiltshire, Oxfordshire, Berkshire and Gloucestershire are also in the top ten counties with airfields. But it was Lincolnshire that had the most, with forty-eight in total covering over 30,000 acres of land (more than the entire country a decade before). The local tourist board now urges us to come to a county branded 'RAF Lincolnshire', a 'perfect way to experience aviation history'. Second World War airfields, alongside the motorways and the creation of whole new towns, were the greatest disruptors and destroyers of our old paths in the twentieth century. In parts of the country, you would need to go back to the railways, a century earlier, to see something which had a greater impact in permanence and scale.[6] With the railways, there was a plan to retain many paths, but in building the airfields hundreds, maybe thousands, of paths were truncated or destroyed altogether.

The Kesteven Uplands are the last place of relatively high ground before the land flattens out to the Fens. Like much of Lincolnshire, this southern part of the county is sparsely populated: small villages clustered around crossroads, scattered farmhouses and a few small towns. On an afternoon's walk with my friend Ed – across silent fields, through quiet woods, on empty tracks – we meet no one else on foot. It's been like this for a long time. The local vicar, in 1887, waged a three-year

6 There were also singular events which changed the landscape, such as at RAF Fauld in Staffordshire. On 27 November 1944, a munitions dump exploded here. The blast, the largest ever recorded on British soil, killed ninety people and destroyed a farm and a gypsum mine. The crater, with a public footpath snaking round one edge, is still there today.

letter-writing campaign 'of constant correspondence with the post-office authorities' to supply the exhausted postman who served these outlying communities with what was described as a 'mounted post' (i.e. to give the man a horse and cart). Further back, to the thirteenth century and earlier, the picture was very different. Lincolnshire was one of the most densely populated counties in England. The Lincolnshire Historic Environment Record lists over 130 abandoned villages across the whole county, with a concentration in the Wolds to the north. Traditional arable farming gave way to the raising of sheep, which needed far fewer people. The climate changed and the Black Death came along – neither of which helped.

We walk through Keisby. An aerial photograph of this area from the 1970s shows lumps and bumps clustered around and spreading out from what is now a hamlet. An abandoned medieval village, now only a handful of houses along a noiseless road. It's the end of summer and, turning on to a farmer's track, the fields are a light biscuit brown. A tall hay bale construction sits at the edge of the field. I stop and count 490 rectangular bales stacked up, a monument to the changing of the seasons. We are on a public footpath which runs east for about four-fifths of a mile. We know it is likely that we are going to retrace our steps, walk back over the same ground. Chatting, we reach the end of the footpath. Over a shallow ditch we emerge on to a long plane of cracked concrete perpendicular to our path. We have found ourselves standing on the runway of an airfield – the former RAF Folkingham.

Within a matter of seconds, a van pulls up, seemingly out of nowhere. 'Can I help you?' asks the driver pointedly. We are being turned back, told that the public was banned here by Parliament in 1939. The surprising speed with which he arrives makes me wonder if there are cameras or sensors somewhere, hidden in the bushes. We have apparently moved to where the public is no longer allowed to go, entered no man's land.

The Emergency Powers (Defence) Acts of 1939 and 1940 gave the government almost unlimited powers to create regulations which were considered 'necessary or expedient for securing the public safety, the defence of the realm, the maintenance of public order and the efficient prosecution of any war . . . and for maintaining supplies and services essential to the life of the community'. The regulations which flowed from these pieces of primary legislation included powers to fully direct industry, the introduction of the death penalty for two new crimes (breaking through roadblocks and looting), food rationing, internment of resident Germans and Austrians, and the legal authorization to interfere with a free press. These regulations also enabled the building of defence infrastructure – permitting entry to any land to undertake any necessary work (used to set up most of the searchlight stations) and requisition of land (used to establish the more permanent structures, such as airfields and ordnance factories). It was under these regulations that the temporary 'stopping up' of public paths and lanes was carried out. The records of these interventions were deposited with local councils, but paperwork was sparsely kept. There must have been such an order at RAF Folkingham, as the agricultural fields were replaced by the airfield that opened in 1940, spreading its wings over a local network of paths from which the public were now barred.

When RAF Folkingham opened, the people of Keisby may have wondered why the skies were silent. The airfield was initially a decoy, a fake installation designed to trick German aircraft away from RAF Spitalgate, seven miles to the north-west near Grantham. This was just one of 230 decoy airfields, called 'Q' sites, which were built during the Second World War.[7] These were masterminded by Colonel Sir John Fisher

7 The Q sites were intended to mimic airfields at night. Alongside these were K sites, smaller operations which were designed to look like airfields

Turner, a man who was never given an official job title (he earned the nickname the 'Dictator of Dummies'), working out of a secret and unnamed department within the Air Ministry (leading it to be simply known as 'Colonel Turner's Department'). Decoy airfields were manned by up to twenty people, who operated a series of lights and moved around dummy planes (supplied, later in the war, by film industry experts from the Sound City studios in Shepperton).

Alongside the fake airfields, dummies were also created for factories, docks and railway yards. An extension of Colonel Turner's work led to the building of Starfish sites, a strange name which came from their official designation 'SF', standing for 'special fires'. These special fires were powered by tanks of paraffin or diesel which were pumped on to burning coal and doused with jets of water. The thick smoke and steam were designed to look like a town or city burning. Placed near real built-up areas, the idea was to convince enemy bombers that this was where their immediate predecessors had hit urban targets, tricking them into dropping bombs where they could be of little harm. It is estimated that over the course of the war these sites avoided 730 air raids and saved at least 2,400 lives.

The airfield at Folkingham didn't remain just a decoy. By 1943, it was a fully functioning RAF base and was then transferred to the US Ninth Air Force by early 1944. Its main role was as a jumping-off point for American troops flying to the war in Europe. From these flat Lincolnshire fields troops were flown to the newly captured Sicily Isles and dropped by parachute or in gliders into France during D-Day and over Holland as part of Operation Market Garden. After a brief and intense burst of activity, by February 1945, RAF Folkingham, like many similar airfields, was no longer required as new airbases were established

---

during the day.

in continental Europe. When the war ended decisions had to be made as what to do with 300,000 acres of airfields. Some were kept as RAF bases, private flying clubs or, over time, transformed into civilian airports.[8] Land and buildings were auctioned off after their original owners were given first refusal. Many airfields returned to agricultural use. Runways served as the foundations of factory farming units or cut across fields with ploughing and sowing taking place right up to the hard surface. Surviving runways serve a myriad of uses now, as hard bases for wind and solar farms, racetracks (such as Silverstone and Goodwood) and kart tracks, power stations, business parks and depots. A good few runways were ripped up for use as hardcore in building the new motorways, while RAF outbuildings and structures found new life as cattle sheds and chemical stores.

The War Works Commission were responsible for deciding what should happen to all these acres of concrete. The Requisitioned Land and War Works Acts of 1945 and 1948 allowed the commission to decide whether to make the temporary stopping-up orders authorized during the war permanent or to return paths to public use (or to permanently divert them). In the early 1950s, the Air Ministry asked the commission for the paths at RAF Folkingham to be closed permanently as they still wanted to use the airfield, but not everyone was on board. In a letter to the commission in 1952, a local landowner furiously questioned whether the commission's secretary was English, because if he was, he would know that 'England is not a Dictatorship, even by officials of the War Commission'. He asserts that the rights of way are enshrined 'by virtue of the position of the land, in the memory and habits of the villagers and drovers'.

8 For instance, RAF Middleton St George became Teesside International Airport, and the former RAF Castle Donington is now East Midlands Airport.

This dispute seemed to have been dragging on for some time at this point, the wing commander of RAF Folkingham detailing in a letter to the commission that in 1950 the same landowner was suspected of repeatedly breaking the locks to the airfield.

The former airfields of Lincolnshire leave a distinctive impression on our current map of the county. Built in standard shapes, the most common being the 'A' (named for the large letter the runways seem to spell), they are hard to miss – ancient field patterns, organic and irregular, interrupted by straight lines and unnaturally smooth curves. Where runways were pulled up and the ground returned to agriculture, a new shape of field was created, inordinately long and narrow. The majority still have no public paths crossing the old airfield boundaries. I count at least ten miles of public rights of way which have been left as dead ends by Lincolnshire airfields – paths to nowhere. These are only the paths which are obvious; many more were completely destroyed, with no trace of them remaining. There are also weird dog-legs and odd diversions, paths which follow a clear ancient desire line and then turn suddenly away at the old airfield boundary. Airfields built in a short ten-year period still leave their mark on our paths eighty years on.

Despite the Air Ministry arguing in 1952 that they needed to use the airfield permanently, the military did leave Folkingham for a short period. In 1947, RAF Folkingham closed and in the late 1940s it served as a racetrack for British Racing Motors; it was where they debuted their new Formula One car.[9] But its civilian use didn't last for long; the Air Ministry got their way

9 A Pathé News film from 1949 heralds this new racing car, 'given its first public workout at Folkingham Aerodrome'. The film tells us that the racing driver, later seen climbing out of his car, cigarette firmly in mouth, is 'like the rest of us, tired of Britain being the world's best losers' and that this BRM car will give Britain 'the same lead on the road, as we have in the air'.

and in 1959 Folkingham came back into active service as part of the innocuously named Project Emily, when Lincolnshire was brought into the dangerous international web of nuclear mutually assured destruction.

Project Emily is a now rather forgotten part of the Cold War in Britain. In 1957, the new British prime minister Harold Macmillan agreed to the placing of sixty Thor intermediate range ballistic missiles at twenty-six airfields in eastern England. Macmillan, a great friend of President Eisenhower, was hoping to bolster the US–UK 'special relationship' which had suffered a knock after the Suez Crisis and the resignation of his predecessor Anthony Eden. These nuclear weapons, which could be fired within fifteen minutes, were the first missiles able to reach the Soviet Union from Europe, bringing the world that bit closer to a deranged, pointless end. During the Cuban Missile Crisis, nearly all the Project Emily missiles were placed on the highest of alerts, ready to launch and strike from the fields of England. Perhaps if it had been twenty years later, the truncated paths around RAF Folkingham would have played reluctant host to a peace camp. Like at RAF Greenham Common, thousands may have come here, to the brown fields of a depopulated Lincolnshire, in anger and determined protest against the madness of nuclear weapons.

In the long life of these medieval earthworks and ancient lanes, RAF Folkingham was a brief interruption. The airfield closed in 1963, one year after the Thor missiles left, and was sold off in 1966. It was fully operational for less than twenty-five years (and for a proportion of that as a decoy and a racetrack) but brought everlasting change to the paths all around it. In addition to the footpath we walked, there are another two and a half miles of nowhere paths around Folkingham, their dead ends defining the boundary of what was once the airfield. We walk a path through the woods to the east of the airfield, past border signs pinned to rusting machinery, reading 'Strictly no access beyond this point' and 'Firearms at use on this site at all times' (maybe with some truth; on the footpath across the fields I scooped up a few discarded shotgun cartridges). Alongside the paths are slabs of broken concrete, the remains of the airfield bomb stores, crumpled and decaying, barely recognizable as buildings any more. These woods are now open-access land managed by the Woodland Trust. The southern end of the wood is in a new upheaval, tree limbs lying everywhere and deep ruts across the ground – woodland management as ash die-back advances here. It is hard to see the path and each step is a negotiation, a decision about where or not to put my feet. From these woods, looking past the alarming signs, we see glimpses of what the runway is used for now: strange distorted shapes on the horizon, jutting metal structures and curved hoods. The former RAF Folkingham is now a storage site for decommis-sioned agricultural machinery, waiting for their spare parts to be harvested. Aerial photographs of the site show hundreds of pieces of equipment and vehicles, like bees at the edge of a hive, lined up along the runways.

At the other side of Britain, on the Pembrokeshire coast in south-west Wales, is a former airfield that has been opened for use by the public, with new life breathed into this military space through the creation of paths. RAF St Davids is named after Britain's smallest city (population: 1,600), which lies a couple of miles west. The airfield saw relatively long service. In the Second World War planes from here searched for submarines in the Battle of the Atlantic and undertook crucial meteorological sur-veys. After the war it served as a base for training flights and as a relief airfield for the nearby RAF Brawdy. RAF St Davids was decommissioned in the 1990s and was bought by the Pembroke-shire National Park Authority with the goal of restoring natural habitats and public access. Part of the airfield has returned to agriculture, where the farmer and the National Park Authority have worked to create a traditional hay meadow, a refuge for ground-nesting skylarks. And as I cross the threshold of the old airfield, I think I hear the skylark's song, caught in the wind coming from the coast.

Paths run round the concrete of the perimeter road and along the runways. Weaving around these are 'spectacle loops', hard-standing where aircraft could turn and stay safely apart to lessen the impact of attack from the air. Between the loops now grow pillowy knolls of impenetrable gorse. From behind the gorse, groups of quiet walkers suddenly emerge. A well-used set of paths trail round and through this former airfield, a stark contrast to the empty dead-end tracks of RAF Folkingham. There is a symbol I rarely see on a path-side signpost, a wheelchair, showing the accessibility of these flat paths for all.[10] In a clearing of sorts between the spiky mounds, I come across a surprise: a stone circle. An ancient monument around which the airfield was thrown up? But one of the stones is stained red-brown by a rusting gate latch; this is not old at all. The circle was constructed as part of the National Eisteddfod of Wales, held here in 2002. The week-long Welsh-language festival of poetry, music, ceremony and celebration brought over 100,000 people here as the abandoned airfield was repurposed as the Maes, the site of the eisteddfod.

In his pioneering book *The Making of the English Landscape*, the historian W. G. Hoskins argues that the only thing uglier than

10 Usually a signpost will only give the designation of the path: footpath, bridleway etc. Sometimes you might find one which gives information about where the path goes with a corresponding distance in miles (uniquely, I think, there are signposts around Haworth in the Pennines that also feature a language other than English or Welsh – with Japanese featuring due to the international popularity of Brontë Country).

an arterial bypass road is an airfield. Standing in the centre of RAF St Davids, I think that Hoskins couldn't be more wrong. The path I took through the airfield to reach this spot, while straight on the map, is a gentle wave on the ground. Soil and plants encroach the hard surface, natural forms returning. On the main runway, moss and grass grow up through cracks in the concrete. The slabs of its original construction show as a green grid stretching into the near distance. The beauty here enhanced by the human surfaces laid down eighty years ago, as a wild world slowly takes over.

14.   The Warpath

Thousands of acorns stand alongside the paths of England and Wales, always dormant and never to grow into oaks. Hammered and carved into wood, the acorn is the symbol of our sixteen National Trails, reassuring and guiding hundreds of thousands of people each year. Supplementing these flagship routes are hundreds of regional long-distance paths, many with their own distinctive waymarkers. These trails bring a strange iconography to our countryside, nailed on gates, stiles and fingerposts. The silhouette of a witch, with spiked hat, atop a broom flies over the Pendle Way. In Conway you follow the image of a bent, wind-smashed tree on the Hiraethog Trail. A fish leaps above clear blue waves on Buckinghamshire's Chess Valley Walk. The Long Distance Walkers Association maintains a grand database of over 1,300 regional and local walking trails across Britain. Of these 550 are signposted and waymarked on the ground and nearly 400 shown and named on the Ordnance Survey maps. These walking routes, which primarily use recorded rights of way and public roads, are semi-official marks on our paths, a network within a network established by communities, ramblers, heritage societies and local councils over the last seventy years. They are intended to celebrate and to memorialize or simply indicate a good walk.[1]

1 In an article for the Cicerone website, Andrew McCloy asks, 'Has England's trail system lost its way?' While many of our trails are well loved and well walked, too many are now lost, fallen out of use and uncared for. Among these are some that were created to celebrate the millennium. How quickly they have fallen.

Many long-distance path names are descriptive of or celebrate local landscapes, such as the Six Dales Trail, Fen Rivers Way
and the Gritstone Trail, or are designed to encircle whole urban
areas, for instance the Penistone Boundary Walk, the Stevenage
Outer Orbital Path (known simply as STOOP), the Aylesbury
Ring and the Wolverhampton Way. There is a small flight of
bird-named paths and trails with cuckoos, ravens and skylarks
swooping over our maps. Nationally and internationally known
names feature: the Brontë Way, Tennyson Trail, Shakespeare's
Way, the John Bunyan Trail and the Gustav Holst Way.

There are some perhaps less well-known figures memorialized, such as Jack Mytton, a regency rake, Member of Parliament
(for, literally, thirty minutes – he found the debates boring and
difficult to hear), horseman and eccentric, who now has a long-
distance path in Shropshire bearing his name. Isaac's Tea Trail in
the north Pennines is named for Isaac Holden, a philanthropist
and itinerant tea-seller, Lady Anne's Way commemorates a
prominent seventeenth-century northern landowner, and great
restorer of churches and ancient castles, and the Stephen Lang-
ton Trail was created for the 800th anniversary of the Magna
Carta and named for a thirteenth-century archbishop who
helped negotiate it. I find the long-distance routes which honour
the heroes of our paths the most touching: the Brenda Parker
Way (named after an inspirational Hampshire Ramblers
volunteer – the path's chaffinch reflecting her passion for bird-
watching), the d'Arcy Dalton Way (in honour of a Colonel
W. P. d'Arcy Dalton who fought for rights of way in Oxfordshire for over half a century) and the John Musgrave Heritage
Trail (in memory of a former chairman of South Devon
Ramblers).

Our trails are also named for war and conflict, paths to celebrate and commemorate military might, bloody battles and the
movement of thousands under arms. You can march the way

that King Harold took from London to Senlac Hill for the Battle of Hastings in 1066, or follow the route of Charles II's flight from parliamentary troops at the conclusion of the English Civil War. You can walk alongside the ghosts of the seventeenth-century artisans and farm labourers who joined the Pitchfork Rebellion in a Protestant attempt to depose James II.[2]

Other trails are less overtly tied to a specific campaign or battle but are connectors between places of martial history. They guide you to walk between twenty-five castles in Kent, twenty castles in Sussex, six in Cumbria and three in Monmouthshire. The Allan King Way links up forts from the Roman, medieval and Victorian ages, while the Battlefields Trail will take you to sites of conflict from the War of the Roses and the English Civil War.[3] While the historical facts are sometimes a little hazy, especially when it comes to identifying the exact routes armies took, these long-distance trails reflect the wider use that our path network has had for military conquest, confrontation, uprisings, resistance and suppression. English and Welsh rulers have long been paranoid, fearing insurrection from below or invaders from outside. The need to deal with these threats (whether real or perceived) has created paths to get troops across the country and to project power.

Some of these military manoeuvres are now legendary. If we look at '1066 and all that', we can see that, as Oliver Rackham points out, in September that year King Harold was able to quickly journey from London to York, picking up an army on the way, to see off the Viking invasion. Two hundred miles in

2 These trails are, in order: 1066 Harold's Way, the Monarch's Way and the Liberty Trail. The Monarch's Way was, until recently, England's second-longest waymarked trail, although it has been pushed into third place by the creation of the England Coast Path.

3 The Allan King Way, also known as the King's Way, is another path named in memory of a Ramblers volunteer.

around four and a half days. Having seen off this threat, he heard of a second invasion, this time by the Normans in the south and was able to travel back to London and on to Kent to almost win the Battle of Hastings. The speed of these events demonstrates the existence of some pretty decent roads to carry these Anglo-Saxon armies.

The Saxons gave a lot to our naming of paths. The word 'way', coming from Anglo-Saxon '*weg*', is applied to paths of many kinds. This suffix was appended to wood, mill, sandy, rough and hay to describe paths and their uses and natures. Alongside words that might be more recognizable to the path aficionado: the holloways and ridgeways. To the Saxon path dictionary we can add a word which means 'army way': the herepath. Academics have made detailed studies of these herepaths, tracing their course through the land, over hills and round rivers. Their findings suggest that these paths didn't just take the most optimal routes but instead were the best fit for linking up Saxon fortifications, part of the system of defence and control.

The Burghal Hidage, a collection of Saxon texts, sets out the creation of burhs across southern England. These were fortified settlements, places for the surrounding population to retreat to and defend, sometimes laid upon pre-existing Iron Age or Roman sites but also established completely from scratch (some of which live on as our modern urban boroughs – from burhs to boroughs over a thousand years). They were secure places to trade, for coins to be minted, goods to be stored and for the populace of the surrounding areas to shelter in times of conflict. Alongside the burhs, two other key parts of the Saxon defensive strategy were beacons (to warn of an incoming threat) and the herepaths themselves. As Alex Langlands has pointed out in his study of the Saxon Wessex network, the herepaths constituted an extensive and efficient network, enabling mustered troops to be easily moved from one burh to another to address any threat.

While they very much form part of a planned Saxon strategy, that isn't to say that they didn't use existing paths and roads, including perhaps the most famous of the warpaths: those established by the Romans in their earlier invasion, conquest and settlement of Britain.

I'm standing next to a wide gate. To my left and right there are lines of trees that meet at this spot, emphasizing the shallow valley in front of me – a gentle green amphitheatre. Soft autumn light moves slowly across the ground, over browned grass with a vivid green track. This is the path I am to follow for the next five miles. Walking this way, I will pass through a patchwork of terrain. An avenue of spiky gorse one mile, a deeply wooded plantation the next. The path runs raised up along a field's edge and then through a collection of stunted hawthorns, the ground under my feet like skin pulled tightly – knuckles of flint and veined with tree roots. Towards the end of my walk, I enter a spectacular holloway, a dark tunnel of worn earth and curled oak and maple. On the train back home, I look at the trace I have made in my Strava app. It shows a straight red stripe, my walks barely deviating from a single line, the course of a Roman road, Stane Street.

In total, the trace of this Roman road, its impression on the land, can be seen for nearly sixty miles – from streets of stone, glass and concrete in South London, through the chalky North and South Downs to Chichester and the sea.[4] The harbour at what is now Chichester was an important site for the Roman

4 Stane Street is the name given to the road by the generations who came after the Romans. It's a name that signifies the solidity of the path, coming from the Old English for 'stone'. Some sections of this road are still the subject of speculation, with competing theories about the exact alignment of its route from the capital to the coast.

military. It offered them a safe landing place in an area under
control of a British tribe who were friendly to the invaders.

In his first volume of *The History of the Decline and Fall of the
Roman Empire*, Edward Gibbon describes the Roman road network as having a 'primary objective . . . to facilitate the marches
of the legions; nor was any country considered completely sub-
dued, till it had been rendered, in all its parts, pervious to the
arms and authority of the conqueror'. And in a talk given a hundred years later about Stane Street itself, the Reverend F. H.
Arnold places the road as one part of an imperial project of conquest and subjugation – compared, in his favourable terms, to
the British Empire: 'the Romans held Britain then, as we hold
India now, by the sword'.

While there is truth in the views of Reverend Arnold and
Edward Gibbon, subsequent historians and archaeologists have
added nuance, developing a more complex and expansive idea of
the purpose Roman roads had and how they were used.[5] As with
prehistoric paths, there is now a recognition that there was a long
lacuna in our understanding of the Roman road network. These
roads were a favourite study of early antiquarians and historians,
but they clutched too tightly to a relatively small number of flagship paved roads, the major arteries across the country. These are
the famous ones, sections of which are now long, straight, tarmacked public roads – Watling Street, the Fosse Way, Ermine
Street, Dere Street and, of course, Stane Street. But as many modern
historians have pointed out, focusing on these only is akin to creating a map of our modern road network with only the motorways
shown. If you look at the uncovered Roman sites (villas, temples
and settlements), they do not line up perfectly along these major

5 As we saw in Chapter 1, the notion that the Romans encountered a pathless
island cannot true; indeed, Julius Caesar mentions finding roads in his
account of his second invasion of Britain in 55 BC.

roads, just as our houses don't share the motorway service station forecourt next to the Little Chef and Wild Bean Café.

Roman Britain wasn't just armies marching across the land on their perfectly straight roads but a place of daily life. Connections were needed to enable everyday trade and travel, which were served by the pre-existing prehistoric tracks and a, perhaps largely unpaved, Roman network. The impulse and need for physical connections in the landscape extended far beyond the demands of great armies, as was the case both for those who came before the Romans and those who followed after them.[6]

The Roman Roads Research Association are using modern technology and looking afresh at the landscape to fill in the gaps. They are building on the work of antiquarians and historians (amateur and professional) of the last several hundred years who have collected, mapped and walked the Roman roads. They are especially standing on the shoulders of that great documenter of Roman roads, Ivan Margary, who created a number system for them in his 1955 book *Roman Roads in Britain*. Much of this early interest in the partially disappeared network of Roman roads, I think, reflects a wider, and seemingly endless, fascination with the promise of modernity in ancient Britain (nostalgia fuelled by the state of roads in earlier centuries, a yearning for when things were 'done properly'). A story is told of a whole 'civilized' nation, with central heating, planned cities formed in neat grids, a sophisticated and efficient centralized bureaucracy and the long, straight, perfect roads – all of which, to varying degrees, have been lost.[7]

This feeling is encapsulated in the now outmoded term to

6 Users of the major roads also extended far beyond military personnel. Stane Street, for instance, was a thoroughfare for goods of all kinds, including timber, pottery and pig iron, plus the luxury goods and treasures the empire could offer, which would arrive in Britain at the harbour in Chichester.

7 As an example, in his *History of England* (published in 1926), G. M. Trevelyan writes of the Roman roads: 'throughout the Dark Ages and in early medieval

describe the post-Roman period: the Dark Ages. This romantic and nostalgic evocation of the Romans and their paths is evident in Richard Jefferies' *The Life of the Fields* in which he comes across a small brook by an orchard. Hanging from a tree is a broken section of a Roman jug and the ground is scattered with further fragments of Roman pottery. From these shards he conjures a whole imagined scene:

> Fifteen centuries before there had been a Roman station at the spot where the lane crossed the brook. There the centurions rested their troops after their weary march across the Downs, for the lane, now bramble-grown and full of ruts, was then a Roman road. There were villas, and baths, and fortifications; these things you may read about in books. They are lost now in the hedges, under the flowering grass, in the ash copses, all forgotten in the lane, and along the footpath where the June roses will bloom after the apple blossom has dropped.

We shouldn't, however, dismiss the Roman military role in forming and using their roads as simple romance and nostalgia. The more refined picture of their roads very much includes the Roman army. The Roman Empire was a military state and it was this military which had the motivation, manpower and the skills to plan and create such a road network. Whereas existing tracks were created through use and built up over time, the Romans employed engineering techniques unfamiliar to the Iron Age inhabitants of Britain. Sophisticated imperial construction methods were used, with aggers (a low ridge to raise the road), ditches and metalled surfaces formed of cobbles, slabs and gravel. The roads and tracks for linking villas and cities, for trade, industry and communication, usually came later. The

---

times, these stone highways still traversed an island otherwise relapsed to disunion and barbarism' and trod by 'wild tribes'.

initial motivation for the Romans to build their roads was conquest. The roads extended further and further as the border of the conquered land moved further north and west: routes for an army on the march, passages for soldiers (and administrators and traders) who journeyed from all over the empire to travel across Britain. Clues can be found of how far people came to set foot on our Roman roads – in Tyneside a tombstone records the death of Regina of the British Catuvellauni tribe, the wife of Barates who came from Palmyra in Syria. We have evidence of soldiers posted to Britain from modern-day Germany, Spain, Belgium, Algeria, Morocco and all the way from the Tigris in what is now Iraq.

The complexity of the Roman road network, for military or civilian use, survives today, piecemeal. It could be said that their roads are the archetypical lost paths. As they were built in 'time immemorial', there is no assumption that their previous public use should carry on today, that we have the right to stride the whole of the Roman network. Of course, after the Roman armies withdrew from Britain in the early years of the fifth century, the following generations didn't simply ignore the roads which had been established. However, without a central power to maintain them, many disappeared. Surfaces sank into the soil, the edges of these roads slowly colonized by creeping and seeding plants. Bridges were washed away, one stone or abutment at a time. But chunks of the Roman network remained, to be used and reused by subsequent generations. When I was encircled by the spectacular holloway on my Stane Street walk, I was walking on a path rechristened as Mill Lane, pointing to its use as the way to the nearby eighteenth-century Halnaker Windmill. The section of Stane Street that I walked is shown on my Ordnance Survey map – the national mapping agency detailing the course of some of the major Roman roads, even if their full length is now buried beneath the accumulated development of the last two thousand years. Hardly any other paths on our historical network are bestowed the honour of being shown in the skeletal lines given to the Roman roads (some of the only others include short pre-historic trackways, such as the Sweet Track).

On the outskirts of Sheffield, I am on the hunt for a lost Roman road. This path is even lost to the map; nothing is shown to suggest it ever ran here. I've just come up a wide track to the moors. As the ground starts to plateau, I walk alongside a wall of coniferous trees. Lady Canning's Plantation, owned by Sheffield City Council, is a small island of woodland with its own internal network of paths on the treeless moor. Gaps in the trees, fire breaks, form popular paths for walking, and a bumpy mountain bike trail has been established through the plantation.[8] I'm on a path called Houndkirk Road, which runs across the moors along the south-east border of the triangular woods. It stretches ahead of me like a stream frozen mid-flow, its surface never flat but rutted and twisting, rivulets of a sandy path which turn around stray hassocks of grass.

Houndkirk Road isn't Roman. This track is a bluff, albeit one with its own history; it was part of the turnpike road from Sheffield to Hathersage in the Derbyshire Peak District. Further along I pass a weathered and crumbling milepost. The letters are faded but I can just make out what it read. On one side is the distance to Sheffield and on the other, the remains of the distances

---

8 It was also, temporarily, home to one of the mirrored monoliths that popped up all over the planet in 2020 and 2021. The first of these objects, standing ten feet tall, was found in a Utah desert canyon in November 2020. Its creator and purpose remain unknown. A physical meme was born, and copycats started appearing in over 120 locations across the globe (from Australia and Iran to Paraguay and Sweden – thirty-three countries in total had their own monoliths).

to Tideswell and Buxton. Beneath these disintegrating letters, the image of a skull, with 'X's for eyes and crossed bones, carved long ago in the grey-green stone. This milestone has only recently been reinstalled on the moor, having been discovered as part of a nearby house's garden rockery. It was removed during the Second World War, alongside many signposts and markers which might have helped an invading German army. During the same war, this moor was home to a whole decoy town, a faux Sheffield designed to confuse enemy planes and steer them away from the city's steelworks. The moors were also used for military training and on boulders in the Burbage Valley can still be seen the scars made by bullets and mortars. After the war, there was a proposal to make Burbage and Houndkirk Moors permanent military-training sites. The plan was strongly opposed by Sheffield City Council and by the Youth Hostels Association (an indication of the value of the land for recreation). Thankfully the scheme was dropped and pretty much the whole area is now open-access land. Had the military stayed, it is likely that there would have been a very different picture of public access.

Turning my attention back to my search for the lost Roman road, I crouch down, my knees brushing a coast of tufty grass which buttresses the sandy-soiled track, moisture seeping into my jeans. The track is busy and passing walkers and cyclists glance at me slightly quizzically. I'm looking for the road's faint trace across the moors, searching for a visible impression on the ground. I examine the valley in the direction of where I have come from. The route I walked to get here went through Ecclesall Woods. Shaded and broad, this path runs alongside the Limb Brook. I was greeted by the words 'Walkers Welcome' and further along I see the signs installed by the Peak and Northern Footpaths Society – handsome slabs of metal. Discs of birch polypore fungi cling to decaying logs at the pathside. There are points where bright orange water, the result of former mining up the slope, seeps across the path and into the Limb Brook, staining the sluggish water. This stream was once an important post-Roman dividing line, the border between the kingdoms of Northumbria and Mercia (and until just under a hundred years ago the separation point for Derbyshire and Yorkshire).

It has been long postulated that there is a Roman road somewhere on the moors to the west of Sheffield, a possible route from the Roman fort, and an accompanying civilian settlement known as the *vicus*, at Navio near Brough-on-Noe in the High Peak. This fort was the destination of the oldest milestone found in Derbyshire. The partial inscription on this Roman marker translates as 'with tribunician power, twice consul, father of his country, from Navio 11 miles'.

The Roman road across Burbage and Houndkirk Moors is proposed as running from Navio to Templeborough, now a suburb of Rotherham on the River Don. Debate about the function and route of this old buried path is ongoing, part of the lively scholarship of Roman roads. It was likely connected to the trade in lead, an important resource for the Romans for lining their drains, coffins and pots.[9] A connection between the lead-mining areas of the Peak District and the River Don (for exportation) – a lead trade and lead road established and controlled by the Roman imperial army.

From the moors, Limb Brook is hidden in the trees, but between me and Ecclesall Woods is a cleft in the ground, the most obvious indication of the course of this lost Roman road. A public right of way runs alongside it, my boots still wet from the path's long grass. I try to follow the line of the indentation towards and behind me, but up on the moors the road isn't obvious – squinting, I try in vain to find an impression it has made on the ground. The Roman Roads Research Association

9 Prompting many internet articles with headlines such as 'Did lead poisoning cause the downfall of the Roman Empire?'

tell the back-and-forth theories about this road. Ivan Margary, picking up on earlier theories, put the road further north, at the centre rather than edge of this moorland world. The first person to question the earlier route was the geographer Tom Welsh, who got out on the ground to look, with more expert eyes than mine, intensively at the landscape. In the late 1970s, he found the lumps and the bumps and the cleft from the Limb Brook, clear signs of a Roman road running up this hillside.

Almost forty years later, researchers looked again at Welsh's theory and used lidar technology to confirm there was definitely something there.[10] David Inglis at the University of Sheffield picked up the baton. Between my vantage point next to Lady Canning's Plantation and the Limb Brook is Sheep Hill Farm. Working alongside a team of archaeology enthusiasts called the Time Travellers, Inglis dug down into the soil. They weren't disappointed. The photos of his trenches show the peeling back of layers of history and the uncovering of a Roman road – right there, just below the surface. This lost way was bigger than anyone expected, twice the width of the standard Roman roads in the area, with tentative evidence of ruts from Roman wheels. It would have left a significant impression on all those who saw it; maybe it was a major boundary in the Roman world, to go along with the one that separated the Northumbrian and Mercian kingdoms in the Limb Brook. A statement in the landscape buried for almost two thousand years.

As I wander on, tracking the yellow line of the path across the moors, I wonder what remains hidden. My feet follow a path

---

10 Lidar technology bounces radar across a surface, showing detail about how it rises and falls. Turning this technology to the hunt for lost roads, the worn passage of old paths can emerge from the background noise or, indeed, the raised agger of a Roman road.

which we can trace back several hundreds of years, but what else is to be found here, how many lines of human communication, how many lost footsteps beneath the soil? The surface of this lost Roman road will never be rewalked; it is now covered up again and returned to the ground. Unlike Watling Street or the Fosse Way, I don't think it will ever be drawn as a ghostly line on our modern Ordnance Survey maps.[11]

These maps do show tracts of land given over to military use. In fact, according to Guy Shrubsole's *Who Owns England?*, the Ministry of Defence is the third-biggest institutional landowner in England after the Forestry Commission and the National Trust (and the fourth biggest if you include all the land owned by local authorities as one). These include areas where live firing takes place, marked out on the maps by alarming red triangles and the words 'Danger Area'. Sixteen large areas and over a hundred smaller ones are scattered across the country. Public rights of way cross these patches of land, but their accessibility can be overridden by military by-laws. Red flags are unfurled and red lamps are lit to indicate that the public shouldn't walk that way – perhaps this would have been the fate of Burbage and Houndkirk Moors if the military had stayed. My search for its lost Roman road would have fallen at the first hurdle. One such place is the closed island of Foulness on the Essex coast. Public rights of way run here but access is severely restricted. These paths include the Broomway, at least 600 years old, which streaks across the sands. Walked and evocatively described by Robert Macfarlane in *The Old Ways*, the Broomway has been called the

---

11 As their name suggests, these maps were themselves born of war. After the Jacobite rising of 1745, there was a clear need for the British army to have better maps of the Scottish Highlands – mapping for the avoidance of similar rebellions, for subjugation. Later that century a detailed mapping effort was expanded to the south coast of England to prepare for possible French invasion in the Seven Years' War.

deadliest path in England, having claimed at least a hundred lives over the centuries (the danger coming from the tides rather than the army).

On other military land, rights of way are almost entirely absent. The villagers of Tyneham in Dorset were cleared out during the Second World War and forbidden to return. No rights of way were legally mapped here in the subsequent decades, only the orange lines of permissive paths, including the course of the England Coast Path, now run through, around and between this abandoned village. People come at weekends to gaze at a landscape frozen in time – a church without parishioners, a silent schoolhouse and a row of crumbling terrace cottages.

15.   Protest and Protection

In 1836, William Wordsworth was travelling in Westmorland with a party of companions, including John Taylor Coleridge (nephew to the poet Samuel). Their destination was a dinner thrown in Wordsworth's honour at the golden-grey turreted lump of Lowther Castle. This opulent country house dressed up as a mock castle, and now tucked just inside the boundaries of the Lake District National Park, was the home of the Viscount Lowther, Earl of Lonsdale and family. In my mind it was a dark and stormy night as Wordsworth and his party left their carriage and set off across the field to the castle. Walking along an old path, they suddenly encountered a wall completely blocking their way. Wordsworth, muttering under his breath, jumped at the obstruction, landing blows on the stone. As he broke the wall down, he cried out, 'This is the way, and an ancient right of way too,' before they continued to dinner. After the meal, Coleridge was chatting to Sir John Wallace, a prominent local landowner whose estate ran close to Lowther Castle, and he mentioned the broken-down wall. Wallace was not happy and wished he could horsewhip the man who did it. At the other end of the table, Wordsworth caught their conversation and rose in anger, shouting, 'I broke down your wall, Sir John. It was obstructing an ancient right of way, and I will do it again.'

Wordsworth was a frequent visitor to Lowther Castle. His host that night was Lonsdale's eldest son, Viscount Lowther, a friend and patron of Wordsworth. He had arranged for the poet to be appointed to the paid position of Distributor of Stamps for the county of Westmorland and later provided a job for

Wordsworth's son. William's sister Dorothy had campaigned for the interests of the Lowther family in the general elections of 1818 and 1820. This close relationship, and in the company of fashionable society and the local elite, makes Wordsworth's outburst even more extraordinary. He obviously wasn't shy in asserting his, and the public's, right to walk the old paths and to take direct action to defend these rights.

The Lake District, that quintessential English walking landscape (moulded in this image in part by Wordsworth), has had its fair share of these fights for public access. In *The Compleat Trespasser*, author and campaigner John Bainbridge recounts the mass trespass on a path called Spooney Green Lane. This rough gravelled path curves round and over Latrigg, a fell half cloaked in woods, rising next to the town of Keswick. The lane regularly features in the numerous Lake District tourist guides written in the 1870s and 80s, many mentioning the helpful guideposts erected on Spooney Green Lane. A well-used path for walks to the low fell of Latrigg itself or as a route to the higher climb up the mountain of Skiddaw. But in 1887, barricades were thrown up by the landowners, the Spedding family. The public was barred from Spooney Green Lane and another path to Latrigg (the so-called 'terrace path' which comes off the lane and winds its way more gently around the fell).

Opposition to the closing of Spooney Green Lane and the terrace path was immediate. The Keswick and District Footpaths Preservation Association had been formed the previous year and was suddenly at the forefront of the fight to reclaim access to Latrigg. This new association was just one of a number of similar organizations which had sprung up independently across England in the early 1880s, including in Sheffield, Blackburn and Reading. In the same decade, a national organization was formed, the National Footpaths Society, which counted among its members John Ruskin and Alfred Tennyson and had

the Duke of Westminster as its patron.[1] These followed an earlier wave of similar societies, such as the Association for the
Protection of Ancient Footpaths in the Vicinity of York
(founded in 1824) and the Manchester Association for the Preservation of Ancient Footpaths (founded in 1826 and which still
thrives as the Peak and Northern Footpaths Society).

The Keswick association quickly agreed to take direct action
to secure access to Latrigg as well as dealing with other obstructions
at Fawe Park, another local estate. In a series of demonstrations
in the late summer and autumn of 1887, members of the association marched to reclaim their local paths. They repeatedly broke
down barricades, formed of rubbish covered in tar, and cut
through locked gates shrouded in barbed wire. They were joined
in their cause by a cross-section of society – tradesmen, hotel
owners, other local landowners, priests and the Member of Parliament for Derby, Samuel Plimsoll.[2] These were not a band of
revolutionaries. As they protested, they sang 'God Save the
Queen' and 'Rule Britannia' (which the landowner's gamekeeper
complained disturbed the grouse). In one of the later actions,
Plimsoll gave a rousing speech on Latrigg where he universalized
the struggle for access to this one Lake District fell. He declared
the need to preserve access to the countryside for the health of the
population and for art:

> It is . . . certain that no intellectual health, no imaginative great-
> ness, no artistic genius, are possible among people who have no
> hill country to walk over, no mountain glens to explore, no lake

1 The National Footpaths Society later merged with the Commons Preservation Society. Today the organization is the Open Spaces Society, dubbed
'Britain's oldest national conservation body'.
2 Samuel Plimsoll was most celebrated in his lifetime for improving the
safety of commercial shipping. He introduced the Plimsoll line, a mark on a
ship that indicates the maximum load, after which the footwear is named.

sides by which to linger . . . the landowner who puts up gates and bars must be allowed to do so at his peril.

In 1888, the owner of Latrigg eventually took the Keswick association to court. Dozens of local people testified that they had used the paths over many years (among them the son of the poet Robert Southey, who had lived in nearby Greta Hall, in the shadow of the fell). The legal proceedings resulted in a partial victory for the people. Spooney Green Lane was declared a right of way and opened back up to the public. In the same year, the *Spectator* declared: 'what a mountain path it was! Small wonder the Keswickians fought hard for such access to Latrigg and Skiddaw'. The lane is still a public bridleway, forming part of the seventy-three-mile Cumbria Way, but the terrace path is destined, for the time being, to remain private. It can still be walked, but only with permission and without the confidence that it will always remain publicly accessible. While disputes over rights of way in the Lake District pepper the local newspapers, it was in the fringes of the Peak District and the Pennines where these battles cemented their most enduring legacy. These were places where industrial towns nestled next to wide-open moors and hills, and where the struggle was decidedly working-class.

In the west Pennines, I am standing on a bank of reeds, wary that any second I'll start to slowly sink into the pillow-soft ground below. I am on the edge of Winter Hill, a moorland world which provides a backdrop for some of the industrial towns of the North West (Bolton, Wigan, Chorley, Bury and Blackburn are all within ten miles of this spot). The ground rises behind me, a bank of bubbling, bursting, restless tussocks, a plane of grass which touches the sky, uninterrupted by trees. Looking out and down there is a wide view, town and country laid out. Past green blocks of field and scrub and tracking hedge-rows, Bolton is a hazy apparition, as seen through a thin gauze.

The post-punk band A Certain Ratio recorded a track about this place, simply called 'Winter Hill'. The music draws you in and unsettles, with driving, rattling drums and a whirring drone which shifts between two high and low tones.[3] Music that suggests the stark beauty, and some of the underlying tragedy, of Winter Hill and its moors – Rivington, Smithills and Wilder's. Alongside ancient paths and prehistoric monuments, sorrow seems to litter the heather and seep from the dark peat of England's moors. Abandoned crumbling buildings slowly descend to the earth and television reports show the burning of the land. There are myths, stories and newspaper reports of death, loss and murder. A flagstone path (the stones perhaps originally from a former mill site in the valley, repurposed and relaid like on other moors) crosses Winter Hill, heading towards the incongruously industrial television mast topping its summit. It is comforting to walk in the sun on this solid path with its reassuring direction, a contrast to what it must be like to be up here alone in the gloom and the dark. Past tragedies of Winter Hill are remembered along its paths. A wrought-iron pillar commemorates a twenty-year-old traveller from Scotland, George Henderson, murdered here in 1838. Two separate plaques record the crash of a Bristol Wayfarer aeroplane in 1958, in which thirty-five people lost their lives. Stone cairns, known as the Two Lads, are said to mark where two men died of exposure here, although the local stories can't agree if this took place in the seventh or sixteenth centuries. The devastating fire which swept through Winter Hill in June 2018 is not memorialized, except in the slow recovery of the moor's ecosystem.

3 These tones were based on a piece of abandoned electronic equipment found on the hill.

Standing on my reed bank on this bright September day, a very different music drifts over Winter Hill. I'm watching the Bolton Clarion Choir sing a song of resistance, solidarity and grassroots action called 'From Below'. The song was written by the Commoners Choir and in their original recording it opens with the sound of a news report on the commemoration of the Kinder Scout trespass. For many the mass trespass at Kinder Scout is *the* access dispute. In April 1932, between 400 and 600 people marched from different directions up this Peak District moorland plateau, a wilful demonstration of their rights to access land which had been enclosed in the nineteenth century. They were led by Benny Rothman, an unemployed mechanic and member of the Young Communist League. Fights broke out as the marchers skirmished with gamekeepers, but they made it to the top for a series of speeches. After leaving Kinder Scout, six of the demonstrators were arrested and later sentenced to prison for between two and six months.[4] The arrests and sentences caused outrage, bringing the trespass to long-lasting national attention.

The events on Kinder Scout have endured, but its direct impact is contested. For some it is a foundational event in the history of the Ramblers, but it took place before the organization formally existed, and many of the Rambling societies were opposed to it, believing that a negotiated and legislated route was the best way to secure access. Journalist and campaigner

---

4 Rothman described facing a 'remarkable group of jurors, comprising, among others, two brigadier generals, three colonels, two captains and two majors, most of whom were landowners'. This was not the first dispute on Kinder Scout. In the 1900s, a path known as Doctor's Gate, first recorded in 1627 as 'Docto Tabotes Gate' (*gate* being derived from the Scandinavian for road), was walked defiantly by rambling clubs from Sheffield and Manchester, climbing over gates and ignoring 'No Road' signs to reclaim the route's public status.

(and first employee of the Ramblers) Tom Stephenson argued that it set back the campaign for greater access by several decades, while Benny Rothman drew a direct line from Kinder Scout to the gains of the 1949 National Parks and Access to the Countryside Act. The story of the mass trespass at Kinder is now celebrated, with commemorative plaques proudly displayed on the path side and annual walks held to honour the event. The emblematic value today of Kinder Scout, and similar historic trespasses and direct action, is important in and of itself. It's a rallying point and an inspiration to protect and expand the public access we currently enjoy.[5]

On Winter Hill, as hundreds of people file past, the Bolton Clarion Choir are singing in praise of a mass trespass which took place at the end of the nineteenth century, overshadowed by later action at Kinder Scout. I have come here with many others from Bolton to this point near the base of Winter Hill in the footsteps of 10,000 who walked the same path in 1896, in what has been called Britain's biggest-ever rights of way dispute. Most of the paths I have trod for this book, indeed most of my walking life, have been walked solo or with a clutch of friends. To be now surrounded by hundreds of people is dizzying, a pleasantly overwhelming experience, but this isn't just a walk; this is a march. It's a celebration of the fight for public access at perhaps its most political. After assembling in the suburb of Halliwell, we stream uphill out of town, people gathering on doorsteps to watch, some joining our ranks. A pub sign proudly proclaims that 'trespassers are welcome'. To the drumbeat of the Public and Commercial Services Union band, we move onwards towards the hill.

The banners carried aloft by the marchers celebrate famous

5 For instance, the spirit of Kinder was directly evoked in 2023 when the long-held tradition of wild camping on Dartmoor was challenged.

local and national names in the struggle for access. I spot Tom Stephenson's name as well as Thomas Leonard, who was instrumental in founding several organizations to enable the working class to enjoy outdoor holidays, including the Co-operative Holidays Association, the Holidays Fellowship and the Youth Hostels Association. As the march progresses towards Winter Hill, we move up a long straight road and the houses drift away and fields emerge to our sides. I make my way to the front of the pack and see the lead banner. At its centre is Gerrard Winstanley, the seventeenth-century radical whose group the True Levellers (more commonly known as the Diggers) reclaimed common land which had been stolen through enclosure. Flanking Winstanley are the portraits and names of Joe Shufflebotham, a socialist, and Solomon Partington, a radical liberal. These men were the principal organizers of the march of 1896 that the crowd is re-enacting today.

We reach the place where the Bolton Clarion Choir are singing at the threshold of the moors. This is where access was denied 125 years earlier. Shufflebotham and Partington organized the original march on Winter Hill because of a newly installed locked gate here, on Coalpit Road. This path had long been used by the people of Bolton to access the moors. A letter to the editor of the *Bolton Evening News* in 1895 decries the blocking of historic rights of way to this open space, describing the Winter Hill moors as the 'breathing ground for a densely populated district, where the inhabitants may fill their lungs with something more congenial than smoke'. I turn to a political slogan, a personal mantra of sorts, to describe this dispute: 'Bread and Roses'. A struggle for social justice and progress that isn't solely focused on improving economic conditions but which passionately asserts the need for dignity and for nature.

It was local landowner Colonel Richard Henry Ainsworth who had ordered the gate to be installed, fulfilling John Ruskin's words that 'of all the mean and wicked things a landlord can do, shutting up his footpath is the nastiest'. The Ainsworth family had bought the Smithills Estate in 1801, which included the medieval manor house of Smithills Hall (with Tudor and Georgian additions), the disputed patch of moor and a bleach works in nearby Halliwell. It was the latter concern which brought the most money into the family coffers.[6]

Colonel Ainsworth took on the family estate in 1870 and became a looming presence in Bolton. He was a bitter opponent of any political reform. The chronicler of the Winter Hill Trespass, Paul Salveson, labels him as 'probably the most rabidly anti-socialist and anti-union employer of any size in the town', therefore it was unsurprising that in particular he clashed with Shufflebotham, a member of the Bolton Socialist Party and an active trade unionist. In a pamphlet called 'Bolton's Augean Stable', Solomon Partington described Ainsworth as:

> . . . a firm believer in the divine right of the squire:
> God bless the squire and his relations
> and teach us all our proper stations:
> this was a charming sentiment of old-time servility and decayed feudalism, behind which lay a festering spirit of ignorance, oppression and want.

There is a portrait of Colonel Ainsworth, painted in 1875, in the collection of Smithills Hall. It shows a haughty figure relaxing in an ornate green-velvet Egyptian Revival chair. He holds a riding crop, is dressed in a red hunting jacket and his black shiny boots are complete with spurs – the very image of a privileged Victorian 'sportsman'. Ainsworth was not only a keen hunter on horseback but a grouse shooter. At the heart of the

6 The Ainsworths were another of those aristocratic families who had made a large fortune on the backs of enslaved people in the West Indies.

dispute on Winter Hill, as in so many places, was the desire of the gentry to keep the public out so they could blast birds out of the sky.[7] The fact that Ainsworth didn't even really live full-time at Smithills Hall – he preferred his residence at faraway Winwick in Northamptonshire – shows that this wasn't anything to do with privacy but simply a rich man wanting to continue his 'sport'.

In a series of actions over September 1896, thousands of people marched to and across Winter Hill, the crowd up to 10,000 strong at points. Among the demonstrators were many of the employees from Ainsworth's own bleach factory, alongside a whole host of other working people. They clashed with gamekeepers and police, tore down the gate and defaced no-trespassing signs. Legal writs were issued by Ainsworth to ten of the main ringleaders. Ordinary people of the area testified to their use of the road over many years, including a bricklayer, a surveyor and a beggar. Despite this, the case was lost and the ringleaders were handed injunctions which forbade them to trespass on Ainsworth's land and public access was denied. It took another hundred years for this access to be legally restored and it was only in 1996 that Bolton County Council declared that Coalpit Road was, after all, a public right of way.

Latrigg, Kinder Scout and Winter Hill are just a few of the innumerable disputes over rights of way that have taken place across England and Wales, some of which have been preserved in local legend whereas others have fallen into obscurity. The

7 The 'sport' of commercial shooting, as well as being ecologically disastrous, has often conflicted with rights of way and public access. Shooting was also a factor in the denial of access to Kinder Scout, as summed up in Ewan MacColl's folk song 'The Manchester Rambler'. In the song, inspired by his own participation in the mass trespass on Kinder, MacColl has a verbal confrontation with a gamekeeper: 'He called me a louse and said, "Think of the grouse".'

names of these disputes tell of the strength of feeling that people had in having the free use of their paths denied. In the 1820s there was the Flixton Footpath Battle in which, just south-west of Manchester, Mr Ralph Wright (nicknamed, in generally insulting terms, as 'Vegetable' by his opponents) blocked off a well-used public right of way called the Bottoms Path. The Manchester Association for the Preservation of Ancient Footpaths swung into action, sawing through the obstructing fence, tramping down the oats that Mr Wright had sown over the path and eventually winning a legal case for the right of the public to use the way. In 1884, what the local papers dubbed the Siege of Knole took place in Kent, where all manner of society rose up to protect a bridleway that ran through the estate of a local aristocrat. Lord Sackville locked the gates and denied the 'existence of any ancient bridle-way and footpath through the park'. Following a lively public meeting of angry locals, chaired by Major German, a Justice of the Peace, a group of 1,400 (led by a local tax collector) tore down the gates and dumped them at Lord Sackville's door. An even bigger crowd gathered the next night to besiege the house itself. Despite prosecutions of trespass being handed out, a right of way was established, though as a footpath rather than a bridleway (the crowd ceremonially led a pony down the path nonetheless).

These disputes all occurred before the National Parks and Access to the Countryside Act of 1949. They sought to prove the public's right to walk these paths, which was essentially carried out retrospectively, when these rights were being subverted or repressed. Lengthy court battles were often fought asymmetrically: local people with little means against powerful and wealthy landowners. These fights show the importance of having rights of way legally recorded, but that doesn't mean that protest and the protection of paths are a thing of the past. Our right to walk the paths of England and Wales can't be taken for granted; there is a need to ensure that not only are our rights of way legally recorded but that the legally recorded network is not chipped away through obstruction, subversion or neglect.

The humblest of paths require as much protection as those which take us up high mountains and to wide-open space. It was the long-running obstruction of an 'ordinary' path which prompted one of the most high-profile campaigns that the Ramblers have fought in recent years. Walking through rural Sussex, it's hard to imagine this as the focus for a bitter access dispute. This is comfortable commuting country. Neat hedges and even neater lines of wheelie bins front the houses. On the footpaths, across fields and paddocks, I encounter more ponies and horses than sheep, and a solar farm takes up more field space than cows. At one point, I walk through a sprawling golf course, with an accompanying hotel and spa complex – an incongruous hodgepodge of conference-centre windows and faux-Tudor chimneys. Away from the greens and clubhouse, this is a landscape of small spaces. The paths cross from one little field to another, through slight woodland and undulating over smooth slopes.

Passing through a modest wooden gate in a country road, I walk into an untended scrubland, a clear path through low banks of messy vegetation. A mat of common fleabane, unassuming in the autumn without its sunny yellow flowers; a tangle of ragged, leaf-pitted brambles; the glossy green leaves of a honeysuckle and the spiked raised fists of teasels. Over to one corner is a mass of red spots, the fruits of a dog rose. This footpath, officially known as Framfield Footpath 9, was shown on the Framfield Manor Enclosure Act map of 1862 and has been legally recorded for many years, but in 1989 a local walker noticed that a barn was being built right across it. Being a member of the Ramblers, he knew what to do and reported the obstruction to East Sussex County Council. However, the council didn't take any action, apparently out of fear of the landowner, property tycoon Nicholas Van Hoogstraten.

Beyond the scrub, through some distant trees, I can see a gaudy glint of coppery gold, a tiny glimpse of Hamilton Palace, the massive £40 million mansion that Van Hoogstraten started building in 1985. Described as 'the ghost house of Sussex', the building remains unfinished to this day. Photographs taken by drone in March 2020 show a lumpy central block with two flapping pink-stoned wings clad in scaffolding. A separate structure, in the same style, stands next to a lake on this fortress estate – a mausoleum for Van Hoogstraten. It is not hard to see why the council may have been wary of Van Hoogstraten, a friend of Robert Mugabe and a man described as 'Britain's most notorious landlord', who, according to Lord Justice Wynn, is 'a sort of self-imagined devil who likes to think of himself as an emissary of Beelzebub'. He is also a criminal, having been convicted of paying for a grenade to be thrown into a rival's house and eight counts of handling stolen goods.

In 1998, the Ramblers took up the campaign to reopen Framfield Footpath 9, leading Van Hoogstraten to brand them as 'scum of the earth'. There were lengthy legal disputes between the Ramblers and Kate Ashbrook (the general secretary of the Open Spaces Society) on one side and the new owners of the land (the oddly named Rarebargain, a company linked to Van Hoogstraten). East Sussex County Council went on to be prosecuted for failing in their duty to uphold the public's rights. In the meantime, the path was becoming more obstructed, with barbed wire and massive shipping containers now blocking its course, and Rarebargain proposed an unnecessary diversion of the path. A clause was added to the Countryside and Rights of Way Act (then going through Parliament) which would give greater powers to magistrates to order obstructions removed.

Many legal twists and turns later, and Rarebargain having gone into liquidation, it was time to tear down the obstructions. In February 2003, Kate Ashbrook cut the lock which barred Framfield Footpath 9, swiftly followed by heavy machinery clearing all the detritus that had been placed in this little path's way. The path could finally be used again by the public after nearly fifteen years.

I'm following a route created by Ramblers volunteer Chris Smith, devised specifically to take in this ordinary path, a walking example of the Streisand effect.[8] I suspect that if it wasn't for these events, it would take me a long time to stumble across this unremarkable 160-year-old path through Sussex scrub and woods, but the case upheld two points of principle: that public rights of way shouldn't be obstructed and that local councils have a responsibility to ensure that the rights of the public are upheld.

Protection of the recorded rights of way is a continuous process; the network is live and constantly subject to change. The Ramblers, along with the British Horse Society, the Open Spaces Society, the Auto-Cycle Union, Cycling UK and the Byways and Bridleways Trust, by law have to be consulted on any proposed changes to our legally recorded paths in England and Wales.[9] Thousands of proposed changes are received a year to be reviewed and responded to by a network of dedicated

8 Defined by knowyourmeme.com as 'the unintended consequence of further publicizing information by trying to have it censored. Instead of successfully removing the information from the public, it becomes even more widely available than before as a backlash against the censorship attempt'. The term originated when Barbra Streisand tried, and failed, to get the California Coastal Records Project to remove a picture of her house from their website, leading to millions more seeing the photo.

9 In addition, some organizations are prescribed as local consultees, such as the Peak and Northern Footpaths Society and the Chiltern Society.

volunteers. Most represent a minor change, especially when seen in the context of 140,000 miles of rights of way, maybe the rerouting of a path around a field edge or away from a farm yard, but they all need to be carefully considered. Small changes add up; they can make our path network less convenient and subvert its beauty, taking away from its historical form.

Alongside safeguarding the shape of the legally recorded network, hundreds of obstructions to our paths are reported every year. There are still too many landowners who deny public access – locked gates, misleading signs, stiles wrapped in barbed wire, paths ploughed completely out or overgrown with crops. There are also those which get blocked out of neglect rather than malice. The majority of rights of way officers at local councils work valiantly to 'assert and protect' the rights of the public, but a decade of austerity has decimated local authorities, their revenue reduced as they are given more responsibilities.[10] Despite their vital importance to health and wellbeing, public rights of way, perhaps understandable, lose out to social care (but less understandable, to me, to potholes).[11] Tens of thousands of voluntary hours are put in each year for paths – clearing them, repairing bridges, fighting unnecessary diversions and closures – but they, and local authorities, need to be backed up with more money. Money that seems to be easily found to build bypasses and stretches of new road but which is sorely absent for preserving and improving our historic path network.

10 The duty is contained within Section 130 of the Highways Act of 1980: 'It is the duty of the highway authority to assert and protect the rights of the public to the use and enjoyment of any highway for which they are the highway authority.'

11 Recent research that the Ramblers commissioned from the New Economics Foundation suggests that the health and wellbeing value of the rights of way network in England and Wales is almost £2 billion per year.

Walking away from Framfield Footpath 9, through the woods to Uckfield station, the backing vocals of 'From Below' play in my head, a repeating chant: 'step, by step, by step, by step, step, by step, by step, by step'. I think about the rights of way defenders of the past. Their singular actions and battles backed up by successive legislation from the 1930s to the early 2000s inched us closer to fulfilling the access to *their* land that the public deserve. Individual men and women fought to protect individual paths and the principle that those paths should absolutely always be open and available for public use.

Today's path volunteers are standing on the shoulders of the access giants, named and unnamed, who came before them. They are engaged in what pilgrim and wayfarer Will Parsons, when speaking of his father's activities with the Ramblers in the 1970s and 80s, called a 'gentle radicalism wrapped into the simple act of walking'.

Leisure

16.   A Challenge

In my mum and dad's house hangs a print of an early nineteenth-century boxer, an ancestor. A young man, shirtless with arm muscles bulging, his fists raised in a fighting pose. He stands in front of a rope strung between staves of wood, a temporary boxing ring on a patch of sand in a large field. Behind him are calmly rolling hills streaked with hedgerows. An anonymous path leads to a gate and beyond to an inviting stand of trees. The portrait puts the boxer right in the English countryside. Across the bottom of the print, the legend proclaims that this is 'Tom Cribb Champion of England'. Flanking this are his achievements, the records of his fights. They make for extraordinary reading, statistics revealing the brutality of these bare-knuckle boxing contests. Most of his fights are over half an hour in length, with dozens of rounds – included is his very first fight against George Maddox on 7 January 1805. The pair fought for over two hours, with Cribb winning after seventy-six rounds of gruelling competition.[1]

Growing up, I heard many stories about Tom. How he was, as the bare-knuckle champion, the first boxer to receive a belt as a prize. How his victory earned him front-page news in *The Times*, pushing the return of the fleet from Trafalgar down the news-paper. How he was employed as an honour guard at the lavish

---

1 Another print of Cribb hangs nearby. In this his fighting days are behind him. This is a portrait of an older man sitting contentedly in retirement. His greying hair is swept back from his head and his hands lie relaxed on the top of a cane, arm resting on a table next to one of his trophies.

coronation of George IV in 1821 (partly, it seems, to ensure that George's estranged wife, Caroline of Brunswick, would not be admitted). Despite the grisly nature of bare-knuckle boxing, when Tom Cribb ruled the sport, it was a fashionable affair – the great chronicler of Georgian boxing, Pierce Egan, jokingly suggested that the Pugilistic Society was an equal of the Royal Society, the Antiquarian Society, the Geological Society and the Society of Arts. Spectators at his fights read like a roll-call of British and European privilege and inherited wealth and power: the Prince of Wales, the Duke of York, Tsar Alexander I and the King of Prussia. To Lord Byron, Cribb was 'an old friend', and the poet used to come to Cribb's pub in Piccadilly to watch the boxers spar in the room above the bar (and even try a little sparring himself). The men that flocked to the boxing and watched, financed and gambled on the sport came to be known collectively as 'the fancy' – an informal group with no membership lists who would gather excitedly at gin houses and training camps and roll up in their carriages at the fights themselves, parking directly alongside the temporary rings.

Although the fancy is most associated with boxing, its wealthy members had a fascination with a whole range of human and animal endurance. They were keen on horse racing and, to a lesser degree, running. But alongside boxing, the most popular sport was one that involved feats of competitive walking, pedestrianism. This wasn't a matter of one competitor directly pitted against another in a straightforward race; but individuals seeking to complete extraordinary walking challenges. Pedestrianism was perfect fodder for lavish gambling, for instance: 'I bet you I can walk 700 miles in fourteen days.' This bet was real. It was laid down, accepted and achieved by a pigman in his mid-fifties called John Batty in 1788 (a gruelling average of fifty miles a day on foot, for a fortnight). He walked a course set out on the Richmond race ground in North Yorkshire, starting off on the first day with a sprightly fifty-nine miles and completing the challenge, walking thirty-six and three-quarter miles on the fourteenth day (all this despite him losing most of the skin on his feet on day one due to his new shoes, which feels like a rookie mistake).

Other early pedestrians ventured beyond the set courses and walked out on the roads and paths, covering vast distances between towns and cities, often marking their progress using the handy turnpike mileposts. In 1765, Mary McMullen went almost from coast to coast in one day, from the village of Blencogo in Cumbria to Newcastle, a total of seventy-two miles. An Inner Temple clerk called Foster Powell was one of the most renowned early pedestrians. His flagship achievement of walking from London to York and back in six days was first carried out in the winter of 1773 and he repeated the feat several times later in his life (incredibly he seemed to have improved his time on each successive occasion). Many people must have made considerable money by betting on Powell, but he was reported not to be motivated by wealth himself; rather he considered that it was 'his wonderful agility . . . from which he derived great glory.' In the late eighteenth century, Donald Macleod walked several times from Inverness to London, then back to Inverness and straight back to London in one go, nearly 1,700 miles – a feat made all the more remarkable by the, frankly unbelievable, reports that he was 100 years old at the time. While these epic walks were not in pursuit of sport (he went to the London to petition the King for his full pension), he went on to undertake a pedestrian challenge in the capital – at the sprightly age of 102.[2]

2 Considerable bets were placed on Macleod's walking challenge – a ten-mile round trip from Hyde Park Corner to the milepost at Turnham Green to be undertaken in under two and half hours. Some of those who bet against him, had assumed that the 'hillocks of road dirt' on the route would stop him from completing his challenge in the allotted time but Macleod simply jumped over them and his walk came in at two hours twenty-three minutes.

And then there was the man of such walking renown that he was simply known as 'the celebrated pedestrian': Captain Barclay. Robert Barclay Allardice was born in 1779 into a venerable and prosperous Scottish family. His father (also called Robert) was the Member of Parliament for Kincardineshire and had a massive 3,500-acre estate at Ury in Aberdeenshire (a member of another branch of the same family started Barclays bank). Walking and boxing were sports that dominated Captain Barclay's life. In the boxing world, he had a keen eye for new talent and was a trainer, imposing strict regimes on those he tutored. One of these men was Tom Cribb, who Barclay trained for his most important fight, a rematch against the African-American Tom Molineaux in 1811.[3] Barclay put Cribb through his paces on thirty-mile walks in the Scottish Highlands and a convoluted process of 'sweating' through which the boxer would run miles dressed in flannel, drink a strange concoction of cider heated with caraway, coriander seeds and liquorice root, and lie in bed under eight blankets.

By the time Captain Barclay was training Tom Cribb, the former had already secured his place as the foremost pedestrian of his age. He undertook the usual challenges of walking large distances across country (such as 150 miles from London to Birmingham via Cambridge in one go in 1799). The accounts of these walks give us glimpses into the state of the paths in the late eighteenth and early nineteenth centuries. Endurance walks through the night on dark, craggy roads (lamps installed and lit only specially for the occasion); treks across the private estates of the gentry, Captain Barclay 'up to his ancles in mud'; and of the

---

3 The events of his fight with Molineaux reveal the darkness of Tom Cribb's story. In the first of his two fights against the American freed slave, the jingoistic English crowd rushed the ring and seemed to have broken Molineaux's hand, after which Cribb won the bout.

numerous inns along the turnpike roads utilized for a quick change of clothes or a glass of brandy.

Captain Barclay's most celebrated walking feat played out not along the roads but, like that of John Batty's at Richmond, going round and round in circles on one site. The venue was to be another racecourse, this time at the home of horse racing, Newmarket in Suffolk. It was here that he was to walk 1,000 miles in 1,000 consecutive hours for a wager of 1,000 guineas. Hundreds of thousands of pounds in bets were also laid by members of the fancy (and it was rumoured that Barclay would increase his own winnings by sixteen times in side bets if he succeeded). The crucial word in this gruelling challenge is 'consecutive'. For each hour over forty-two days, he would have to walk a mile, meaning that his longest period of rest in over six weeks could only be for around an hour and a half at a time. A beautifully simple but seemingly crazy task.

Just after midnight on 1 June 1809, Captain Barclay set out for his first mile walk. Toothache, wind, dust and a strained ligament plagued him over the weeks, but he continued on and in the six weeks thousands of people flocked to Newmarket to watch him walking up and down the half-mile course. A tense excitement built as he approached the end of his challenge. All the hotels and inns around Newmarket were fully booked and 'every horse and every vehicle engaged'. On the final day of his epic walk, despite the newly installed ropes to keep them away, the crowd gathered around him, squeezing and jostling, 'so great that he could scarcely find room to walk'. He strolled his final mile on 12 July, according to the *Statesman* newspaper, 'with perfect ease and great spirits'.

Captain Barclay had successfully completed his walk, a little tired and over two stone lighter. Others took up the challenge of 'the Barclay match' in subsequent decades and often tried to one-up his achievement. There was Josiah Eaton who in 1816 walked 1,998 half-miles in 1,998 successive half-hours on the Brixton Causeway. This feat took place on what is now the busy south London road of Brixton Hill, at the time a much more rural setting, leading to complaints from the magistrates about the crowds that gathered there. Two of the most remarkable successors brought pizzazz to pedestrianism. Madame Angelo (born Margaret Atkinson) completed Captain Barclay's original challenge on multiple occasions and toured the music halls to sing her 'Walking Song' and 'astonish all creation by her graceful style of walking' (Madame Angelo was biracial and appeared in what the newspapers called 'native costume'). And the celebrated Ada Anderson, dubbed 'The Champion Lady Walker of the World', who achieved the Barclay match at Leeds in 1878 and then sought fame in America, where she walked 2,700 quarter-miles in 2,700 quarter-hours.[4] This meant that her longest rest period was a mind-boggling nine minutes over the twenty-eight days, and she didn't just use these precious moments to sleep. Anderson was a natural performer, using her breaks to entertain the crowd with singing, pranks and speeches.

By the 1880s, crowds were no longer gathering at racecourses and music halls or at the roadside to watch extraordinary walking feats. The interest in pedestrianism had died out, polite society now finding the spectacle of men and women exerting themselves to exhaustion simply distasteful. But the generations of pedestrians had established that the paths of England and Wales were not just a transport network but could also be a place of sport and repurposed for challenge.[5] While pedestrianism no

4 Madame Angelo was given a similar moniker; she was referred to in the newspapers as 'The Champion Female Walker of the World'.
5 I don't think it is too much of a stretch to say that the pedestrians pounding the pavement were the forebears of today's marathon and ultra runners. It's said that the actual length of the modern marathon was determined by the streets of London (and royal whim). In the first Olympic Games held in

longer exists as a recognizable sport, thousands of people a year still ply our highways and byways, pushing themselves to their personal limits or seeking victory in competitions.[6] Alongside 5ks, 10ks, marathons and ultra marathons and a plethora of road cycling events, testing multi-mile walks haven't disappeared. The Long Distance Walkers Association, which celebrated its fiftieth anniversary in 2022, organize the annual '100', walking 100 miles in forty-eight hours. Raising money for charity, you can also choose to walk 100 kilometres on rural paths and country lanes between London and Brighton or the same distance on the Thames Path National Trail or the England Coast Path on Dorset's Jurassic Coast. These are group events, camaraderie sustaining tired legs, but in the last hundred years there has also been a revival of the personal walking challenge, more often than not involving a walk across the whole island.

In a Pathé News film from 1960, a slight, determined woman dressed in black marches confidently towards the camera. She is followed by a policeman on a motorbike, a couple of cars and a few fellow walkers, skipping as they try to keep up. She strides past enthusiastically waving crowds. The news film heralds this fast-walking woman:

> A mere twenty odd miles to go and the amazing Dr Babs would reach her goal: Land's End. One thousand and twenty-eight miles spread over twenty-three days and all done on salad, grapefruit, cream, bananas, fruit juices, honey, and that great drink: hot water. Dr Barbara set out to prove that's the diet if

---

London in 1908 the marathon route was laid out to run from the lawns of Windsor Castle to finish, 26.2 miles later, at the royal box in the stadium at White City.

6 Though the sport of pedestrianism did live on in a sense, morphing into the modern sport of race walking.

you want to be healthy and energetic, as undoubtably she must be. But what's John O'Groats to Land's End? Just a stroll to Barbara. With short rests and a bite now and then, she is going to walk across America, three times the distance.

Dr Barbara Moore, filmed on the last stretches of her walk across Britain, had already had an extraordinary life. Born Anya Cherkasova in 1903, she was one of the first female engineers trained in the Soviet Union after the Russian Revolution. Before coming to England in 1939 and marrying an English teacher, she became the Soviet Union's long-distance motorcycling champion. Following her walk from John O'Groats to Land's End, in the very same year, Dr Moore did indeed walk the breadth of the American continent, completing her 3,387-mile walk from New York to San Francisco on 6 July (a trip which she had to break from to successfully sue a British newspaper for libel).[7]

I've scanned the film of Dr Moore's entry into Land's End several times, looking for sections that I recognize from when I set off on my own walk across Britain in 2017. However, Dr Moore was set on taking the quickest route, striding directly on the roads which would enable her to achieve her walk in as fast a time as possible, whereas I took a more leisurely approach. Before embarking on my 'big walk', I was a pretty novice rural walker, mostly wandering the streets of London. Setting off from the tip of Cornwall felt like, in the words of the title of a book by philosopher and broadcaster C. E. M. Joad, 'an untutored townsman's invasion of the country'. I had Ordnance Survey maps on my phone, a pack on my back and a desire to, slightly self-indulgently, walk every day for four or so months. Old routines were quickly forgotten, to be replaced with a new

7 They had asserted that she did her walks for personal gain.

way of living; all I needed to do was work out where to stay, roughly tracing my finger over the maps and making a snap judgement about which path to take. Time became a strange, distant thing, without deadlines and relatively comfortable about delays. Miles became more important than minutes or hours, and each day was governed by those green lines and dashes snaking across the country ahead of me.

Perhaps the seminal modern account of a walk from Land's End to John O'Groats was written by John Hillaby in 1968, *Journey Through Britain*. Hillaby started out with a clear aim: to walk only on footpaths, bridleways and byways – to leave cars and traffic behind, avoiding roads entirely. He quickly abandons this idea, finding too many of the 'ancient by-ways' overgrown, obstructed and ploughed up. Less than two decades after public rights of way started to be legally mapped for the first time, Hillaby found that the paths sometimes weren't there at all, and they didn't take him where he wanted to go. In the introduction he cites a specific example of trying to walk across the Welsh border into the English Midlands, when the lack of cross-border paths sends him back time and time again to the roads. Looking at the modern Ordnance Survey map now, I still find many paths which terminate at the two nations' border. These footpaths, bridleways and byways don't connect with another right of way or road, don't even stop at some natural feature like a river; they simply hang, severed at that imaginary line between England and Wales. And it isn't just the border between nations which creates paths to nowhere – at many county and parish boundaries there are dozens of dead ends.

This highlights one of the problems in how rights of way were recorded in the 1950s, 60s and 70s. When each county was faced with the task of drawing up their first-ever definitive maps, they turned to parish councils to see what should be recorded. Many local communities only looked as far as their borders, and in numerous instances a parish or county recorded a path but the parish or county on the other side of the border simply forgot to do so (or, in some cases, deliberately left it off). Paths which follow the border itself could be even more neglected, forgotten by bodies both sides of the boundary. This is just one of the reasons we don't have a map which can be called truly definitive – sections of possibly ancient paths are lost, adrift and unrecorded.[8] Incomplete paths, stubs, gaps and anomalies litter our definitive maps – our heritage lacking protection simply because of a quirk of bureaucracy from half a century ago.

When you walk across the country, the landscape changes almost imperceptibly. A soft slide from gentle, field-filled valleys to open, purple-burnished moor and heath. Carefully managed, bench-spotted wood becomes wind-torn mountain almost without noticing. Starker are the differences in the ability of the public to access this land. A day's walking on what seems to be a continuous thread of paths is suddenly broken. On the Ordnance Survey map some parishes shine brightly with green rights of way, whereas right next door there may be a parish which seems to have hardly any. Putting the recording of rights of way, which may have been in existence for hundreds of years, in the hands of the few people sitting in a parish council meeting at one point in time in the 1950s or 1960s was bound to lead to problems.

The Open Spaces Society have collected examples of irregularities in how parishes managed this process. A common issue

8 In some cases historical evidence which was unavailable or inaccessible at the time can help make the case that paths were public. For instance, the maps produced under the 1910 Finance Act (often called the Lloyd George Domesday Survey) show public roads and some public footpaths and bridleways, but weren't easily available for inspection in the 1950s.

was that parishes only focused on recording the paths that were in use at the time. For instance, in Barley in Hertfordshire, a path went unrecorded just on the say so of the local pub landlord who stated that it was little used. This was taken to the extreme in Suffolk where Hitcham Parish Council wrote to the county surveyor, stating that there were 'scores of footpaths which have not been used for at least twenty-five years', suggesting that they were only going to survey those in use rather than 'wasting time going over the whole parish'. Amazingly the county surveyor agreed, saying that to record all rights of way would be 'tedious and expensive' and that the parish should 'only include those paths which it considers desirable to preserve and maintain'.

John Hillaby and Dr Moore were not the first people to feel the pull of the walk from the tip of Scotland to the furthest reach of England (or vice versa). The first recorded continuous walk between these famous points was made by two brothers, Robert and John Naylor, who, after walking from London to Lancashire in 1870, set out to walk 'from the top of the map to the bottom' the following year.[9] Their account of their travels was published in 1916. A first edition sits on my shelves. A blue bound lump of a book, weighing nearly 2.5 kilograms. The forty-or-so-year gap between the Naylor brothers walking the paths and writing their account can be sensed on the page. It is a book infused with nostalgia, a longing for a lost Victorian age

9 The Naylors were influenced by Elihu Burritt, an American peace activist and abolitionist who briefly served as the United States consul in Birmingham under Abraham Lincoln. Burritt, who is mentioned in the Naylors' book, was a keen long-distance walker. Two of his books placed the most north-easterly and south-westerly points in Britain as walking destinations: *A Walk from London to John O'Groats's* and *A Walk from London to Land's End and Back*.

before the arrival of the motor car. In the foreword they reflect on changes in travel and paths in the preceding decades. They reminisce about a time when railways were replacing the stage-coaches, when cobbled roads were becoming macadamized and when 'toll-gates still barred the highways' and 'the bulk of trav-elling in the country was done on foot or horseback, as the light-wheeled vehicles so common in later times had not yet come into vogue'. When seasonal Irish workers would arrive in Liverpool and walk as far as the 'great corn-growing county' of Lincolnshire for work. Workers in bare feet and with their shoes slung over their shoulders, described by the Naylors as 'good and steady walkers . . . with a military step and a four-mile-per-hour record'.

The Naylor brothers were wealthy Victorian gentlemen and they set about their walk in a very proper manner. They never walked on a Sunday and they devote many pages to detailing the church services that they attended on the day of rest (often more than one service a day). They are also keen to point out that on their walk they 'were also to abstain from all intoxicating drink, not to smoke cigars or tobacco'. In some ways their abstemious lifestyle set a template for those who would follow in their foot-steps. The idea of using the walk from Land's End to John O'Groats to prove a point about health or to promote a particu-lar view about diet comes up again and again.

In the early twentieth century, there was a competition of sorts between two men, which came about over the eating of meat. 'Dr' Deighton at sixty-one years old was something of a celebrated walker and the athletic instructor at Durham Univer-sity. He strode out from Cornwall in February 1904 dressed in 'grey knickers, a white sweater and a soft hat', walking the roads to cries of 'good luck', 'he's a jolly good fellow' and the rather more pointed: 'you've got a long way to go'. He completed his challenge twenty-four days later, carrying his trainer on his back for the last fifty yards (which feels like unnecessary showboating). He declared to journalists that when it came to diet 'he never restricts himself in any way. He eats when he wants to, and heartily, but drinks sparingly'. However, following a sponsorship deal, he always made sure to tell everyone that 'the Doctor only trains on Bovril' (the company took out adverts featuring Dr Deighton to make sure that no one missed the point).

Dr Deighton's reliance on the magical powers of beef extract did not go down well with George Allen, a man often referred to in the newspapers as the 'well-known Vegetarian long-distance walker'.[10] While already a seasoned challenge walker, it was Dr Deighton's Bovril-fuelled walk which spurred Allen to undertake the Land's End to John O'Groats challenge in 1905. He wanted to prove that not only was it possible to walk the 900 miles on a vegetarian diet but that he could beat Dr Deighton's time; he also got his own sponsorship deal, with a tonic wine called Phosferine. In fact, he smashed Deighton's time, completing the walk in under sixteen days (compared to his rival's twenty-four days).[11]

10 Dr Moore was also a famous vegetarian. The newsreel announcing her arrival in Cornwall confidently asserts that 'we all laugh at her diet as we enjoy our steak and boiled puddings'. Barbara Moore specifically went out on long walks to extol the benefits of a meat-free diet, which she believed, along with abstention from alcohol, smoking and sex, would lead to a lifespan of 200 years. It is sometimes claimed that she became a breatharian, shunning food entirely, and that this was part of the cause of her death in 1977 at the age of seventy-three.

11 Allen was not only an advocate for the health benefits of a vegetarian diet but was also a proponent of land reform, telling a meeting of the Gloucester branch of the Independent Labour Party that 'all that was needed to secure the permanent prosperity of this country was free access to the land and security of tenure'. He envisioned a nation where all could farm and put their

While Deighton and Allen were racing to complete their walk in as little time as possible, most Land's End to John O'Groats walkers today, like Hillaby, undertake their challenge for pleasure. The usual itinerary for walking links up, as far as possible, National Trails and other named long-distance paths. For my version, I hopped from town to town, from one city to another. I didn't set out to avoid roads like John Hillaby but tried to walk the paths less travelled, the 'ordinary' paths. Like Hillaby, I encountered problems. Our National Trails are generally in pretty good nick, but they make up less than two per cent of the network. The other ninety-eight per cent of paths are often the most important to communities, but as places for everyday walking rather than a holiday they can easily be overlooked. Especially in less populated areas, perhaps if they aren't used for a while, they become overgrown or someone encounters a locked gate but doesn't get round to reporting it. The paths can easily fall out of use. But it is this network which sets our rights of way apart from other countries where walking is focused on a small number of flagship trails. After the rush of walking those final footsteps to the signpost at John O'Groats (accompanied by the cheering and clapping of a coach of American tourists who happened to have pulled up just before), I felt achievement wash through me, the satisfaction of a challenge conquered. I had discovered corners of the country, beautiful, wonderful and odd corners, which I need to return to. But I wasn't expecting to find beauty in the utility and form of the infrastructure itself. I had fallen in love with the hyperlocal path network, a spider's web of history, laid on the land.

---

labour into cultivating the soil (which included, presumably, a significant reduction in farming for meat).

17. Rambling

Under the wrought-iron ribcage of Paddington station's grand roof, a mass of people, mostly in their twenties and thirties, squeezed on to the platforms. Decked out in 'sensible' skirts, mackintoshes, plus fours and trench boots, they jostled for a place on a special train service – a trip to an unknown destination. The crowds were larger than anticipated – 1,600 had turned up – and another train had to be quickly made up. In the train carriages they beseeched the driver and conductor for information about where they were going but to no avail (apparently, they didn't know either). They didn't need to wait long. Shortly after departure, a representative of the trip's organizers, Great Western Railway, squeezed through the passengers like 'a drop of oil between sardines' and ceremoniously pulled out an envelope to reveal their destination. Ahead of them lay an adventure on foot, a 'mystery hike' in Berkshire, where they would be 'dotting the Thames Valley like daisies' on Good Friday 1932.

The mystery hikers weren't the only ones enjoying the outdoors over that bank holiday: the newspapers declared the whole weekend a resounding 'open-air success'. Crowds gathered for whippet racing on the North Sea sands, an Easter parade in Sunderland, a hockey festival in Folkestone and at dozens of football matches (one out of every fifty people saw a match on Good Friday). The roads out of towns and cities, especially to the coast, were jammed with buses and cars, including 1,000 motorcoaches taking 100,000 day-trippers to Blackpool for the delights of the Golden Mile. Meanwhile, in the skies, private aeroplane owners jetted around for a day of pleasure – one amateur pilot thought nothing of flying from the Midlands to Brighton for a bathe and lounge on the pebble beaches before winging it back home for a late dinner. But alongside the seaside jaunts and the highs and lows of the sporting contests, the most popular activity over that Easter bank holiday weekend was walking.

Today, the idea of walking for pleasure is firmly embedded. Twenty-three million people, almost half the adult population, walk for leisure at least once a month in England. And leisure walking is increasing in popularity: every year, for the past five years, a million more recreational walkers have been added to the paths of England. A great upswing of interest in walking – dubbed the 'hiking craze' – was also taking place in 1932. The year before, six regional federations of rambling clubs had joined together to form the National Council of Ramblers Federations (which, in 1935, would go on to become the Ramblers Association), and a month later the Kinder Scout mass trespass would take place. This burst of interest in hiking came during the depths of the Great Depression. Unemployment was to reach its height in the summer of 1932, and a little later in the year, the National Hunger March would take place, with 3,000 people converging on London from across the country, demanding jobs and the alleviation of poverty. The dire economic circumstances meant that, for most people, long holidays and foreign travel were out of the question, and hiking was growing 'more popular every year as taxes [went] up'.[1]

1 One unnamed civil servant attributed, extraordinarily, some of these economic woes to the new craze for hiking. Apparently, cheap walking holidays were to be blamed for over-consumption, leading to inflationary pressure. The official pointed to the origins of the hiking movement in Germany, where 'when it got to the height of its popularity there the German economic crash came'.

The *Sheffield Daily Telegraph* reported 'hordes seeking health and pleasure where it is most easy to find, on moorland, mountain and lakeside, not to mention the dusty roadside itself, that may lead anywhere or nowhere in particular'. Its Steel City rival, the *Sheffield Independent*, in a somewhat satirical column, bemoaned these new walkers as a plague of locusts descending on 'the once peaceful land'. Walkers from 'nine to ninety' fanned out across the moors and disturbed quiet corners of the countryside, where previously 'a fellow and girl could have a little communion of the hearts without being noticed'. It wasn't just day hikes that were popular: the *Leeds Mercury* reported that 'the hiking fraternity' were setting out with kit for four days' walking, seeking accommodation in the many new youth hostels which were popping up across the country.[2]

This early-1930s hiking craze was framed as one of reconnection between the younger generation and rural Britain through walking its ancient paths. An adventure and a rediscovery of the country 'by multitudes to whom it was formerly merely a place on the map'. Newspapers urged readers to trace 'the old . . . trackways' and learn about 'the minor placenames [which] go straight back to [the] Domesday Book'. The *Hampshire Advertiser* proposed that there were 'a thousand experiments' to be undertaken in following the old paths – by way of example, it suggested that its readers might like to walk the route from the New Forest to Winchester, down which the body of William Rufus (son of William the Conqueror) was carried. According to the *Leicester Mercury*, 'young Britain is beginning . . . to realize that only afoot can one really get first-hand knowledge of

2 The Youth Hostels Association of England and Wales had been established in 1930, inspired by the network of accommodation established in Germany, which by the early 1930s had over 2,000 hostels.

those treasured beauties of our Isles which lie off the beaten
track and in retreats the wheel seldom traverses'.

Almost ninety years after the 1930s hiking craze, I stand outside
Cromford station in the Derbyshire Dales, a day's walking
ahead. Like the young interwar hikers encouraged to retrace the
passage of eleventh-century kings, I am attempting to reconstruct a mystery hike which started here on 10 July 1932. For the
Good Friday trip from Paddington to Berkshire was not a singular event. Mystery hiking was a craze within a craze. In 1932
alone, a particular boom year, Great Western Railway laid on
these hikes every fortnight in the summer months from cities
such as London, Cardiff and Birmingham. Independent walking clubs and youth groups joined in and organized their own
mystery hikes. Walking on the paths in that year, you could have
bumped into the Wayfarers Rambling Club in Cardiff on their
expedition (its invitation read: 'Bring tea, opportunity for bathing') or see groups of boys from Scout troops or the Junior
Imperial Club roaming the paths of Hampshire, Kent and
Oxfordshire on mystery hikes.[3]

The July 1932 mystery hike was organized by the Derby-
based Trent Motor Traction Company – their slogan: 'HOLIDAY
TOURS ARE BRITISH' (public or cheap private transport
was a great facilitator of the boom in hiking; trains, trams and
buses enabled the masses to come to the paths). For me, this hike
is still mysterious, as with so many of these events there are no
printed maps or detailed descriptions of the routes the walkers
took. I am following a simple list of places that they visited on

3 The craze also spread overseas and was particularly strong in New Zealand
and Australia. In July 1932, 8,000 walkers caught a train from Sydney for a
mystery hike along the Hawkesbury River. The hike included lunch at Kan-
garoo Point and, it being a Sunday, an open-air church service.

their ten-mile ramble. In the words of the *Derby Daily Telegraph*: 'The secret route unfolded to the hikers was as follows: Cromford, Bonsall, Bonsall Moor, Rowter Rocks at Birchover, Stanton Moor and Rowsley.'

My train has swept me into a part of Derbyshire dubbed 'the Switzerland of England'. Alongside the remains of dormant industry, the Derwent Valley holds a set of spectacular rock formations, valleys, edges and hills. The drama of the landscape hits me quickly. Minutes after stepping off my train, my path takes me along the bottom of a massive cliff face. Trees grow up high, directly out of breaks in the rocks, their leaves rusting and falling to the ground. On the way to the first stop on my bare list of instructions, I pass the shell of Sir Richard Arkwright's cotton-spinning factory – it is just a façade, and there seems to be a multistorey car park behind the red bricks. Peering through the open windows of one building confirms it is empty now, its use as a shopping centre, promising over sixty 'retail concepts', a casualty of the pandemic. I turn up an almost hidden old path running past a row of small, neat cottages. The stone steps taking me upwards are worn, their middles sinking from the passage of thousands over dozens of years. As the steps peter out, the path climbs a bank, and from the earth emerge pieces of pottery and ceramic, studded jewel fragments crystallized in the dark loam. I pick up a handful of these shards as I walk, wiping the dirt away. Tiny broken images emerge: the bright red of a single apple, blue filigree vines and ferns, and a glimpse of a scene – what looks like a flight of steps leading up from a riverbank.

Without my Ordnance Survey clearly showing me the way, I might have missed this path entirely. In 1944, the Ramblers published a booklet entitled 'Right of Way: Footpath Law for Everyone'. The advice in this publication neatly demonstrates the situation the hikers of the 1930s would have faced when

navigating unfamiliar countryside.[4] Just finding public rights of
way was fraught with misstep. Some footpath maps were published by councils and by the Ramblers, but, as the 1944 booklet
says, these 'at present . . . cover only a small area of the country'.
Although an article in the *Hampshire Advertiser* from March 1932
suggests that the latest Ordnance Survey maps would only show
publicly accessible paths, I'm not sure that this would have been
accepted by landowners at the time. Users hoping to navigate
without a map were in even more trouble, as they 'cannot expect
to find a sign "Public Footpath"' – physical signage is very much
'the exception not the rule'. The *Cornish Guardian* in 1946
pleaded for the preservation of that county's footpaths and bridleways. The erection of fingerposts on these historic paths was
deemed necessary so that tourists could truly 'gain an experien-
tial knowledge of Cornwall and our rural people'.[5] The lack of
easily accessible information in the 1930s, whether on maps or
on the ground, points to the need for events like the mystery
hikes. Walkers required a trusted guide to help them negotiate
the countryside, especially when venturing out into unknown
territory. The mystery hikers of July 1932 were led through this
landscape by a representative of the Trent Motor Traction Company, described as 'a hiker of experience'.

But I don't need such help now; I can walk alone and at my
own pace because our public rights of way have been captured
on the map. My path climbs higher, the tarmacked roads are
long behind and I'm bathed in green. From one side an arch of

4 The booklet and its importance for shining a light on the pre-National
Parks and Access to the Countryside Act situation was explored in an article,
authored by Rodney Whittaker, for the Ramblers' *Walk* magazine.
5 Even with public rights of way recorded and shown on Ordnance Survey
maps, the need to signpost these paths where they leave a road was only
introduced at the prompting of the Ramblers and the Open Spaces Society
in the Countryside Act of 1968.

vegetation, a draped canopy of tree branches, and from the other a glowing lichen-covered stone wall that shines luridly in the semi-gloom. Heading north, the path becomes more informal as it rises into the woods. A smattering of rotting wooden treads, fallen branches and protruding rocks provide points for my boots to cling to. On the flat top of Harp's Edge, the path skirts Ball Eye Quarry, a deep, wide scar on the side of the hill. A little way on, I get a view of a village nestling perfectly in the valley below – my first waypoint: Bonsall.[6]

All is quiet as I walk through the village, a peaceful and prosperous Dales community. At its heart, solid grey buildings form an irregularly shaped courtyard, a meeting point with a cross at the road junction, elevated high on a round base of twelve steps. I slip between two houses up a footpath called Stepping Lane, which traverses a gentle incline. Two straight, neat drystone walls clearly define its direction. An amazingly detailed map of the area displayed in the village tells me that the ground I'm walking was laid down after the mystery hikers came through Bonsall, having been resurfaced by German prisoners of war in the 1940s. There is a short break in the wall-lined path, crossing a small field guarded by an upstanding squeeze stile. The weather is shifting, waves of drizzle coming over, and washing hangs in a nearby garden, limp and damp. On my quest to walk in the footsteps of the mystery hikers, I am yet to meet any other walkers, although at the top of Stepping Lane, I stop to chat to some metal detectorists digging into a green paddock, where two horses stare into the neat little holes.

This area of the White Peak is interlaced with green on my

6 Down below is a valley and road both called Via Gellia, named in bizarre faux Latin after Phillip Eyre Gell, a local eighteenth-century aristocrat who owned lead mines. The road and valley inspired the name of a long communication trench outside the village of Kemmel in Belgium during the First World War and of a fabric produced here in Derbyshire, a blend of wool and cotton trademarked as Viyella.

Ordnance Survey map. A plethora of rights of way, an abundance of footpaths, bridleways and byways spiral out from here and across Bonsall Moor to the north-west. But even here there are gaps, lanes across moors and valleys and between the patchwork quilt of fields, which are simply unrecorded. Other rights of way meet and branch off these lanes, but they remain a legal no man's land. This network of coloured public rights of way has appeared on the Ordnance Survey map since the legal recording of paths from the 1950s; my copy bears the statement, 'Public rights of way shown on OS maps have been taken from local authority definitive maps and later amendments'. These lines give me some certainty about where I can walk, and an expectation that the path will be clear and usable (sometimes this is more the case in theory than in practice, as thousands of our public rights of way are overgrown or illegally obstructed). The rather formal, protected status of these paths belies the joy they bring. We are accustomed to the path-wound countryside being a space for leisure. This was the playground of the interwar outdoors movement, a place to experience the wonders and the simple pleasures of a good walk. But this conception wasn't entirely new then; it was one that had its first blush over a hundred years earlier.

It was on the paths of the Lake District that the concept of walking for pleasure first truly found its feet, by those seeking the beauty and spectacle of its vistas and ancient monuments. The antiquarian Thomas West, in his 1778 *A Guide to the Lakes in Cumberland, Westmorland and Lancashire*, was among the first to write about the Lake District as a place for tourists. In West's account, the Lakes were an alternative to, or at the very least a training ground for, the European grand tour, providing 'in miniature an idea of what they are to meet . . . in traversing the Alps and Apennines, to which our northern mountains are not inferior in beauty of line, or variety of summit, number of lakes, and transparency of water, not in colouring of rock, or softness of turf, but in height and extent only'. But for West there was one big advantage that the Lakes had over their French and Italian cousins: 'The mountains here are all accessible to the summit.'

Poets followed in the wake of Thomas West. Samuel Taylor Coleridge, Dorothy and William Wordsworth, and Robert Southey were drawn to the wild (although not too wild) nature of the Lakes, to gaze upon the picturesque and experience the sublime. The tourists who joined them at this time were primarily those who could afford aimless leisure, 'respectable' people with the time to enjoy non-essential pursuits. Many books guided the early tourists around the most scenic viewpoints and vistas (including a celebrated guidebook from William Wordsworth himself in 1810).[7]

In our images of the poets striding the Lake District, they are alone, deep in their own philosophical thoughts, or walking perhaps with one other companion, engaged in intellectual conversation. But walking is, for many of us, a communal activity. The 500 local groups of the Ramblers organize tens of thousands of walks a year, alongside those laid on by hundreds of other community groups and local walking clubs. These group walks offer a social experience but also play a key role in people being able to explore new places on foot, to discover land they wouldn't venture alone.

Clubs for walking started to emerge in the half-century before the 1930s hiking craze. These groups are often characterized by a class divide. For instance, there were the middle- and upper-class clubs like the Sunday Tramps, established in 1879. Organized by literary critic and journalist Leslie Stephen and

---

7 To further appreciate the 'formally' beautiful scenes, a mirrored Claude glass was recommended. The tourist would turn their back on the view and observe it through the mirror, which would simplify the tones and create a painterly effect.

comprising primarily intellectuals, the Sunday Tramps would take the train out into the Home Counties for invigorating and stimulating rambles of up to twenty-five miles a day.[8] There were clubs which were very much working class and sometimes avowedly socialist, such as the Sheffield Clarion Ramblers, founded by G. H. B. Ward in 1900.[9] A Sheffield Clarion Ramblers publication from the early 1920s gives an indication of the importance of their excursions in providing education and enjoyment for those joining the walks. Walk leaders are reminded to follow the agreed route come rain or shine, and to 'give useful information along the way (place names, etc.) from Ramblers booklets and other sources, and to see that some song is sung during the day'.[10] It is from many of these working-class walking groups that many of the trespassers and rights of way activists of the 1930s onwards sprang (Ward also founded another organization specifically dedicated to protecting rights of way – the Hallamshire Footpaths Preservation Society).[11]

---

8 Stephen had fallen in love with walking and mountaineering while a fellow at Trinity Hall, Cambridge, and on regular walking holidays in Europe (fellow mountaineer Douglas Freshfield remarked that 'the Alps were for Stephen a playground but . . . also a cathedral').

9 The socialist rambler became an archetype and the subject of some mockery. In Orwell's 1936 novel *Keep the Aspidistra Flying*, socialism is described by Gordon Comstock as: 'Some kind of Aldous Huxley Brave New World: only not so amusing. Four hours a day in a model factory, tightening up bolt number 6003. Rations served out in grease-proof paper at the communal kitchen. Community-hikes from Marx Hostel to Lenin Hostel and back.'

10 These instructions from the early 1920s, shared anew by Tomo Thompson on Twitter, tell walk leaders to ensure that they are wearing 'a distinctive badge' and to 'see that new members do not leave waste paper or orange peel to defile either field or moorland'.

11 Other early clubs included the Manchester YMCA Rambling Club (1880), the London-focused Forest Ramblers' Club (1884) and the Yorkshire Ramblers' Club (1892).

I think of the camaraderie of these clubs on my walk in the Derbyshire Dales, passing a group of six walkers coming the other way, seeing how they laugh as one slips in the newly formed mud. I reach the area labelled as 'Bonsall Moor' on my map. It is not the sort of moorland I have come to expect; there are no uninterrupted carpets of heather or dark bogs. A pattern of tiny geometric fields divides the area. Here I join the Limestone Way, a regional trail devised by the Rotary Club of Matlock in the 1980s. The trail dissects the small enclosures, from path to stile and stile to path.

As it reaches the Bonsall Road, I stop to check my phone. I'm after a place to stop and buy a snack, so I look up what might be open in Winster, the village that I know is somewhere below me. It is then that I notice something on Google Maps: the next section of the trail, a continuation of the public footpath, is labelled 'Winster to Bonsall Path'. This is unusual; while some National Trails appear on Google Maps, only a tiny fraction of our extensive network of ordinary public rights of way are recorded on the most widely used app for navigation. Ordnance Survey maps have their own entrancing beauty, their symbols, lines and colours recognizable to seasoned walkers. However, knowing that these maps exist and what they show – and, of course, buying the maps – represents a barrier to getting more people walking. Putting our 140,000 miles of rights of way in the hands of the public, on Google Maps, could revolutionize connection to public paths. It would show the hyperlocal network that is there to be discovered, right on our doorsteps – as well as demonstrating how our paths, especially in towns and cities, can provide the quickest options for getting from A to B.[12]

I branch off the Limestone Way to go down into the winding

12 The wonderful Open Street Map community have made great efforts to bring our path network to everyone for free, but for the foreseeable future it

alleys that mass on the south side of Winster and then head on, towards the extraordinary formations of Rowtor Rocks and the high plateau of Stanton Moor. If I were to continue on the Limestone Way, on another twenty-three miles of footpaths, bridleways, byways and roads of the Peak District, I would arrive at Castleton. This would place me less than two miles from the start of the nation's first National Trail. The Pennine Way was originally proposed by Tom Stephenson in an article for the *Daily Herald* in the 1930s. Britain was rather late to the party when it came to long-distance trails: Germany had had them since the early 1900s, and across the Atlantic the Long Trail in Vermont had begun construction in 1910. Stephenson had a vision of England's first such path as 'akin to the Appalachian Trail' (the flagship American route, established in the early 1920s). It was to be 'no Euclidean line, but a meandering way deviating as needs be to include the best of that long range of moor and fell . . . a faint line on the Ordnance Maps which the feet of grateful pilgrims would, with the passing years, engrave on the face of the land'.

The National Trails, like the National Parks and the legal recording of rights of way, came from the 1949 National Parks and Access to the Countryside Act. Introducing the bill, the Minister of Town and Country planning, Lewis Silkin, described it as a 'people's charter . . . for everyone who lives to get out into the open air and enjoy the countryside'. Note the emphasis on enjoyment – with this Act and with the Pennine Way the idea of paths for leisure was set in legislation for the first time.

While the 1949 Act practically codified our paths as spaces for pleasure, just a few decades earlier the walking craze was not well

---

is unlikely that these maps will be as widely used as the ubiquitous Google Maps.

received by all. For many of the older generation of walkers, the words 'hikers' and 'hiking' were simply too much – uncouth Americanisms which signified a perceived amateurism in the younger generation's exploration and embrace of countryside walking. In their 1931 handbook, the Manchester and District Ramblers' Federation described 'hiking' as a 'detestable word'; and in 1932 the Member of Parliament William Mabane launched an incredible diatribe in the *Leeds Mercury*, declaring his hatred for the word 'hiking' (although he admitted he couldn't find anything better).

The Berkshire mystery hikers were two-thirds women, and many of the attacks on the hiking craze were gendered and misogynist (with a good dose of classism too). Mabane writes that hiking was 'in danger of degradation by its constant use to describe the suburban activities of forward young ladies in ill-fitting flannel trousers or hideous shorts and, of course, high-heeled shoes'. A proper walk, in Mabane's eyes, is 'a serious business and a strenuous business' which 'requires a map, a rucksack, strong boots and an objective . . . it is a revolt against the shrieking promenades, the piers and palaces, the soda-fountains and side-shows of an ordinary holiday'.[13] His 'final rule' was that 'women are better left at home'.

Above Mabane's words the editor had attached the rather pointed warning: 'This challenging article may not command general approval. We shall welcome letters to the Editor stating other points of view.' It's heartening to see rebuffs to Mabane in the following editions. A letter signed by 'Four Working Girls from Bradford' puts him straight: 'We are afraid Mr William Mabane takes his hiking too seriously . . . Girls are just as good at walking as men, and we are just as entitled as men to dress suitably. We consider ourselves just as much hikers as Mr Mabane.'

13 I wonder if Mabane continued to hold this attitude when, in the 1960s, he became chairman and then president of the British Travel Association?

In a bleak echo from the past, there are still people who see the countryside as 'theirs', who want to exclude others from the pleasures that come from walking in nature. As people discovered new paths during the Covid pandemic, news stories focused on unsuitable clothing (again, we see shades of Mabane's invective – just replace 'ill-fitting flannel trousers' with 'jeans'), litter and increased erosion from more feet, rather than the good news story: more people were getting out walking. In 2021, the Muslim Hikers group, founded by Haroon Mota, organized a Christmas Day walk up Mam Tor in the Peak District (where a white supremacist group had unfurled a White Lives Matter banner some seventeen months earlier). A post about the walk on a local Facebook page attracted abuse, lobbed from behind the safety of the keyboard – comments, some negative and others plainly racist, and more bizarre Mabane-esque accusations of them not being 'proper walkers'.

There is still a way to go before our paths are seen as a place for all. Only one per cent of visitors to a National Park are from a black and ethnic minority background. In 2019, the chief executive of the Lake District National Park commented that these landmark areas needed to be for 'everybody in Britain, all society' and warned that they were in danger of losing their relevance if there were places 'exclusive to one single use group'. Alongside the Muslim Hikers, a glorious profusion of new groups has sprung up, welcoming a wider representation of our society, in all its diversity, to our paths. Groups such as Black Girls Hike, Steppers UK, the Wanderlust Women and Peaks of Colour. They join longer-established groups such as the Gay Outdoor Club, Hiking Dykes London and 100 Black Men Walk for Health (the latter of which has recently changed its name to Walk4Health to reflect the many women and younger people joining).

Writing in an article for the *Inkcap Journal*, Maxwell Ayamba, the founder of 100 Black Men Walk for Health, describes his walking as a political statement. A reconnection with black rural history and a reversal of a historical narrative that says that rural spaces have only ever been for white people. Confidence in being accepted and 'belonging' in rural walking Britain is often cited by their founders as a reason to set up these new groups. In the words of Sophie Brown, founder of Bristol Steppin Sistas: 'There has been a reluctance for women of colour to venture into unfamiliar spaces where they feel exposed, judged and remarked on. This has led to our staying in our lanes.' In the *Guardian*, V. V. Brown writes of the countryside as 'a territorial place, full of imperial nostalgia . . . the very concept of British-ness is wrapped up in images of the fields of England – and I do not represent that concept. Yet, as part of a dual-heritage family leaving an overpriced city to set up life beyond the smoke, I am now a representation of the countryside's future.' This is a future in which all should be welcomed to walking. Rhiane Fatinikun, founder of Black Girls Hike, writes that, perhaps, things are changing: 'You do get people with old-fashioned values and set ideas about what a traditional walker is and some-times you just have to forget about bringing them into 2022. But a lot of people are just happy to see you in the countryside. They enjoy it, so why would they not want you to enjoy it?'

The exclusion of people in the countryside goes beyond race. The Queer Rural Connections project is reclaiming history and challenging 'the idea that being queer means being urban' by uncovering the stories of LGBTQIA+ people in rural Britain. Exclusive, systematic and oppressive barriers to access can be counted on a multitude of different levels. Our countryside is littered with unnecessary infrastructure which prevent our paths from being physically accessible – fields which haven't seen a cow or sheep for half a century, but which are guarded by pointless wooden stiles. There is a dearth of toilets and places to change – vital facilities which would enable more people to get out on our paths. Walking in the countryside is still presented as only doable by those with 'the right kit' – an economic barrier (despite the fact that most ordinary countryside walking, at least in decent-ish weather, can be undertaken in jeans and trainers). The decimation of rural public transport also makes much of our countryside inaccessible for those without a car.

As I stand at the bus stop at Rowsley, at the end of my Derbyshire Dales walk, I think about the ways behind me. Our paths, urban and rural, are for people. They were mapped and recorded by communities, and many were formed and reaffirmed simply by the act of people, the mystery hikers among them, moving through the landscape. In an article for the *Guardian*, Professor Glen O'Hara calls for a 'cultural shift . . . away from the idea of "access" and towards the idea of equal rights that we all enjoy together' and 'imagining our huge network of paths, byways and bridleways as a collective resource, in trust for all of us'.[14] But work lies ahead to ensure that the path network is for everyone, that all feel that our paths are places for them, that they belong. So that Silkin's 'People's Charter' can be fulfilled, and that we truly and honestly say that they are *public* rights of way.

14 Glen O'Hara, along with Dr Clare Hickman, led the In All Our Footsteps project, which seeks to demonstrate the importance of the mapping, development, use and experience of twentieth- and twenty-first century rights of way.

Urban

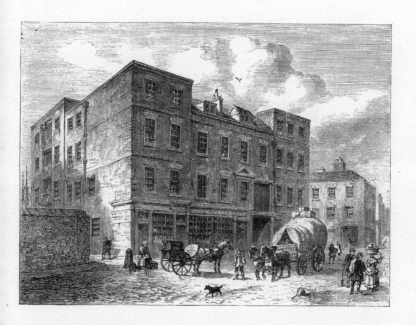

18.   The New Towns

A small smile of satisfaction must have crawled across the Reverend Walter Loveband's face as he surveyed his congregation. The pews were full as, in the presence of the Archbishop, he presided over the consecration of a brand-new church for his flock. The old chapel hadn't been big enough to accommodate the burgeoning population of the rural community of Ifield in Sussex – recent years had seen standing-room only at the harvest festival. So, St Peter's had been built, at the site of a Saxon crossroads in the village's West Green area. What the Reverend Loveband couldn't have foreseen was just how much his community would grow in the future. His church would come to mark a boundary – a transition from Victorian village to post-war new town.

For a moment I stand in the shade of St Peter's and of a monumental tree which towers above it – bowling-pin shaped, a voluminous bottom narrowing towards the top, a giant redwood. Crossing the road, I walk into Smalls Mead, a street of brown-bricked houses with little box porches, set back from the road by wide green verges. Smalls Mead was built in 1949, across from a former field. It was the first street of a master plan which transformed this Sussex landscape, the creation of the new town of Crawley.

For much of British history, the growth of our towns and cities has taken place piecemeal, with individual houses contributing to an organic growth outwards or small neighbourhoods developing as urban annexes. The National Library of Scotland has digitized, as seamless layers, Ordnance Survey maps from the

1880s to the 1960s. I can spend hours on the website, with a click and a swipe, jumping through time. Seeing hamlets turn into villages, which grow into towns and develop into cities. Suburbs are added, town centres redesigned and infilled with new housing. Settlements which, as they grow larger and larger, usually follow the underlying structure of the landscape. Development creeps along existing roads, houses clustering along them as urban Britain slowly expands, and then further roads are built off these with houses, shops and factories. Old footpaths and tracks are transformed into alleyways between homes or become solid roads and streets serving new developments. It's a process of gradual change described negatively by one MP in the 1940s:

> It starts, perhaps, with Acacia Road spreading out a tentacle into the green and pleasant land surrounding it, but it has numerous and prolific progeny. In turn, it brings forth Acacia Grove, Acacia Street, Acacia Avenue, Acacia Crescent and Acacia Court, until the whole country is engulfed by these tentacles in one uniform mass of undistinguished bricks and mortar.

Supplementing this incremental development, England and Wales have seen some attempts, in fits and spurts, to create whole new communities, to take a swathe of land and (pretty much) start from scratch. The Romans, the island's first urbanists, established forts and planned towns which are still urban centres today: Chester, Gloucester, York, Lincoln and Cirencester among others. After the Romans left, many of their towns remained, but the habit of building completely new planned settlements seems to have been lost for generations. In the ninth and tenth centuries, Alfred the Great and his daughter Æthelflæd fortified existing settlements and built new towns, the burhs, across the English south and Midlands. Much later, towns were established for industry and commerce, places such as Barrow-in-Furness for its docks, steel production and shipbuilding, or model villages for workers such as Saltaire near Bradford, Bournville in Birmingham and Port Sunlight on the Wirral.

The genesis of the post-war new towns such as Crawley came from the garden city movement a generation before, set out by Ebenezer Howard at the end of the nineteenth century in *Tomorrow: A Peaceful Path to Real Reform* (republished, in 1902, as *Garden Cities of To-morrow*). These towns would relieve the pressure on what Howard called the 'crowded, ill-ventilated, unplanned, unwieldy, unhealthy cities', places he regarded as 'ulcers on the very face of our beautiful island'. He wanted these new towns to draw people away from the cities, leading to a fall in urban land values that would trigger the redevelopment of city slums and bring better living standards. At the same time Howard argued that the flow of people from rural areas to the cities would be stemmed by offering them work in the newly created green and pleasant planned communities. Howard's ideal garden city would be self-contained, with housing and industry for all in the town, replete with wide boulevards, green open space and public parks. An idealized plan in the first edition of *To-morrow* apes Da Vinci's *Vitruvian Man*. The core garden city sits in the centre, with six radial cities around it, forming what Howard called the 'social city'. In between are large farms, allotments, forests and reservoirs. There are institutions, notably separated from the towns, described in the language of the Edwardian age as 'home for inebriates', 'epileptic farm', 'insane asylum' and 'home for waifs'. Old paths are conspicuously absent from Howard's plan; instead new roads link the towns in straight lines, as well as 'grand' and 'inter municipal' canals and a circular 'inter municipal railroad'.

Although a utopian, Howard was not just a theorist, and in 1903 4,000 acres of land was bought (though not with his money) to build the first garden city at Letchworth, a place to demonstrate the practicability of his ideas. As a privately developed

scheme without the full support and power of the state, Letchworth didn't quite match Howard's vision. Grand boulevards
were built, but there were no new canals or railways. A few older
footpaths, crossing fields and along forgotten hedgerows, were
destroyed when Letchworth was built, their existence wiped off
the map. A skeleton of the old road network survived. The bones
of Durham's Lane, winding gently to the south. A section of the
ancient Icknield Way, which at the end of the nineteenth century
was just a track. This venerable thoroughfare was incorporated
into the plan for the town and reborn as a road at the centre of its
new industrial area. It became home to many of Letchworth's
biggest employers, including the Spirella Corset Company
(whose factory was disguised as a sprawling country house) and
the British Tabulating Machine Company (who manufactured
the mechanical 'bombes' which helped crack the Enigma code).
In *The New Town Story*, Frank Schaffer describes Howard as
having 'the vision of the prophet in his plans for a better way of
life'. The devotional language is somewhat typical of earlier followers of Howard's ideas. It was a fervour which sustained the
movement through a period when Letchworth, alongside
Welwyn Garden City (started in 1919), stood alone as new
planned towns, a fervour which propelled the building of new
towns after the Second World War.

Considering that the Attlee government was in office for only
seventy-five months, in a Britain which was recovering from the
ravages of war, its achievements are startling. In this time it created the National Health Service; nationalized whole industrial
sectors including coal, steel, the railways, civil aviation, road
haulage, canals, electricity and gas; strengthened workers' rights;
implemented a social welfare programme which significantly
expanded sickness, unemployment and pension benefits; and
implemented expansive support for agricultural communities

with the provision of water, gas and electricity, secure tenures, rural bus services and minimum wages for agricultural workers. On the foreign policy front, it oversaw the decolonization of India, Pakistan, Burma, Sri Lanka and Jordan; helped found NATO; and developed Britain as a nuclear power. Many of the ministers from that time are still remembered names – Aneurin Bevan, Ernest Bevin, Herbert Morrison, Hugh Gaitskell, Harold Wilson.

One perhaps overlooked figure in Attlee's team is Lewis Silkin, the Minister of Town and Country Planning. Silkin was a London boy, born in 1889 to Jewish Lithuanian parents who had recently emigrated to Britain. He was a keen countryside walker, influenced by journalist and writer Robert Blatchford, whose book *Merrie England* lionized a pre-industrial Britain and rural cooperatives.[1] In 1925, Silkin was elected to represent south-east Southwark on the London County Council and as a councillor he championed the creation of the green belt around the city. In May 1936, he was elected to be the Member of Parliament for Peckham and was made a minister after the formation of the Attlee government in 1945. In just four years, Silkin marshalled three Acts through Parliament that changed the lens through which we see land, and the countryside, in England and Wales to this day.

As we have seen, the National Parks and Access to the Countryside Act (1949) created the responsibility for most councils to map their public rights of way as well as establishing, for the first time, National Trails, National Parks and Areas of

---

1 Blatchford was the editor of the socialist newspaper *The Clarion*, which inspired many social clubs, including for cycling and walking. The most famous of these was probably the Sheffield Clarion Ramblers, founded by G. H. B. Ward. While the clubs he inspired lived on, in later years Blatchford moved away from socialism, becoming a First World War jingoist and spiritualist.

Outstanding Natural Beauty, and perhaps it was Silkin's love of walking which led him to describe this legislation as 'the most exciting Act of the post-war Parliament'. But before this came the New Towns Act (1946). Introducing the Bill in the Commons, Silkin firmly placed the proposed generation of new towns in a historical context, as an effort to combat piecemeal urban development, stating that his research went 'back to the time of Sir Thomas More. He was the first person I have discovered to deplore the "suburban sprawl".' Then came the Town and Country Planning Act in 1947, which Silkin described in Parliament as 'the most comprehensive and far-reaching planning measure which has ever been placed before this House'. Although amended on several occasions in the subsequent five decades, this Act established the framework for much post-war development. In all, 147 planning authorities were established which oversaw the new requirement for planning permission, created development plans for building and rebuilding, and were given compulsory purchase powers to acquire land (backed up by large government grants). The Act sought to limit unfettered development, introducing listing for historic buildings, protecting woodlands and curtailing outdoor advertising.[2]

The first wave of new towns, unleashed by the 1946 Act, were primarily concentrated in a ring around London beyond the capital's green belt (including Basildon, Bracknell, Crawley, Harlow, Hemel Hempstead and Stevenage), along with Corby in Northamptonshire and Newton Aycliffe and Peterlee in

---

2 Outdoor advertising was a big point of contention in the first half of the twentieth century. Organizations such as the Campaign to Protect Rural England and the Society for Checking Abuses of Public Advertising campaigned against the blight of advertising in the countryside. There were also worries about advertising in the sky – on planes themselves and through messages the aircraft could write using smoke ('sky-writing' was banned in the 1960s, although it is now permitted since a change in regulations in 2020).

County Durham, all serving as new towns to relieve populations in industrial areas. Future developments, in the 1960s, focused on similar places in the Midlands and north – places such as Runcorn, Redditch, Washington, Warrington and Telford. Of the twenty or so new towns, Crawley was the second designated (just pipped to the post by Stevenage, designated fifty-nine days earlier). Crawley is a sometimes-overlooked new town, regarded by some as simply an appendage to Gatwick Airport, which lies to the north, and described by Robert Smith of the Cure (a Crawley boy) as 'grey and uninspiring with an undercurrent of violence'. Crawley doesn't have the visionary public art of Harlow or the intense civic pride of Milton Keynes; it was also not an entirely new town. The newly formed Development Corporation took the historic market town of Crawley, along with the Reverend Loveband's Ifield and the village of Three Bridges, and filled in the agricultural land between to create their new town.

Old Crawley town was the halfway stop on the coaching route between Brighton and London, an important node in the transport system of the south. Historical maps show the unplanned older town clustered around the High Street, with coaching inns such as the George, the White Hart and the Rising Sun (the latter providing one half of the set-up for the old Crawley quip that the town had the longest high street in the world, stretching as it did from the Rising Sun to the Half Moon pub). The fate of these inns shows the changing face of the town. Built in the seventeenth century and then rebuilt a century later, the White Hart was, at one point, the main town post office and still survives as a pub. The Rising Sun once stood near the North Toll Gate at the beginning of the turnpike where it left Crawley. As the stagecoach era ended in the late nineteenth century, the business went under and the building was split between a cafe and a boarding school. It was demolished in the 1980s and in its place now stands the local headquarters of NatWest (in Turnpike House). The most physically impressive is the George Inn, red-bricked and black-and-white-panelled, still running along the wide high street. This Grade II listed seventeenth-century inn has now been clunkily rebranded as 'Ramada by Wyndham Crawley Gatwick'.

At the time of the coaching inns, Crawley was still a small town with under a thousand residents. The arrival of the Mid-Sussex railway in 1848 connected the town to the London to Brighton line, which was built seven years earlier, and Crawley came within commuting distance of the capital.[3] Its rail connection and proximity to London made it a prime candidate for a new overspill town. The Crawley Development Corporation was formed to 'design, build and administer a self-contained industrial town of 50,000 within fifteen years, and weld this on to the existing scattered haphazard development' of Ifield, Crawley and Three Bridges. The corporation initially appointed Thomas Sharp to plan the new town, but he resigned after submitting his plan and it fell to Anthony Minoprio to create the masterplan for Crawley (he later used what he learned on this Sussex new town on plans for Kuwait, Baghdad and Dhaka).[4] Minoprio planned Crawley with an expanded town centre, an industrial zone and nine neighbourhoods each with a variety of housing and a school, church and parade of shops. These

3 An early commuter was the founder of *Punch*, Mark Lemon, who moved to the town in 1858 and set up at Vines Cottage, now swallowed up by an Asda Superstore.
4 An often-overlooked part of the history of British new towns is the role the state, in concert with private enterprise, had in creating whole new settlements abroad as part of the colonial project – settlements which saw the theory and ideals of town planning becoming, in the words of John Delafons, writing in the journal of the Town and Country Planning Association, 'instruments of imperialism and racial prejudice'.

residential developments were intended to be places where all classes mixed, where, in the words of Lewis Silkin, people leaving work would not see 'the better off people to go to the right and the less well-off to go to the left. I want them to ask each other, "Are you going my way?"'

During the early 1940s, academics were arguing for the need for the state to take over land in order to direct the planning of new towns and redevelopment in cities. In a letter to *The Builder* in 1941, A. W. Crampton argued that private ownership of land was 'the cause that fetters modern development', a sentiment echoed by C. S. Orwin, writing for the same publication a year later: 'whatever way the problem is regarded, it seems impossible to be fair to the community so long as private property in land persists'. A committee was formed during the Second World War to investigate 'compensation and betterment' and consider the legal ramifications of building new communities. Their recommendations were for the state to build on 'undeveloped land' (how much land in Britain can truly be described as undeveloped?), with appropriate compensation. This wasn't the abolition of private property, but it did enable the state (through development corporations) to direct land use and remake the landscape, a power which hadn't been available to the earlier builders of new towns.

The Crawley Development Corporation not only had the power to build houses, and industrial and civic buildings but also took control of all aspects of the infrastructure needed for a modern new town. It planned where the gas, electric and waste services would go. It was given almost unprecedented powers, exercised through the Minister, to remake paths and roads within their area.[5] Since the only grounds needed to justify these changes

5 Similar powers were later granted over land vested in or acquired by urban development corporations formed in the 1980s. These bodies set about

came through the land being designated for a new town, the public had little legal scope for the retention of their traditional paths. Changes to the old ways could not be fought through the usual local pressure. Crawley Urban District Council was only created in 1956; before then the area of the new town was split between three boroughs – Surrey, East Sussex and West Sussex. Even after the creation of this new local government body, power was concentrated in the development corporation – an undemocratic position which was deemed necessary for establishing a whole new successful community.

It is not surprising that the creation of new towns generated considerable opposition from the people who already lived there – an uprooting of the life, and land, they had come to know. The establishment of the new Crawley was delayed as the original order designating it was challenged in the courts. When it did get underway, Mr D. A. Butterfield, chairman of the (Old) Crawley and District Residents' Association, railed against the plans, calling for what he described as an 'unwanted, ill-conceived scheme' to 'be put away so that the expensive talents of the members of the Development Corporation and their large staff can be diverted to productive channels'. Mr Butterfield wasn't a fan of the planners, who 'with their pretty pictures and paper schemes frequently, I fear, overlook human nature and the unhappiness and uncertainty they bring into the lives of people whose homes and businesses they threaten with their boulevards and public buildings and campuses and what not.' Anger was directed at Lewis Silkin and his ministry who, in the opinion of Mr Butterfield, had selected an area 'wholly

---

transforming city landscapes, creating areas such as London's Docklands (and the Canary Wharf area as we see it today), Cardiff Bay and the 'regeneration' of Liverpool's docks.

unsuitable for a new town' (although, like many people who instinctively oppose new housing now, no clear alternative was offered up). Criticism of Silkin wasn't uncommon. As John Grindrod recounts in *Concretopia*, when the Minister visited the village which would become the first new town, at Stevenage, he was welcomed by road and railway station signs daubed with the words 'Silkingrad' and found that his tyres had been let down and his car engine filled with sand.

Laying the current plan of Crawley over the historical maps reveals how much of the physical pattern of rural life was swallowed up by the new town. Buildings from the old map of Crawley disappear. A tile works is replaced by a small housing block. Little Buckwood Farm is today a roundabout, and Scallows Farm is now only remembered in the name of a few new roads where it once stood: Farm Close, Scallows Close and Scallows Road. Small areas of woodland, like Punch Copse and Butts Copse, are replaced with cul-de-sac housing. In 1952, officially through the Minister of Housing and Local Government, notice was given of an order to 'extinguish' public rights of way between Three Bridges Road, Crawley and North Road. This single order removed public rights over a mile and a half of footpaths, and a largely new road system was implemented, with a ring road and roads radiating from the centre. There were some nods to the old, with a handful of streets and lanes being retained, particularly around the High Street at the core of Crawley old town. Where more outlying roads were kept, their names were often changed to give a gentle pastoral flavour to the newly urbanized environments. Blackdog Lane was split into Hollybush Road and Barnfield Road, though Hog's Hill became, simply, Brighton Road.

It wasn't only Crawley where the old paths were swept away. The new towns feature prominently in the councils which have lost most rights of way over the past 120 years. Stevenage tops the list and is joined in the top ten by Milton Keynes, Harlow, Welwyn Garden City and Hatfield. That isn't to say that alternative paths weren't created; many planners of new towns wanted to find a way of making life possible and enjoyable on foot. Stevenage became 'internationally famous' for being 'the first modern town with a completely pedestrianised precinct'.[6] In Basildon, a new town which didn't lose quite so many of its old paths, a new walking infrastructure was created – passages between houses and roads laced with footbridges and tunnels.[7]

I think the best way to see Crawley is still on foot, weaving through the town's neighbourhoods. These areas were designed to discourage through traffic, and long straight roads were avoided. In Crawley the guiding principles, as described by Osborn and Whittick, were 'unity, variety, quietness and safety from traffic'. Late on a summer's afternoon I walk around Langley Green to the north-west of the town, barely encountering any moving cars. Most houses are in cul-de-sacs, set back behind verges and around greens, now dotted with mature trees. Many of the original workers who built Crawley found homes in this neighbourhood. Having lived on site in huts, after nine months they became entitled to council accommodation, settling in the very houses they helped to build. The street names spring from nature. From Juniper Road branches Pine Close, Chestnut Walk, Maple Close and Walnut Lane. Flocking together are Swift Lane, Robin Close, Lark Rise and Raven Lane. Squirrels, hares, leverets, foxes and moles are joined in a menagerie of

6 Frederic Osborn and Arnold Whittick in their influential book *The New Towns: The Answer to Megalopolis*.

7 Twenty years after Basildon was founded it was noted that there had only been two fatal accidents involving pedestrians on the main highways and only one accident in a residential street, described as 'moderately serious'.

lanes and closes, round the corner from Warren Drive. Taking a route through a myriad of alleyways and cut-throughs, it's a walk of exploration. Most of these pedestrian paths are not shown on Google Maps or recorded as rights of way – a hidden walking network not given the prominence it deserves.

It is in neighbourhoods like Langley Green that you can see why Crawley was popular with those who settled there. In oral histories gathered from the early residents by Crawley Museum, there is much talk of community spirit and the openness their new environment offered them. David Stoker tells the story of his family moving to Crawley when he was a toddler, replacing their 'cramped second floor garret at 208 East Lane, Walworth' with a 'brand new three-bedroomed house' in the Northgate neighbourhood (named for where the old turnpike road ran). He recalls the freedom he had to roam the town and an 'adventure playground' where children were free to try out and play with 'picks, shovels, wheelbarrows, carpentry tools and loads of scrap wood, largely unsupervised'. Many residents speak of how easy the town was to navigate on foot and bike. In their account *Why We Moved to Crawley – and Loved It*, Brian and Rita Burton describe living in Arundel Close in the Pound Hill neighbour-hood: 'we had wonderful neighbours with young children, and so near shops, school and doctors. Didn't need to use the bus, pushed the pram into Town' (an almost perfect description of what we might now call fifteen-minute neighbourhoods – an excellent concept which, bizarrely, has become controversial). David Stoker also describes people travelling to work by bike; the factories had large bike sheds and the cycle tracks which ran beside the main roads were crowded at the beginning and end of each working day.

Walking from the first street in Crawley new town, Smalls Mead, I explore the rest of the West Green neighbourhood. I'm here in search of the landscape which came before. It's the middle of a June heatwave, the sort of intense heat I associate with a suburban summer – a continuous hot breath on the back of the neck. Warmth bounces off the pavements, buildings and from the front gardens, some of which remain clothed in grass and clipped shrubs, many more now paved over. There is a smell of unseen barbeques. It's too early in the year for the grass to be browned by the summer sun, and the light intensifies the green of the vegetation. Trees offer welcome shade, especially the specimens seemingly much older than the houses around them. Occasional oaks and beeches, which could be survivors from a lost field boundary, appear as centrepieces in mown verges or tower up from behind back-garden fences.

Wandering through West Green, I see the results of Minoprio's plan – a varied mix of housing. There are small streets of detached and semi-detached houses, buildings are set at an angle or stepped back from the line of the road, opening up the spaces in between. Some houses stare at each other across small greens. Scattered around are bungalows and small blocks of flats. Closest to the centre of town are the Sunnymead flats, three-sided Y-shaped blocks built, according to the conservation area description, in 'Festival of Britain style'. The dusky pink sides of these flats glows through the leaves of tall weeping willows growing close by. Coming to the edge of the neighbourhood, I'm standing by one of the verges which pepper West Green and looking down an incongruous track, gently curving so its end is out of sight. The path runs to the historic high street core of Crawley and is bordered by old trees and what looks like the remains of an ancient hedgerow.

This path is at least a hundred years older than the housing around it. It was recorded on the 1839 tithe map as 'The Driftway', a path for driving animals (analogous to a drove road). From the Driftway used to run a footpath to Ifield Lodge, a connection from the lost countryside into the old town. In the 1990s the Driftway was legally converted to a cycle track, part of an effort to make Crawley 'a cycling mecca'.[8] The path is certainly broad enough for walkers and cyclists: a wide green urban lane. Strong branching oaks of some age define its boundaries alongside a scrubby wild undergrowth of hawthorn, maple seedlings and hornbeam. Small paths feed the Driftway: ways and entrances to the surrounding cul-de-sacs. One side path has a homemade sign – 'Shelia Tyson Ramp' – a simple piece of modern path naming.[9] Quite why the Driftway survived the planner's pen is a mystery – perhaps it was in just the right place for a connection from the first new neighbourhood to the town centre – but survive it does, a connection to a past landscape in this new world.

8 Efforts which didn't seem to work. According to Department of Transport statistics, Crawley has lower than the national average rates of people walking or cycling regularly and is the lowest of any district in West Sussex.
9 A less pleasant example of modern path-naming has been applied to the Driftway. On Strava the path is known as 'dog turd alley', which seems like an unfair downgrading of this historical path.

19.   The City and the Suburbs

I'm walking up stairs of polished concrete. There are four flights, partially enclosed, embedded in the side of an office building. No one else is coming this way; it's unloved – the treads stained with grime, a urine tang in the air. This office block, with its external staircase, is in a strangely isolated bit of the City of London. A run of riverside buildings, cut off from the rest of the city by an unusually fast central London road, sandwiched between traffic and water. Thames Street has always been a busy thoroughfare, albeit in previous centuries the vehicles moved much slower.[1] There were once grand residences along here such as Coldharbour House, a many-storeyed mansion that was home to a succession of the elite – the Duke of Exeter, the Earls of Shrewsbury, Lady Margaret Beaufort (mother of Henry VII) and the Lord Mayor of London. At the westerly end of the street, where the Thames met the Fleet (a river now buried and hidden, relegated to a sewer), stood a Dominican priory, giving its name to the area and subsequently the railway station, of Blackfriars.

Alongside its mansions and religious institutions, Thames Street was a place of commerce and trade. Just downstream was the Pool of London, a section of river where ships came to have their cargoes checked and customs levied. Warehouses and wharves flanked much of this part of the Thames, bringing in and storing goods from all over the world. When Coldharbour

1 Thames Street has now been split, in name only, to Upper and Lower Thames Street.

House stood on Thames Street, it looked out on the old London Bridge, a crossing covered in buildings with, at its centre, a chapel dedicated to St Thomas Becket, which served as the starting point for a pilgrimage route to Becket's shrine in Canterbury. For centuries this was the only bridge in central London, and Thames Street was swelled by Londoners walking on foot to take one of the many ferries across the Thames, operated by thousands of rivermen.[2] Part of the busyness of Thames Street came from Londoners walking on foot to take one of the many ferries across the river, operated by thousands of rivermen.

Above Thames Street, I have reached the top of the stairs, with my back to the river, and there is nowhere to go. A strange triangular landing overlooks the constant stream of cars thundering below, the taste of traffic in the air. This hasn't always been a dead end. This landing once continued on, as a walkway that spanned the road, leading to a building which has long since been knocked down. This stub of a path is a remnant of a lost pedway, a missing chain in a pedestrian network that sought to separate people from cars, concrete paths, which rose from the wreckage of the Second World War.

*

2 Long before the famous old London Bridge, the Romans built bridges across the river in what is now central London, as did the Normans in the twelfth century. Before the riverside was built up and embanked it would have been possible to be forded. In the 1950s, an eccentric peer called Lord Noel-Buxton attempted to walk across the Thames near Parliament to 'prove' the existence of an old Roman ford. He struck out into the river wearing corduroy trousers, tennis shoes, shirt and pullover, and soon found that he had to swim to reach the other side. He seemed undaunted, however, declaring to the assembled press that 'There was much more water than I expected. I should say it has been raining pretty heavily in the Cotswolds. The ford is undoubtedly there. The little bit of extra water made all the difference, but I feel I have proved my point.'

In 1946, an eight-foot-wide drawing called *A Tribute to London* was shown at the Royal Academy. It was the work of Cecil Brown, the assistant surveyor of St Paul's Cathedral and a senior architect to the Diocese of London, who had started on this mammoth piece in 1942, as the Blitz still raged. His completed drawing shows the destruction wreaked on the city after more than five years of war.[3] Whole city blocks have been reduced to a scribble of rubble, their footprints only defined by the streets which run between them. St Paul's Cathedral emerges from a sea of broken-down buildings. Nearby is Christopher Wren's Christ Church Greyfriars, largely destroyed, walls standing but the roof entirely missing.[4] A depiction of a battered London, vividly described by the artist Frank Auerbach as 'pittered with bomb sites . . . survivors scurrying among a ruined city . . . a landscape with precipice and mountain and crags'.

The visceral experience of devastation lingers long in London's deep memory. The early city had been sacked and razed by Boudica and the Iceni. The Great Fire of Southwark of 1212 had destroyed much of the old Borough High Street and leapt across the river to the heart of the City itself. And then, of

---

3 The full title of the work, scrolled across the top, is 'A Prospect of the City of London from the south east in the year 1945 shewing [sic] its architecture, the destruction caused by the King's enemies during the previous five years and some of the means whereby the safety of the citizens was maintained'.
4 In 1944 *The Times* wrote of the church: 'The time will come – much sooner than most of us to-day can visualise – when no trace of death from the air will be left in the streets of rebuilt London. At such a time the story of the blitz may begin to seem unreal not only to visiting tourists but to a new generation of Londoners. It is the purpose of war memorials to remind posterity of the reality of the sacrifices upon which its apparent security has been built. These church ruins, we suggest, would do this with realism and gravity.' They got their wish and the semi-ruined church still stands, its shell repurposed as a public garden.

course, the Great Fire swept through in 1666, burning down more than 13,000 houses over 436 acres of the city. Excited visionaries saw opportunities in the cooling embers of 1666 and in the craggy rumble of 1945, a chance to rethink the city anew. The seventeenth-century ideas included those of the prolific writer, diarist and member of the committee to repair St Paul's, John Evelyn, whose ambitious plan would replace the old chaotic city streets with a largely uniform grid, while Christopher Wren's vision was for radiating avenues and blocks (not unlike what Georges-Eugène Haussmann implemented in Paris in the latter half of the nineteenth century).[5] Twentieth-century plans for a new London were not too dissimilar. Months after the Blitz had finished, but when the war was still very much going on, the Royal Academy Planning Committee proposed a Wren-like scheme: a London of new and enlarged grand public spaces, many circuses and squares connected by long boulevards. Equally impatient were members of the Modern Architectural Research Group, who proposed in the June 1942 issue of the *Architectural Review* that the city should be split into defined zones with new linear neighbourhoods stretching in perpendicular lines from the river. Walking through today's City of London, with its maze of alleyways, and surprising hidden nooks and corners, it's difficult not to be thankful that this was not all swept away in the excitement of new ideas.

It was the vision of the architect Charles Holden and planner William Holford, contained in *The City of London: A Record of Destruction and Survival*, that imagined the beginning of the pedway network in London. Like many others, their plan called

---

5 These grand plans were not implemented, partly because of their exorbitant cost but also because Londoners were in uproar at the idea that they wouldn't get to rebuild their houses and businesses on the same footprints.

for the clearing of damaged and some undamaged buildings. The new footprint of London would see buildings with 'really efficient lifts and other connections between the ground floor and basement and the upper floors' and pedestrian walkways in the sky which would be 'as fit for the traffic it carries as any of the main streets'. Perhaps with their knowledge of the grand plans for London which had failed before, Holden and Holford recognized that they might have to graft their ideas on to 'the myriad paths and circulations both horizontal and vertical that have come into being in the course of centuries'. Despite this acknowledgement of what came before, their plan seemed to include a walkway running through the centre of St Paul's Cathedral, the very symbol of national resilience, and it is perhaps unsurprising that their expansive vision wasn't realized.

Modernists had long seen the streets, where people, vehicles and buildings come together, as 'chaotic, dysfunctional and obsolete'. In the 1920s, the German architect Ludwig Hilberseimer had visions for an otherworldly city which would remake the street. His design for the Hochhausstadt or 'Highrise City' saw slabs of uniform tall buildings around which weaves a network of straight angular unfenced pedestrian walkways and wide avenues for cars far below. The visuals remind me of a 90s platform video game – the people divorced from the land beneath their feet.[6] In 1963, the town planner Colin Buchanan led a team who published a report called 'Traffic in Towns', which the *Architectural Review* called 'perhaps the most significant planning document of the twentieth century', which started to turn, albeit somewhat covertly, modernist theory of

6 A similar approach – the city as a machine, the high walkways between buildings – can be seen in Fritz Lang's ground-breaking science-fiction film of 1927, *Metropolis*.

the city into real-world practice in the form of London's pedways.[7]

The report goes to the heart of one of the key issues that worried planners in the post-war years: the proliferation of cars. When Buchanan published his report there were 10.5 million vehicles registered in Britain. He predicted that this number would quadruple by 2010, a rise which would cripple our urban streets. He wrote that 'it is impossible to spend any time on the study of the future of traffic in towns without at once being appalled by the magnitude of the emergency that is coming upon us. We are nourishing at immense cost a monster of great potential destructiveness, and yet we love him dearly'. There turned out to be 34 million vehicles in the year 2010, so he wasn't far off.

The introduction to Buchanan's report called for a modernization of the city which would 'touch a chord of pride in the British public and help give them the economic and spiritual uplift of which they were in need'. It's wide-ranging, touching on parking policy, the development of new urban areas and public transport. It also considers, in wonderful 60s fashion, the future of personal jet propulsion, monorails and hovercraft in cities. But at the heart of the report is the provision for, as far as possible, total separation of pedestrians and vehicles – paths for people and paths for cars.

It was the Barbican Estate, completed in 1976, with its many paths and walkways which came closest to fulfilling and sustaining Buchanan's vision in London. In 1965, the year the Barbican's construction began, the first official mention was apparently made of the pedway scheme in a City of London Corporation drawing (this document is cited many times, but no one can seem to find the original). At the Barbican, paths march out into wide-open plazas, along public balconies with lines of beaten

7 The report proved so popular it was published as a Penguin book.

concrete columns stretching into the distance.[8] Passageways are
tunnelled assertively through buildings, or wind smoothly
down from one elevation to another. This is a social space,
dozens of people sitting out on ledges and benches, next to long
pools of green water. Reading, drinking, talking. Wandering
round the complex (and it certainly is complex) with some
friends from the Ramblers, we are very much elevated above
and away from the traffic.[9]

The pedways don't just exist within the estate; there is a
revival of sorts as new pedways reach out from the Barbican to
the outside world. These reflect a modern aesthetic, the concrete replaced with snaking wooden panels inside and brushed
rusting metal on the outside. A couple more pedways are
planned, but I am sceptical that any sort of extensive network
will emerge. The same issues pertain today as with the original
scheme. The London County Council's pedways were driven by
incentive and cajoling rather than enforceable planning. If a
new development included provision for a pedway around or
through the building, then it could use this space as temporary
offices until a neighbouring building provided the connection.
Unsurprisingly this left many unrealized paths, with the temporary offices becoming permanent. Where a pedway was
established, all it took was one of the buildings to be redeveloped and the path would be severed. The market was left to

8 The rough finish on the concrete was achieved by hand. Workers would
wait for several weeks until the concrete was completely dry and then labori-
ously chip away at the surface with hand-held pick hammers. The effect
works well, providing texture, as raking light is caught projecting miniature
shadows across the concrete's surface.
9 One feature, which helps somewhat in the negotiating of this complexity,
is a yellow line painted on the floor that winds its way through the Barbican.
If you follow the cheerful line, you eventually find yourself at the Barbican
Centre, the arts and entertainment complex at the heart of the estate.

itself and it failed. The newly proposed pedways follow a similar model, although this time led by the developers themselves. Legally unprotected, they are likely to follow a similar pattern of loss in years to come, especially in a city where some buildings seem almost to be temporary, pulled down and replaced within the space of a few decades.

The brief appearance of pedways, and the total separation of people and cars, was certainly a new concept for London. Throughout most of its history, people and vehicles have shared the same spaces, all mixed up on the city streets. Up until the seventeenth century, these streets were usually surfaced with cobbles set into the ground and mortared in. For much of this time London was mostly to be found in two areas formally designated as cities: the City of London and the City of Westminster. From the 1660s and throughout the eighteenth century, London started to expand significantly, filling in the gaps between the two historic cities. These new-built, infilled areas saw the introduction of new surfaces: granite setts (superficially similar to cobbles but more uniform and easier on hooves) and wooden blocks (these had the unfortunate habit of soaking up copious amounts of horse urine, which would squirt out if a heavy load ran over them or simply stink on hot days). Asphalt and tarmac eventually buried these surfaces, but lost sections can still be seen in London; there are granite setts in the Seven Dials area near Covent Garden and wooden blocks on Chequer Street opposite the old Bunhill Fields burial ground. In just fifteen words of his poem 'Trivia, or the Art of Walking the Streets of London', John Gay encapsulates what it was like to walk in these busy streets jostling with horses, people and coaches:

> Thy foot will slide upon the miry stone,
> And passing coaches crush thy tortur'd bone . . .

Alongside new surfaces, the physical division of the streets between people and traffic began on both the old and new roads. Prints from the time show the introduction of bollards on the medieval Leadenhall Street and in the newly constructed St James's Square, demarcating the roadway from the footway. As pavements became more common in the nineteenth century, in the last years of the Georgian age, the first legal distinction of specific places for people on the city streets was introduced.

The Highways Act of 1835 is a rare piece of legislation which, in its language, reveals the depth and richness of real life. The Act defines what can and can't be done on the pavement or footway. It makes it an offence to 'wilfully ride upon any Footpath or Causeway by the Side of any Road made or set apart for the Use or Accommodation of Foot Passengers' and to 'wilfully lead or drive any Horse, Ass, Sheep, Mule, Swine, or Cattle, or Carriage of any Description, or any Truck or Sledge upon any such Footpath or Causeway'. Other things are outlawed as well, such as the playing of 'Football or any other Game on any Part of the said Highways, to the Annoyance of any Passenger'; the pitching of a 'Tent, Booth, Stall, or Stand' by 'any Hawker, Higgler, Gipsy, or other Person travelling'; and firing of 'any Squib, Rocket, Serpent, or other Firework whatsoever'.

The legal framework of paths, in urban and rural environments, is still that people on foot, in theory, are supreme. Our streets and roads are primarily for people, a reflection of a network developed over centuries, where motorized vehicles are simply recent interlopers. People are allowed to walk on 99.5 per cent of our road and path network, whereas cars are only there, on the road, with permission and by licence. There is only one class of road from which people are banned, the one that has been established in the age of the car: motorways (and their slip roads).[10] The American concept of illegal walking across and along roads, the offence of jaywalking, has never taken hold on British streets.[11] While there are few legal restrictions in Britain, physical infrastructure which either impedes pedestrian access or attempts to channel it have proliferated – pelican and zebra crossings, staggered crossings, metal barriers – interventions which consciously place cars above people.[12] They turn our city streets, in practice, from a shared public space to one in which people are allowed in limited circumstances. On Thames Street these pedestrian obstacles are very much in evidence. Down the central reservation runs an almost continuous black barrier, stopping people crossing where the city doesn't want them to. Sanctioned crossing places are at periodic traffic lights, and a few pedways which, unlike the walkway to nowhere, still bridge the street.

For about ten years now I have been attempting to walk every street in London, a probably futile endeavour. I strike off at the weekend to wander around a far-flung London neighbourhood or take a different route to the pub or shops to discover and explore, to find new streets. I really *know* the roads, paths and alleys of central London. I find myself pulled through a mental memory map of connections and cut-throughs. In my quest to

10 There are 2,025 miles of motorways in England and Wales. There are 208,673 miles of other roads and more than 140,000 miles of other public rights of way.

11 The term 'jay' comes from the early days of America where it meant a rustic – an indication of the status of pedestrians in modern American cities. The American jaywalking laws were, unsurprisingly, the result of motorcar lobbyists in the 1920s.

12 To add to this, too many of our town and city streets have become places to keep cars – private property stored on public highways (which all too often encroach on the spaces where the pedestrian should be the undisputed king: the pavements).

discover the pedways, I walk along the Thames Path between the Blackfriars and Millennium Bridges.[13] I've been along this stretch hundreds of times, and yet I've never noticed the smooth rampway turning away from the river. Perhaps I've been subconsciously put off venturing further by the words emblazoned across its entrance: ACCESS ONLY NO THROUGH ROUTE.

Walking up this path, as it gently twists and turns and runs through whole buildings, is disconcerting. It's the uncertainty of not knowing if I will have to turn back, but also the feeling of being in a part of a city I thought I knew so well but in a totally new space, on a path I never knew existed. Somewhere under my feet is Thames Street, the cars completely hidden from view, and then, suddenly, I emerge into a concrete courtyard. Standing at its centre is a bizarre sculpture, a totemic stack of heads, which starts from wide-eyed baby to skeletal old man, a representation of Shakespeare's Seven Ages of Man. Across the plaza is a little-used entrance to Blackfriars station, the whole courtyard elevated above another busy road, Queen Victoria Street. This surviving pedway seems to have been largely forgotten. At my laptop, I flick through the maps – Google, Ordnance Survey, Bing, Apple. It doesn't appear at all. Its record, its reality, is lost in a tangle of central London roads.

This area was redeveloped in the 1960s and 1970s, with Thames Street turned into a busy dual carriageway running through the heart of London. What resulted was the 'Traffic in Towns' report writ large, cars relatively unfettered and people encouraged to cross on their own walkways. The redevelopment also marked

13 The avenue which runs from the Millennium Bridge to St Paul's Cathedral, the view captured on millions of photographs, is actually a pedway itself, just not one that is elevated.

the end of river traffic for the docks on this part of the Thames. This change was lamented in the *Illustrated London News* in 1971: 'Just ten years ago, a barge was moored in Puddle Dock . . . now this is an underpass slip-road. The walk along Upper Thames Street was once a voyage through nineteenth-century commercial history . . . with frequent glimpses of the dark river between the buildings . . . in a few years traffic will roar along where previously barges lay at anchor.'

The cessation of boats stopping at Puddle Dock (and at its fellows – Anzac Wharf, Paul's Pier Wharf, Sunlight Wharf and Vitrea Wharf), was part of a wider decline in freight and passenger transport on the Thames. The towpath upriver was largely abandoned, a path seemingly without a purpose. In the late 1970s the River Thames Society and the Ramblers put forward a proposal for a new long-distance path along the river.[14] An idea which the Countryside Commission (now Natural England) made a reality. The Thames Path National Trail was opened in 1996: 194 miles long, from the source of the Thames in an unassuming Gloucestershire field, to the metallic shells of the Thames Barrier in Greenwich.

The Thames Path was just one of many leisure routes created in London in the second half of the twentieth century, new paths through this great big city. The Silver Jubilee Walkway, opened in 1977 to celebrate the anniversary of Queen Elizabeth's accession to the throne, is a fifteen-mile loop of the central London tourist sites.[15] Joining the Jubilee Walkway are two of the landmark walking routes in London, paths which

14 A Thames Path had first been proposed in the Hobhouse report of 1947 (which led to the National Parks and Access to the Countryside Act 1949). It was Ramblers volunteer David Sharp at the forefront of reviving the idea in the 1970s, mapping it out and writing the first guidebook for the trail.
15 The route was renamed simply 'The Jubilee Walkway' in 2002 to celebrate the fiftieth anniversary of Elizabeth II's accession.

encircle the whole city. The seventy-eight-mile Capital Ring,
fully opened in 2005, is a girdle round Greater London's mid-
point. And in 1998, as the *Kingston Informer* reported, there was
news of a 'new M25' which had 'environmentalists rubbing
their hands with glee – because this one is a path'. The London
Outer Orbital Path, usually known as the London LOOP, was
opened in 2001. It's perhaps surprising as a London path. While
staying mostly in the city's boroughs, it is largely a rural walk
through fields, woods and commons. A reflection of how the
city stretches out into the countryside (it could be said that the
Capital Ring goes through the city and the LOOP around it).
The London path for which I have the most affection is the
path of my childhood, the Green Chain Walk, which weaves
its way through south-east London. Unlike the other leisure
routes of London, the Green Chain is not just a linear trail but
a network. Fifty miles of paths link up hundreds of green
spaces across four London boroughs, the outer boroughs of
Bromley and Bexley, and the inner boroughs of Greenwich
and Lewisham.

What these leisure trails bring to London are new ways of
seeing and exploring the city on foot. They create links in the
capital city with the most parks in Europe, in a city of a thousand villages. Along these trails can be found the history of
London, grand and small. But many of these routes do not use
recorded public rights of way. Twelve of the thirty-two London
boroughs are statutorily defined as constituting 'Inner London'
(plus the City of London itself) and these are the only parts of
England and Wales (with the exception of the Isles of Scilly)
which are not required to have a legal map of public paths.[16]

16 The inner London boroughs are: Camden, Greenwich, Hackney, Ham-
mersmith and Fulham, Islington, Kensington and Chelsea, Lambeth,
Lewisham, Southwark, Tower Hamlets, Wandsworth and Westminster.

Local authorities in inner London *can* have a definitive map, but unsurprisingly none have voluntarily decided to create one so far. Public rights of way exist in inner London but they are not mapped, so every path has to be legally defended if and when an issue arises – the position that the rest of England and Wales faced before 1949. Paths across 123 square miles which do not have the same level of protection as the rest of the country.

Shooter's Hill sits right on the line between inner and outer London. Here the Green Chain Walk meets the Capital Ring at one of London's highest points. The hill for most of its history has been a place outside or on the very edge of the city, only brought within the Greater London fold 130 years ago (a mere fraction of time in the long history of London). Shooter's Hill has served as an entrance and a viewing platform, a place to reflect upon the sprawling metropolis and a steep thumb pointing the way to the capital. In Byron's epic poem, Don Juan gets out at Shooter's Hill:

> Sunset the time, the place the same declivity
> Which looks along that vale of good and ill
> Where London streets ferment in full activity . . .

Streets of suburban houses now curl and sprawl down the northern side of Shooter's Hill, but its southern flank is largely free from the march of what Thomas Macaulay called 'the long villas, embowered in lilacs and laburnums'. This side is a patchwork of ancient woodland, meadows and parkland crossed by dozens of paths.

On the slopes of Shooter's Hill is Shrewsbury Barrow, the sole survivor of a series of Bronze Age burial mounds; it is now enclosed behind neat railings, a small public green space among streets of 1930s semi-detached houses. A tantalizing possibility that prehistoric tracks once ran over the hill before the Romans built Watling Street from the ports of Kent to London (and beyond into the rest of England). This road, now the A207, runs dead straight over Shooter's Hill. It was the probable route that the pilgrims took in Chaucer's *Canterbury Tales*. It remained a key path into London, although a dangerous place, where 'ferocious footpads, cutpurses, highwaymen, cut-throats, and gentry of allied professions' would emerge from 'leafy coverts' to take 'liberal toll from wayfarers' (Henry IV ordered the clearing of some of the trees to protect those passing from 'violent practices'). As such an important artery into the city, Shooter's Hill was a place where the bodies of executed highwaymen were hanged (Samuel Pepys mentions this grisly sight in his diaries when he took this road on the 11 April 1661).

Perhaps some respectability, or at least improvement in the road itself, came from the turnpike trust established here in 1718 (just down the hill in Welling is the New Cross Turnpike, a pub and regular teenage haunt of mine), although the mail coach still struggled when going up the hill in the opening to Dickens's *A Tale of Two Cities*. Later still, it was part of the Second World War stop-line defences, including a flame fougasse – a forty-gallon drum of oil and petrol disguised in a fake shopfront, which could be ignited as the enemy came up the hill. Across the area can still be found strange concrete blocks and shapes, the remnants of the 1940s defence of London.[17]

Climbing to the top of Severndroog Castle, an eighteenth-century folly near the apex of the hill, I look down on home turf. South to my childhood home across the tarmac arteries of

17 In 2012, during the Olympics, another weapon of war, a Rapier missile battery was placed on the open ground of Shooter's Hill, on the meadows which adjoin Oxleas Woods.

the A2 and A20 and east to the Capability Brown landscaped gardens, and now public park, of Danson House. To the north is the Thames and the churchyard of St Mary Magdalene, Woolwich, where an aloof stone lion marks the grave of my boxing ancestor Tom Cribb, and to the west is where I have made my home in Lewisham. The view from Severndroog Castle may have looked very different. There have been multiple threats to the green spaces of Shooter's Hill – Oxleas Woods, Jack Wood, Shepherdleas Woods and Eltham Common. In the mid-nineteenth century, there was a proposal to create a military cemetery across large parts of the hill. The wild ancient woods would be cut down to be replaced by sensible avenues of yew and cypress. All the paths, the public rights of way, were to be severed or destroyed entirely to create 'The Shooters Hill Necropolis and United Services Mausoleum'. After this idea was abandoned, the next destructive proposal for Shooter's Hill came from its prominence and position as the gateway to London. In the 1860s, there was to be a military fort across the hill, with ditches dug, ramparts thrown up and all the trees felled to give a clear line of sight in a possible war with France on the soil of south-east London.

A much more recent threat to these woods and fields came in the 1980s. The Thatcher government, as part of its Roads for Prosperity plan (proudly billed as 'the largest road building programme since the Romans'), proposed the East London River Crossing, in part to aid in the regeneration of the Docklands on the north side of the Thames. From the river a six-lane motorway was planned to run right through the woods of Shooter's Hill. Opposition to the scheme, which rumbled on long after Thatcher had tearfully left Downing Street, was strong, chaotic, eclectic and wonderful. The Greater London Council, Greenwich Council and, eventually, the European Commission were all opposed. Traditional conservation and campaigning organizations lined up against the proposal, including CPRE, the Ramblers, the RSPB, the Wildlife Trusts and Friends of the Earth (they were even joined eventually in opposition by the British Road Federation). The greatest resistance came from local people, arranged under the banner People Against the River Crossing. But the cause also attracted a collection of tiny, strange groups. The Dragon, a pagan collective of 'witches, Odinists, druids [and] magicians', threw a magical protective ring around the site and the Fellowship of Isis, having received a spiritual message from W. B. Yeats, undertook a series of complex rituals to save the woods. Protest songs rang out from Shooter's Hill:

> I shall not cease from mental fight,
> Nor shall my sword sleep in my hand,
> Till we have saved old Oxleas Wood
> For England's green and pleasant land.

Each tree was adopted by a local, with the plan being that they would each physically defend 'their tree' from the path of the bulldozer. A series of legal battles ensued with the Department of Transport (nine local people put their houses on the line to fund their legal costs). Eventually on 7 July 1993, after more than eight years of fight, the Thames crossing and motorway proposals were dropped and Oxleas Woods were safe.

The paths of Shooter's Hill – from prehistory to the Romans, through pilgrimage and the coaching age to the pleasures of a simple stroll in the woods – are important; they really mean something. Millennia of continuity and change were almost swept away in the modern obsession with building more roads (which apparently, somehow, will suddenly lead to traffic disappearing).[18] Despite their lack of formal legal designation as

18 A battle is being fought in this regard over the Silvertown Tunnel, currently under construction. This underground crossing of the Thames will

public rights of way, people saved the paths of Shooter's Hill, their paths. I have the same territorial feeling. This last chapter has focused on London, my home. I can see myself, back through time, on Shooter's Hill. Walking through the woods' lower reaches, where it touches suburban fencing, as an awkward teenager on the way to school. A Christmas Day with my family at the top of the hill, footsteps on the ground coated with a rare festive snowfall. Drinking in the Bull, tucked away in streets flanking the straight Roman road. Despite my connection with this place, I am still not sure I completely understand its geography: how this path leads to the next, where it might break out into a clearing or a meadow. I can still get lost in the woods, seemingly finding endless new paths through the trees.

---

run between the Greenwich Peninsula (a stone's throw from Shooter's Hill) to Silvertown in the London Borough of Newham. The building programme of over £1 billion will bring even more cars into London, with yet more pollution, but without any facilities for walking or cycling.

Epilogue

The last few years have seen a revival in campaigning for greater and deeper public access to the countryside. In particular, a new generation of campaigners have joined the ranks of long-standing activists to seek, and to fight for, an expanded freedom to roam. They look to countries such as Norway, Estonia, Sweden and Scotland for examples of how greater freedom brings greater connection to the land. The Ramblers and the recently formed Right to Roam campaign want us to be able to explore more and have the opportunity to freely wander through woodland, along riversides and over the grasslands of England. An expanded freedom to roam leads to an uncovering of the hidden corners of our land – land from which we have too long been denied access, barred by the all too familiar sign: 'Private: Keep Out'.

Roaming freely we are invited to step off the path, but the importance of these linear routes, of the ways old and new, mustn't get lost in the noise and excitement of all these fresh possibilities. For paths, even where there is a freedom to roam, are crucial. For proof of this we only need look to Scotland. In a country where the freedom to wander is so deeply and rightly cherished, there is still the need and a clamour for paths. When the Land Reform (Scotland) Act 2003 confirmed in law a near universal right of access to land and inland waters, it also required all local authorities to designate a network of Core Paths in recognition of the fact that these would be essential to enable most people to enjoy their rights. Ramblers Scotland have incorporated this network, alongside other data, into a

Scottish Paths Map. This now records over 40,000 miles of paths in the most comprehensive map of its kind ever compiled. ScotWays (the Scottish Rights of Way and Access Society) is a doughty defender of access to Scotland's paths and has researched and mapped the most historically significant routes. In England and Wales, as in Scotland and across the globe, the practical importance of paths is still evident. These routes, with their clear ways, sometimes with stout signposts and the reassuring marks of walkers who have gone before, are still the primary means by which people experience the wider world on foot. They facilitate access for those who are unable to clamber over gates and through uncertain ground. They are physical guides in familiar and unfamiliar lands. In the words of H. G. Wells: 'There will be many footpaths in Utopia.'

From city streets to the mountainside, paths are being created and improved and new ways being charted, sometimes on the oldest of paths. Thousands of volunteers from the Ramblers, the British Horse Society, the Open Spaces Society, alongside a myriad of other voluntary and governmental organizations are working on such projects right now. In London and Manchester new green routes are emerging – calm and leafy ways which offer a respite from the drone and thunder of traffic. On the slopes and peaks of our National Parks the British Mountaineering Council is mending our mountains, repairing paths to ensure that people can continue to experience some of our wildest lands. Whether out in the open air or sitting behind a computer screen, volunteers safeguard and improve our paths for everyone, securing a public resource. The Slow Ways project is creating a grassroots movement of walkers, plotting routes between the settlements of Britain. Created by Dan Raven-Ellison, this initiative has been founded with the simple principle that 'people should be able to walk reasonably directly, safely and enjoyably between any two neighbouring villages, towns or cities' and is showing anew how this land can be experienced by putting one foot in front of the other. I hope that by reaching this epilogue, you have seen that paths are not simply utilitarian but infinitely more than that. They are connections not just from one place to another but from the present to the past – connections that deserve to endure long into the future.

Across Britain policy makers and legislators have sought to lay a protective cloak over our physical history – recorded, monitored and enforced through a patchwork of legislation and regulations. From the 1880s onwards we have safeguarded our most ancient history through the 'scheduled monument' designation, securing sites such as Stonehenge, West Kennet Long Barrow and the Lake District's Castlerigg Stone Circle. There are now half a million listed buildings in England and Wales, from medieval farmhouses, sixteenth-century stately homes and Victorian factories to Second World War pillboxes, futuristic petrol stations and twentieth-century office blocks. On land we protect almost fifty battlefields with their own special designation and at sea the same number of wreck sites are shielded from modern interference. The Blaenavon Industrial Landscape in south Wales, Oxfordshire's Blenheim Palace and the Jodrell Bank Observatory in Cheshire are just three of over twenty UNESCO World Heritage Sites in England and Wales, joining over a thousand places of natural, cultural and scientific importance around the globe.

The 1949 National Parks and Access to the Countryside Act is not usually placed alongside legislation such as the Ancient Monuments Protection Act (1882) or the Protection of Wrecks Act (1973), but, as Britain recovered from war, in the throes of nationalizing industries and creating the National Health Service, the Attlee government decided to protect our paths. The creation of the definitive map and the recording of rights of way not only secured public access to the countryside in England and

Wales but also helped to preserve our collective heritage. The 140,000 miles of footpaths, bridleways and byways now found on the definitive map are – as much as enigmatic stone circles, manor houses and fancy Georgian terraces – markers of a long material and physical history, which have survived through centuries of change and upheaval.

The ways I've walked, the Droitwich salt way, the quarrymen's path through the Dinorwic Quarry and the pilgrimage routes to Chittlehampton, alongside thousands of other paths across England and Wales, represent a great open-air museum of movement – created and used for a myriad of different functions but all part of one whole. This network of paths was formed and solidified by generations making and remaking their landscape on foot and horseback, their actions now fixed in time. The story of how paths were created or destroyed, or where we fought to protect them, is fundamental to our working-class history. They are living expressions of 'the ordinary' over generations.

The nineteenth-century American diplomat Elihu Burritt described the paths of Britain as spaces that 'thread pasture, park, and field, seemingly permeating her whole green world with dusky veins for the circulation of human life'. This network of threads, of veins, is worth fighting for. In February 2022, the UK government announced its intention to repeal the deadline by which historical rights of way need to be recorded in England (the same was announced by the Welsh government in 2018). It looked, for a brief time, that our paths would be reprieved. However, following lobbying from vested interests, from landowners, a U-turn came. The government backtracked, only delaying the date to 2031. The Ramblers have identified over 49,000 miles of potentially lost paths which are now at risk, paths which face being swept away for ever.

We are all brief stewards of our world, with a duty to leave it better than we came into it. To face up to the climate emergency which will ravage the globe, to restore and cherish nature and to protect our history. Paths can't be divorced from this history; they deserve recording and protecting. Each application to save an unrecorded right of way is a mini research project. An exploration of the stories of individual paths which shine brightly when the light of enquiry is turned upon them. Stories of our paths which can then be passed to the next generation.

I hope that this book serves as a call to arms. Our paths were legally mapped from the 1950s onwards by ordinary people, and it was a great work of the citizenry to record their right to access the land. I hope that you now want to join thousands of citizen volunteers in delving into the archives, tracing time back through the records to reconstruct a history of public use in order to apply for more of our paths, for more of our history, to go back on the map. And, beyond that, we must fight to secure and improve what we already have. We can't preserve our paths in aspic; we have seen how our network has evolved, but every single change that reroutes or destroys a path needs to be made only when completely necessary and fought against when it isn't. So join the movement to protect and reclaim our history on foot. And walk – walk in celebration and in a continual reassertion of our history, so that our paths can live on long into the future.

Further Reading

While writing about our paths, I had the pleasure of delving into many aspects of the UK's past and present. My research led me down many avenues and introduced me to wonderful scholarship in areas including anthropology, mathematics, poetry, science, religion, cartography, law and history (from prehistory up to the present day).

Below are some of my key sources and suggestions for further reading. In addition to the chapter-specific notes, the following sources were crucial to the writing of this book:

British History Online, www.british-history.ac.uk

The British Newspaper Archive, www.britishnewspaperarchive. co.uk

Sarah Bucks and Phil Wadey, *Rights of Way: Restoring the Record* (2017) (the definitive handbook for reclaiming lost paths)

'Cof Cymru – National Historic Assets of Wales', Cadw, cadw.gov. wales/advice-support/cof-cymru

C. W. Scott-Giles, *The Road Goes On: A Literary and Historical Account of the Highways, Byways, and Bridges of Great Britain* (1946) (which took me to many other historical sources)

'Designated Sites View', Natural England, designatedsites.naturalengland.org.uk

'The National Heritage List for England', Historic England, historicengland.org.uk/listing/the-list

National Library of Scotland, maps.nls.uk

Richard Oliver, *Ordnance Survey Maps: A Concise Guide for Historians* (2013)

Oxford Dictionary of National Biography, www.oxforddnb.com

Survey of English Place-Names, epns.nottingham.ac.uk

A Vision of Britain Through Time, www.visionofbritain.org.uk

I also want to recognize two authors who I fell back in love with while writing this book and whose words periodically pepper its pages: Richard Jefferies and Thomas Hardy.

LAND

1. Ancient Highways

Martin Bell, *Making One's Way in the World: The Footprints and Track-ways of Prehistoric People* (2020)

Martin Bell and Jim Leary, 'Pathways to Past Ways: A Positive Approach to Routeways and Mobility', *Antiquity* 94, no. 377 (2020): 1349–59

Alan Cooper, 'Once a Highway, Always a Highway: Roads and English Law, *c.* 1150–1300', in *Roadworks: Medieval Britain, Medieval Roads*, eds. Valarie Allen and Ruth Evans (2016)

D. J. Garner, *The Neolithic and Bronze Age Settlement at Oversley Farm, Styal, Cheshire: Excavations in Advance of Manchester Airport's Second Runway* (2007)

Sarah Harrison, 'The Icknield Way: Some Queries', *Archaeological Journal* 160, no.1 (2003): 1–22

Tim Ingold, *Being Alive: Essays on Movement, Knowledge and Description* (2011) (the quote on p. 8 comes from this tremendous collection of essays)

Rhiannon Philp, 'Changing Tides: The Archaeological Context of Sea Level Change in Prehistoric South Wales' (PhD diss., Cardiff University, 2018)

Paul Richard Preston and Thomas Kador, 'Approaches to Interpreting Mesolithic Mobility and Settlement in Britain and Ireland',

Journal of World Prehistory 31, no. 3 (2018): 321–45

Andrew Reynolds and Alexander Langlands, 'Travel as Communication: A Consideration of Overland Journeys in Anglo-Saxon England', *World Archaeology* 43, no. 3 (2011): 410–27

Philip Strange, 'The Dorsetshire Gap – A Special Place', *Philip Strange Science and Nature Writing*, 2014

2. Animals

K. J. Bonser, *The Drovers* (1970)

Idris Evans, *Hard Road to London: A Graphic Account of the Lives of the Welsh Drovers* (2008)

Michael R. Evans, *Inventing Eleanor: The Medieval and Post-Medieval Image of Eleanor of Aquitaine* (2014)

Ruth Fasnach, *A History of the City of Oxford* (1954)

Jonathan Glancey, 'Outrage Revisited – from Northampton to Daventry', *Guardian*, 2010

William Page, ed., *A History of the County of Oxford: Volume 2* (1907)

Bruce Smith, Local Drove Roads, localdroveroads.co.uk

John Steane, 'Bernwood Forest – Past, Present and Future', *Arboricultural Journal* 9, no. 1 (1985): 39–55

Shirley Toulson, *The Drovers* (2011)

Shirley Toulson with photographs by Fay Godwin, *The Drovers' Roads of Wales* (1977)

University of Sheffield, 'Showmanship, Magic and Illusion', 'The Fairground Bioscope Shows' and 'The History of the Fairground', National Fairground and Circus Archive

Andrew Venner, *Wotton Underwood: 1881–1990* (1976)

3. The Parish Road and Turnpike

Dan Bogart, 'The Turnpike Roads of England and Wales', in *The Online Historical Atlas of Transport, Urbanization and Economic Development in England and Wales c. 1680–1911*, eds. L. Shaw-Taylor, D. Bogart and M. Satchel (2017)

Alan Cooper, *Bridges, Law and Power in Medieval England, 700–1400* (2006)

R. Sharpe France, 'William Yates: Cartographer', *Transactions of The Historic Society of Lancashire and Cheshire* 109, (1957)

J. B. Harley, 'William Yates and Peter Burdett: Their Role in the Mapping of Lancashire and Cheshire in the Late Eighteenth Century', *Transactions of The Historic Society of Lancashire and Cheshire* 115, (1962)

David Harrison, Peter McKeague and Bruce Watson, *The Bridge Chapels of Medieval Britain: A New Gazetteer* (2019)

Brian Jones, *The Old Roads and Trackways through Carnforth* (2022)

Joan Parkes, *Travel in England in the Seventeenth Century* (1925)

Eric Pawson, *Transport and Economy: The Turnpike Roads of Eighteenth Century Britain* (1977)

Linda Porter, *Mary Tudor: The First Queen* (2007)

Michael Shrubb, *The Lapwing* (2007)

Timur Guran Tatlioglu, 'Biographies of People and Place: The Harewood Estate, 1698–1813' (PhD diss., University of York, 2010)

William Makepeace Thackeray, *Roundabout Papers* (1860) (the quote on p. 64 is from this title)

Andrew White, 'The Garstang-Heron Syke Turnpike Road: Two Examples of Modernisation in the Nineteenth Century', *Contrebis* 28, (2004): 30–32

Sidney Webb and Beatrice Webb, *English Local Government: The Story of The King's Highway* (1913)

Geoffrey N. Wright, *Turnpike Roads* (1992)

4. Railway Mania

Fernando Ascensão and César Capinha, 'Aliens on the Move: Transportation Networks and Non-native Species', in *Railway Ecology*, eds. Luís Borda-de-Água, Rafael Barrientos, Pedro Beja and Henrique Miguel Pereira (2017)

Robin Atthill, *The Somerset & Dorset Railway* (1968)

Mike Beale, '150 Years of the Somerset & Dorset Railway', *BackTrack Magazine*, 2008

Simon Bradley, *The Railways: Nation, Network and People* (2016)

Anthony Burton, *Walking the Line: Enjoying Disused Railways and Tramways in Britain* (1985)

Tim Deacon, *The Somerset & Dorset Aftermath of the Beeching Axe* (1996)

Nicholas Faith, *The World the Railways Made* (1990)

Steph Gillet, *The Somerset & Dorset Railway Through Time* (2016)

Paul Readman, *Storied Ground: Landscape and the Shaping of English National Identity* (2018)

Leigh Shaw-Taylor and Xuesheng You, 'The Development of the Railway Network in Britain 1825–1911', in *The Online Historical Atlas of Transport, Urbanization and Economic Development in England and Wales c. 1680–1911*, eds. L. Shaw-Taylor, D. Bogart and M. Satchel (2017)

Christian Wolmar, *Fire and Steam: A New History of the Railways in Britain* (2007)

5. From the Ground

Daphne du Maurier, *Vanishing Cornwall* (1967) (the quote on p. 85 is from this title)

Michael Freeman, Sublime Wales, sublimewales.wordpress.com (an extraordinary collection of early impressions of Wales from tourists, scientists and writers from the seventeenth century onwards, including those early explorers of Yr Wyddfa)

Gillian Hutton, 'Roads and Routeways in County Durham: 1530–1730' (PhD diss., Durham University, 2011)

National Slate Museum in Llanberis

Ted Nield, *Underland: A Journey Through Britain's Lost Landscape* (2014)

Oliver Rackham, *The History of the Countryside* (1986) (also for Chapter 6 on hedge planting and enclosure)

Arthur Raistrick, *A History of Lead Mining in the Pennines* (1965)

Alun John Richards, *Slate Quarrying in Wales* (2006)

6. Enclosure

Corianne Fowler, *Green Unpleasant Land* (2020)

Jon Gregory and Sarah Spooner, 'Mapping a Changing Landscape: Breckland c. 1750–1920', *Journal of Breckland Studies* (2020)

Nick Hayes, *The Book of Trespass* (2020) (also for chapter 15 on Kinder Scout)

Christopher Hill, *Reformation to Industrial Revolution: A Social and Economic History of Britain, 1530–1780* (1969) (the quote on p. 105 is from this title)

Amanda Claire Jones, ' "Commotion Time": the English Risings of 1549' (PhD diss., University of Warwick, 2003)

Eric L. Jones, *Landed Estates and Rural Inequality in English History* (2018) (in particular, the chapter on road capture)

Christina Bosco Langert, 'Hedgerows and Petticoats: Sartorial Subversion and Anti-Enclosure Protest in Seventeenth-Century England', *Early Theatre* 12, no. 1 (2009): 119–35

G. E. Mingay, *Parliamentary Enclosure in England: An Introduction to its Causes, Incidence and Impact, 1750–1850* (1997)

Katrina Navickas, A History of Public Space, www.historyofpublic-space.uk

Marion Shoard, *This Land is Our Land* (1997) (in particular on the extent of parliamentary enclosures)

Marion Shoard, *The Theft of the Countryside* (1982)

Guy Shrubsole, *Who Owns England?* (2019)

E. P. Thompson, *The Making of the English Working Class* (1991) (in my early twenties, this was my introduction to land justice, and it still sparkles upon rereading)

LIFE AND DEATH

7. In Work and Poverty

Burton Latimer Heritage Society, www.burtonlatimer.info

Nicholas Crowson, ' "Tramps" Tales: Discovering the History of Homelessness in Britain', YouTube, 2017

Peter Higginbotham, *On the Road: First-Hand Accounts of Visits to Workhouse Casual Wards from Somerset to Yorkshire (1928–35)* (2017)

Peter Higginbotham, The Workhouse: A Story of an Institution, www.workhouses.org.uk (an invaluable website – Peter Higginbotham's contribution to the history of the workhouse cannot be overstated)

Julie Hipperson, ' "Efficiency on Foot"? The Well-Run Estate of Nineteenth-Century England', in *Walking Histories, 1800–1914*, eds. Chad Bryant, Arthur Burns and Paul Readman (2016) (for the story of the Gloucestershire carpenter who walked fourteen miles a day to and from work)

E. J. Hobsbawm, 'The Tramping Artisan', *Economic History Review* 3, no. 3 (1951): 299–320

Tony Ireson, *Northamptonshire* (1954)

North Mymms History Project, www.northmymmshistory.uk

Humphrey Southall, 'The Tramping Artisan Revisits: Labour Mobility and Economic Distress in Early Victorian England', *Economic History Review* 44, no. 2 (1991): 272–96

8. The Church, Death and Taxes

Mick Aston, *Monasteries in the Landscape* (2009)

Professor Janet Burton, The Cistercians in Wales, www.monas-ticwales.org

Alan Cleaver and Lesley Park, *The Corpse Roads of Cumbria* (2018) (a wonderful book about these deathly paths)

Paul Devereux, *Spirit Roads* (2003)

Eric J. Evans, *A History of the Tithe System in England* (1970)

W. G. Hoskins, *The Age of Plunder: King Henry's England, 1500–1547* (1976)

Emilia Jamroziak, 'Centres and Peripheries', and Constance Hoffman Berman, 'Agriculture and Economies', in *The Cambridge Companion to the Cistercian Order*, ed. Mette Birkedal Bruun (2013)

W. H. Matthews, *Mazes and Labyrinths* (1907)

Jan Morris, *Wales: Epic Views of a Small Country* (1998) (the quote on p. 145 is from this title)

Nick Peyton, 'The Dissolution of the English Monasteries: A Quantitative Investigation' (PhD diss., LSE, 2020)

Eddie Procter, Landscapism, www.landscapism.blogspot.com (a beautiful and expert documentation of the Cistercians' paths of South Wales)

Eddie Procter, 'The Topographical Legacy of the Medieval Monastery: Evolving Perceptions and Realities of Monastic Landscapes in the Southern Welsh Marches' (PhD diss., University of Exeter, 2019)

Nicholas Rudd-Jones and David Stewart, *Pathways* (2011)

Kim Taplin, *The English Path* (1979) (a magnificent stroll of a book looking at our paths in literature and art)

Edward Trollope, 'Notices of Ancient and Mediæval labyrinths', *Archaeological Journal* 15, no. 1 (1858): 216–35 (and the addendum 'Additional Notes on Mazes in England' by Albert Way)

The World-Wide Labyrinth Locator, www.labyrinthlocator.com

9. Pilgrims' Paths

Matthew R. Anderson, 'Luther and the Trajectories of Western Pilgrimage', *International Journal of Religious Tourism and Pilgrimage* 7, no. 1 (2019): 52–61

Peter Beacham with photographs by James Ravilious, *Down the Deep Lanes* (2018)

Hilaire Belloc, *The Old Road* (1904)

Derek Bright, *The Pilgrim's Way: Fact and Fiction of an Ancient Trackway* (2011)

Reverend J. F. Chanter, 'St. Urith of Chittlehampton: A Study in an Obscure Devon Saint', *The Transactions of The Devonshire Association*, 1914

F. C. Elliston Erwood, 'The "Pilgrim's Way": Its Antiquity and its Alleged Mediæval Use', *Archaeologia Cantiana* 37, (1925): 43831

The Gough Map Research Project, www.goughmap.org

Kathryn Hurlock, *Medieval Welsh Pilgrimage, c. 1100–1500* (2018)

Martin D. Locker, 'Landscapes of Pilgrimage in Medieval Britain' (PhD diss., UCL, 2012)

Mark Rosen, 'A New Chronology of the Construction and Restoration of the Medici Guardaroba in the Palazzo Vecchio, Florence', *Mitteilungen Des Kunsthistorischen Institutes in Florenz* 53, no. 2/3 (2009)

Diana Webb, *Pilgrimage in Medieval England* (2000)

WATER

10. Salt Ways

Jane M. Adams, *Healing with Water: English Spas and the Water Cure, 1840–1960* (2015)

S. A. M. Adshead, *Salt and Civilization* (1992)

Andy Evans, Wonders of Britain, www.wondersofbritain.org (an excellent compendium of Nennius' wonders and their various interpretations)

G. B. Grundy, 'The Ancient Highways and Tracks of Worcestershire and the Middle Severn basin', *Archaeological Journal* 91, no. 1 (1934): 66–96

Peter J. Neville Havins, *The Spas of England* (1976) (for some of the later history of the town and the wider context of spa towns)

W. G. Hoskins, *The Making of the English Landscape* (2013)

J. D. Hurst, *Savouring the Past: The Droitwich Salt Industry* (1992)

Pierre Laszlo, *Salt: Grain of Life* (2001)

Tony Marsh, Blisworth, www.blisworth.org.uk

Barbara Middlemass, *John Corbett: Pillar of Salt 1817–1901* (2017)

The Salt Museum at the Droitwich Spa Heritage Centre

11. The Climate Coast

Patrick Barkham, *Coastlines: The Story of Our Shore* (2015)

James Gleick, *Chaos: Making a New Science* (1987) (for the coastline paradox and an enthralling read on randomness and un-randomness in the universe)

Sophia Kingshill and Jennifer Westwood, *The Fabled Coast: Legends & Traditions from Around the Shores of Britain & Ireland* (2012)

Phil Mathison, *The Legendary Lost Town of Ravenser: On the Trail of Yorkshire's Famous Vanished Seaport* (2015)

Stephen Neale, *The England Coast Path: 1,000 Mini Adventures Around the World's Longest Coastal Path* (2020)

Jules Pretty, *This Luminous Coast: Walking England's Eastern Edge* (2011) (the quote on p. 206 is from this title)

12. Drainage

Bryony Coles and John Coles, *Sweet Track to Glastonbury: The Somerset Levels in Prehistory* (1986)

Susanna Wade Martins, *Farmers, Landlords and Landscapes: Rural Britain, 1720 to 1870* (2004)

Stephen Minnitt, 'The Iron-Age Wetlands of Central Somerset', in *Somerset Archaeology: Papers to Mark 150 years of the Somerset Archaeological and Natural History Society*, ed. C. J. Webster (2000)

Stephen Minnitt and John Coles, *Lake Villages of Somerset* (2006)

Michael Williams, *The Draining of the Somerset Levels* (1970)

Michael Williams, 'The Enclosure of Waste Land in Somerset, 1700–1900', *Transactions of the Institute of British Geographers* 57, (1972): 99–123

Robin Williams and Romey Williams, *The Somerset Levels* (2003)

CONFLICT

13. The War at Home

Bomber County Aviation Resource, www.bcar.org.uk

Council for British Archaeology, Defence of Britain Archive (2002), archaeologydataservice.ac.uk/archives/view/dob

William Foot, *Beaches, Fields, Streets, and Hills: The Anti-Invasion Landscapes of England, 1940* (2006)

Paul Francis, Richard Flagg and Graham Crisp, *Nine Thousand Miles of Concrete: A Review of Second World War Temporary Airfields in England* (2016)

Mairi Robertson and John Schofield, 'Monuments in Wartime: Conservation Policy in Practice, 1939–45', *Conservation Bulletin*, no. 37 (2000): 16–19

South Keveston District Council, *Heritage of flight in South Lincolnshire*

L. Parker Temple III and Peter L. Portanova, 'Project Emily and Thor IRBM Readiness in the United Kingdom, 1955–1960', *Air Power History* 56, no. 3 (2009): 26–51

14. *The Warpath*

Reverend F. H. Arnold, 'The Corn Supply of the South Coast in British and Roman Times', *Sussex Archaeological Collections* 39, (1894): 154–60

Hugh Davies, *Roads in Roman Britain* (2002)

Mike Haken, 'Navio (Brough on Noe) to Templeborough (2018)', Roman Roads Research Association, roadsofromanbritain.org (the association's whole website is an excellent resource)

David Inglis, *The Roman Road Project: Excavation and Geophysical Survey of Linear Features at Sheep Hill Farm, Sheffield, South Yorkshire* (2016)

Alexander Langlands, *The Ancient Ways of Wessex: Travel and Communication in an Early Medieval Landscape* (2019)

Long Distance Walkers Association, Long Distance Paths (database)

Meredith Leigh Wiggins, 'Roman Households: Space, Status and Identity' (PhD diss., University of London, 2014)

15. *Protest and Protection*

About Rivington: Two Lads, www.about-rivington.co.uk

Kate Ashbrook, Framfield Footpath Story, campaignerkate.wordpress.com

William Atkins, *The Moor: Lives, Landscape, Literature* (2014)

John Bainbridge, *The Compleat Trespasser: Journeys into Forbidden Britain* (2020)

David Hey, 'Kinder Scout and the Legend of the Mass Trespass', *Agricultural History Review* 59, no. 2 (2011): 199–216

David Killingray, 'Rights, "Riot" and Ritual: The Knole Park Access

Dispute, Sevenoaks, Kent, 1883–5', *Rural History* 5, no. 1 (1994): 63–79

Nicholas Kingsley, 'Ainsworth of Smithills Hall and Moss Bank', *Landed Families of Britain and Ireland*, 2013, www.landedfamilies. blogspot.com

Donald W. Lee, *The Flixton Footpath Battle* (1976)

Mike Parker, *The Wild Rover: A Blistering Journey Along Britain's Footpaths* (2011)

The Ramblers, *Kinder 60* (1992)

Paul Salveson, *Will Yo' Come O' Sunday Morning: The 1896 Battle for Winter Hill* (1996)

Chris Smith, Mr Van Hoogstraten's Path, Uckfield, travelloglewes. co.uk

LEISURE

16. A Challenge

John Hillaby, *Journey Through Britain* (1986)

John Hurley, *Tom Cribb: The Life of the Black Diamond* (2009) (I'd also recommend a pint or two at the Tom Cribb pub just off London's Haymarket to gaze at the walls of early boxing memorabilia)

Geoff Nicholson, *The Lost Art of Walking: The History, Science, Philosophy, Literature, Theory and Practice of Pedestrianism* (2011) (quite possibly my favourite book about walking)

Peter Radford, *The Celebrated Captain Barclay: Sport, Money and Fame in Regency Britain* (2001)

Walter Thom, *Pedestrianism; or, An Account of the Performances of Celebrated Pedestrians during the Last and Present Century* (1813)

17. Rambling

Maxwell Ayamba, ' "Our hikes were a political statement": The Sheffield Walkers Reclaiming 2,000 Years of Rural History', *Inkcap Journal*, 2021

V. V. Brown, 'To Be Black in the British Countryside Means Being an Outsider', *Guardian*, 2020

Rhiane Fatinikun, 'The Trail Blazer: The Rewards of Setting up a Walking Group', *Guardian*, 2022

Amelia Hill, ' "We Didn't Feel It Was for Us": The UK's Minority Ethnic Walking Groups Tearing Down Barriers', *Guardian*, 2022 (the quote from Sophie Brown on p. 303 appears in this article)

Professor Glen O'Hara, 'Roaming the Countryside is Our Right – We Must Fight to Preserve It', *Guardian*, 2021

Professor Glen O'Hara, Dr Claire Hickman, Dr Tom Breen and Dr Abbi Flint, In All Our Footsteps: Tracking, Mapping and Experiencing Rights of Way in Post-War Britain, allourfootsteps.uk

Rebecca Solnit, *Wanderlust: A History of Walking* (2002) (also for Chapter 8 on labyrinths and Chapter 15 for the history of early path protection societies)

Simon Robert Thompson, 'The Fashioning of a New World: Youth Culture and the Origins of the Mass Outdoor Movement in Interwar Britain' (PhD diss., Kings College London, 2018)

Rodney Whittaker, 'Before 1949, "In a confused state" ', in *Walk*, 2019 (as part of the wider article 'A Rambling Revolution' by Andrew McCloy)

Andy Wright, 'Rowdy "Mystery Hikes" to Undisclosed Locations Were All the Rage in the '30s', in *Atlas Obscura*, 2017

URBAN

18. The New Towns

Roger Bastable, *Then and Now, Crawley* (2004)

Christopher Beanland, 'Just Like Starting Over: When Britain (Briefly) Fell in Love with New Towns', *The Long + Short*, 2017

Dr Alex Chapman, *Routes to Nature: Unlocking Local Access in England and Wales* (2023)

Dr Alex Chapman, *Who Has a Public Right of Way? An Analysis of Provision and Inequity in England and Wales* (2022)

Mark Clapson, 'The English New Towns Since 1946: What are the Lessons of their History for their Future?', *Histoire Urbaine* 50, no. 3 (2017): 87–105

John Grindrod, *Concretopia: A Journey Around the Rebuilding of Postwar Britain* (2014)

Peter Gwynne, *A History of Crawley* (1990)

T. P. Hudson, ed., *A History of the County of Sussex: Volume 6 Part 3, Bramber Rape (North-Eastern Part) Including Crawley New Town* (1987)

Oral histories at Crawley Museum, crawleymuseums.org

Guy Ortolano, *Thatcher's Progress: From Social Democracy to Market Liberalism through an English New Town* (2019)

Frederic Osborn, *New Towns After the War* (1942)

Frederic Osborn and Arnold Whittick, *The New Towns: The Answer to Megalopolis* (1963)

Frank Schaffer, *The New Town Story* (1970)

19. The City and the Suburbs

Simon Bradley and Nikolaus Pevsner, *Buildings of England, London 1: The City of London* (1997)

Charles George Harper, *The Dover Road: Annals of an Ancient Turnpike* (1895)

The Landscape Architects' Association, *London Loop & Capital Ring Walks: History and Landscape Planning* (2016)

Chris Bevan Lee, *The Pedway: Elevating London* (2013)

David Sharp, *Thames Path* (2010)

Oliver Wainwright, 'Walkways in the Sky: The Return of London's Forgotten "pedways"', *Guardian*, 2017

Owen Ward, 'A Forgotten Part of London's Heritage', Save Bloomsbury, savebloomsbury.co.uk

Tom Wareham, *Oxleas: History, Conservation and Connection in a Suburban Woodland* (2020)

Acknowledgements

It has been a privilege and a joy to write this book. My huge thanks go to those who helped from the beginning, with my very first footsteps through the writing world. To my agent, Adam Gauntlett, for his always wise counsel (and all at Peters Fraser + Dunlop); the whole team at Penguin Michael Joseph, in particular my wonderful editor, Jill Taylor, who has kept me buoyed up and improved the text immeasurably; Jonny Ainslie for his invaluable research skills, on everything from tithes and turnpikes to pedways and pilgrimage; and Richard King, who very helpfully steered me through whole new lands. My endless thanks, friendship and love go to Ewan Harrison, who has been there with me on this journey from the very start.

My thanks and appreciation go to all the volunteers I have worked with at the Ramblers. Their dedication and enthusiasm for protecting our paths and ensuring access to the countryside continues to inspire me every week. To all my Ramblers colleagues for their good humour and commitment to a truly great cause – you are all amazing. In particular, for their words of encouragement and support, I would like to thank Tom Platt, Stephen Russell, Sophia Khan and the fabulous Paths team – Eugene Suggett, Sophie Reindorp, Kate Jury, Helen Bates, Heather Clatworthy and Josie Mizen.

I'm indebted to those who shared with me their knowledge, passion and scholarship; there is nothing more joyful than talking to someone about a subject they love. To Brian Jones for his immense help in untangling the many lines of human communication through the valleys of Lancashire; Sarah Bucks for her expertise and enthusiasm for the sometimes overlooked paths and landscape of the Somerset Levels, and for her ongoing support (and to Phil Wadey, her co-writer on *Rights of Way: Restoring the Record*); Bruce Smith for our extremely helpful chats about the Oxford Road (and his excellent website Local Drove Roads); Jim Leary for casting an expert eye over an early draft of the 'Ancient Highways' chapter; Tony Davy for sharing his books and knowledge on the ecology of the Brecklands; Chris Smith, whose walk guided me through the fields of Sussex to Framfield Footpath 9; Brendan Paddy for his always insightful Scottish perspectives; John Bainbridge and Kate Ashbrook for sharing their knowledge of the history of protest and protection of public paths; John Rowlands for his insights on flood adaption; Ian Mitchell for providing leads and information on the enclosure roads of Norfolk and to Sarah Spooner for giving me a sneak preview of her and Jon Gregory's work on the paths of the same county; Paul Wood for his tree identification skills; and to those involved in the In All Footsteps project, for their encouragement and passion for paths – Claire Hickman, Glen O'Hara, Abi Flint and Tom Breen. To these names, I would like to add a mark of appreciation to all those passionate about their communities, who delve into the past to uncover local history – the unsung writers of information boards, leaflets, plaques and parish websites which have been so helpful in writing this book.

Some wonderful friends rambled the lost paths of this book with me: I discovered the beauty of the Dorsetshire Gap with Liv Freeman and had an excellent day exploring a boiling hot Buckinghamshire with Anna Lidgate (despite our run-in with a particularly frisky herd of cows). Ed Jennings was exceptional company, as always, on our rather circuitous wander around rural Lincolnshire, and I loved marching in inspirational joy with Lil Ratcliffe and all the commemorators of the 1896 Winter Hill Trespass. At the risk of accidentally leaving out some names,

I want to thank my glorious friends. Writing this book at the weekends and in the evenings, I haven't always seen as much of you as I'd like, but you mean the world to me. I have already mentioned some of these magnificent people, but to add to this list and in appreciation of all the drinks, dinners and distractions when I was deep in writing: Eve Castle, Harriet Curtis, Jessica Benson-Egglenton, Chloë Arnold, Jamie Smallbone, Katie Traver, Ben Gridley, Tim Silman, Tom Mclenachan, Laura Cassidy, Sam King, Roy Ashman, Lauren King, Katie Clifford, Toby Roycroft, Rosamund West, Kate Miles, Dave Drew, Frances Ryan, Sarah Crocker, Claire Le Houx and Paul Kociucki. And to the 'lads', because I wouldn't hear the end of it: Dan, Dean, Phil, Will, James and Ollie.

Last, but by no means least, I want to thank my family. To my amazing mum, dad, my brother Sam and to Bryony for their continuing support and love. And to my nan, who died before this book was published, and my two nephews, Max and Charlie, to whom this book is dedicated.

Picture Credits

Appendix

The Ramblers

The Ramblers is Britain's largest walking charity, founded on 1 January 1935 as the Ramblers Association, which is still the formal name of the organization. The 1930s saw a hiking boom sweep across the country, but it was a time when many people's access to paths and open country was challenged (perhaps most memorably on Kinder Scout in the Peak District). In its earliest days, the Ramblers was most associated with advocating for access to the moors and the mountains, primarily in the north of England, and with the creation of long-distance trails. But the Ramblers soon became a force for action and campaigning for our paths everywhere, to ensure that we have a network of paths, tracks and trails which reach into every community, whether out in wild open country, through farmland or in our towns and cities. The spirit of the 1930s still lives on in the Ramblers – it can be seen in the charity's work to secure and protect access for the public and in fostering and enabling a love of walking across Britain.

Looking back on the last nine decades, we can see a step change in the public's ability to access our wonderful natural landscapes. Successive legislation has enabled people to walk and wander further, with greater confidence and with their rights protected. The Ramblers, including Ramblers Cymru and Ramblers Scotland, has played a crucial role in securing these Acts of Parliament and they naturally pepper and help define the history of the organization. At the heart of this book is one of those signature victories: the National Parks and Access to the Countryside Act 1949. Proudly declared by Lewis Silkin as a 'people's charter . . . for everyone who lives to get out into the open air and enjoy the countryside', it created our National Parks and National Trails and, vitally, ensured that our historic paths are recorded and protected for everyone.

The Ramblers was instrumental in the passing of the Countryside and Rights of Way Act 2000, which opened up for the public vast open country and registered common land in England and Wales, and the Land Reform (Scotland) Act 2003, which gave the public the legal right of responsible access to nearly all land and inland water in Scotland. Similar campaigning by the Ramblers led to the creation of the Wales Coast Path and the passing of the Marine and Coastal Access Act 2009, which created the England Coast Path (when the establishment of this 2,700-mile long-distance path was seen to be in danger, the Ramblers memorably chivvied it on by pitching up in Parliament Square in an ice cream van). Behind and alongside these legislative victories is the perhaps less flashy work: influencing policy and regulations, demonstrations, countering Private Members' bills which could erode people's rights of access, and fostering relationships with partners and politicians.

But the Ramblers are not just looking back with satisfaction on what has been achieved in the past; they are looking forward for the next big step to unlock the outdoors, especially for the almost 40 per cent of people who are more than fifteen minutes' walk from green space. Recent research from the New Economics Foundation, commissioned by the Ramblers, showed that the public path network in England and Wales is worth almost £2 billion in health and wellbeing value per year but that access is unequal.[19] The Ramblers are advocating for an Access to

19 The research can be read in full on the Ramblers website at ramblers.org. uk/paths

Nature Bill, to set legally binding targets for expanding and improving our path network. This would set quality standards and ensure that more of our paths are genuinely open for all. It would build on the successes of the Countryside and Rights of Way Act 2000 by expanding the freedom to walk freely to woodlands and watersides whilst also ensuring that our historic paths can be reclaimed long into the future.

In celebrating the Ramblers' fiftieth anniversary, Tom Stephenson, the Ramblers' first full-time employee and leading light for so many years, wrote that it had been five decades of 'fellowship with men and women who found beauty in the land and strove that others may enjoy that beauty'. There is a power in this fellowship and in collective action, which runs through the history of the Ramblers and which thrives to the present day. The Ramblers now has over 100,000 members and 22,000 volunteers, and these people are the charity's beating heart. Volunteers in the 500 local Ramblers groups share their passion and enthusiasm for walking by leading 50,000 walks a year. Ramblers Wellbeing Walks, led by volunteers, are free, short walks that take place all across England. They're designed to help people take their first step towards better health and wellbeing. Ramblers volunteers have been at the forefront of creating many of the much-loved regional and National Trails which lace the country, and members and volunteers have created a library of over 4,000 routes on the 'ordinary' (but really extraordinary) path network for those who want to discover the beauty of our paths by themselves.

None of these activities, indeed any good walk in the country, would be possible without the work that the thousands of volunteers do to protect, improve and expand the fundamental infrastructure for walking. Every day, the volunteers lobby, campaign and advocate for their local paths and respond to any threats to the network. Any proposed change to the path network in England and Wales (around 1,200 a year) is carefully scrutinized by volunteers to safeguard the interests of the walking public. Teams of footpath wardens walk the paths in their communities, checking that the public can use them and reporting any problems, and 150 path maintenance and improvement teams are out on the ground – clearing paths of vegetation, improving path surfaces, removing physical barriers such as stiles and, in some cases, literally building bridges. And almost a thousand Don't Lose Your Way volunteers are combing through the archives to find the evidence to ensure that our lost paths – our history – are put back on the map to stand for generations to come (you can see which paths might be lost in your area and join this inspirational band of volunteers at dontloseyourway.ramblers.org.uk).

The vital work of Ramblers volunteers is supported by a staff team of around a hundred. In addition to ensuring that volunteers have the tools, training and support they need, staff oversee legal work to protect the rights of the public so paths can be there for all. And they deliver projects such as Paths to Wellbeing, which has put walking at the heart of eighteen communities in Wales; the Ramblers Path Accessibility Fund, which is making public paths more physically accessible; the creation and auditing of Scotland's best-ever map of paths; and the Out There Award, which is helping young adults in Scotland to get outdoors, irrespective of background, budget or experience.

It is a real privilege to work for an organization with such a proud and rich history but also with such a crucial mission today. Hundreds of thousands of people over the past eighty-nine years have achieved so much but there is more work to be done, and Ramblers volunteers and staff are taking action every day for the public, so that everyone can enjoy the wonder that is walking.

Index